BEYOND THE FINISH LINE

JONATHAN FINN

BEYOND THE FINISH LINE

Images, Evidence, and the History of the Photo-Finish

McGill-Queen's University Press
Montreal & Kingston • London • Chicago

ISBN 978-0-2280-0343-4 (cloth)
ISBN 978-0-2280-0451-6 (ePDF)
ISBN 978-0-2280-0452-3 (ePUB)

Legal deposit third quarter 2020
Bibliothèque nationale du Québec

Printed in Canada on acid-free paper that is 100% ancient forest free (100% post-consumer recycled), processed chlorine free

This book has been published with the help of a grant from the Canadian Federation for the Humanities and Social Sciences, through the Awards to Scholarly Publications Program, using funds provided by the Social Sciences and Humanities Research Council of Canada.

Funded by the Government of Canada | Financé par le gouvernement du Canada | Canada

Canada Council for the Arts | Conseil des arts du Canada

We acknowledge the support of the Canada Council for the Arts.

Nous remercions le Conseil des arts du Canada de son soutien.

Library and Archives Canada Cataloguing in Publication

Title: Beyond the finish line : images, evidence, and the history of the photo-finish / Jonathan Finn.
Names: Finn, Jonathan M. (Jonathan Mathew), 1972– author.
Description: Includes bibliographical references and index.
Identifiers: Canadiana (print) 20200251414 | Canadiana (ebook) 2020025152X | ISBN 9780228003434 (hardcover) | ISBN 9780228004516 (PDF) | ISBN 9780228004523 (EPUB)
Subjects: LCSH: Photography of sports—History. | LCSH: Photography of sports—Technological innovations—History. | LCSH: Sports—History.
Classification: LCC TR821 .F56 2020 | DDC 778.9/9796—dc23

Contents

Tables and Figures

Tables

Figures

Acknowledgments

There are numerous people who directly and indirectly helped make this book a reality. First and foremost, thank you to my home team: my partner Janice Maarhuis, and our two wonderful daughters, Naomi and Neve. Thanks for putting up with me, laughing with and at me, cheering me on at races, and just generally making everything better.

Significant portions of the book are based on research at the Historical Archives of the International Olympic Committee in Lausanne, Switzerland. Stéphanie Moreno of the Olympic Studies Centre was especially helpful in accessing the vast collections of the IOC. Thank you to Roda Ferraro of the Keeneland Library (Lexington, Kentucky) for helping me navigate and begin to understand the intersection of photography and horse racing (a topic I knew little about). Roda's clear passion for the topic and a shared interest in the photographs of John C. Hemment made for excellent conversation and some fascinating finds. Thank you to Ross Knapper, Elizabeth Chiang, Deborah Mohr, and Virginia Dodier of the George Eastman House Museum and Library (Rochester, New York) for access to images and texts from the early history of photography.

The book would not exist without the support of the Social Sciences and Humanities Research Council of Canada. An Insight Grant enabled me to do archival research, present research findings at conferences and workshops, and work with numerous graduate students throughout the project. A grant through the Awards to Scholarly Publications Program from SSHRC aided with the publication of the book.

Thank you to Ira Wagman at Carleton University for extensive feedback on a draft of the manuscript. Thanks to Jonathan Crago and the staff at

McGill-Queen's University Press for taking on the project and helping it across the finish line, and thank you to Grace Seybold for her excellent copy-editing. The peer reviewers offered thorough and substantial feedback on the manuscript which enabled me to address some of the gaps in the project and to foreground its contributions. I was fortunate to be able to work with numerous graduate students on the project – thank you to Nicole Boulet, Alexandra Howie, Lauren Judge, Dylan Kalloo, Laura Neil, Amara Pope, Maria Proulx, and Megan Voll. And thank you to the many undergraduate students in my media and sport courses who listened patiently as I talked at length and a little too excitedly about the photo-finish. My hope is that you will continue asking the deep questions about why we do what we do in the world of sport. Thanks to my colleagues in Communication Studies, and especially to Peter Urquhart and the late Paul Heyer for their many comments and suggestions. Paul was eager to see the book completed and his enthusiasm for the project sometimes outweighed my own, serving as a constant source of support. FinishLynx was helpful and generous in providing images and permissions. And thank you to John Marsden of Speed River Timing for the conversations, recommendations, links, and race times.

Research presented here appeared previously in "Timing and Imaging Evidence in Sport: Objectivity, Intervention, and the Limits of Technology," *Journal of Sport and Social Issues* 40, no. 6 (2016): 459–76; and "Anatomy of a Dead Heat: Visual Evidence at the 2012 US Olympic Trials," *International Journal of the History of Sport* 31, no. 9 (2014): 976–93.

BEYOND THE FINISH LINE

CHAPTER ONE

Images, Objectivity, and Visual Evidence in Sport

On 18 February 2018, Martin Fourcade of France and Simon Schempp of Germany finished the 15km mass start Olympic biathlon in a time of 35:47.3 (35 minutes, 47 seconds, 3 tenths of a second). Both athletes received the same time, calculated to a tenth of a second, but Fourcade was awarded the gold medal and Schempp the silver. Placing was awarded based on a photo-finish image that showed Fourcade crossing ahead of Schempp. The next day, 19 February, Canadians Justin Kripps and Alexander Kopacz won an Olympic gold medal in the two-man bobsleigh with a time of 3:16.86. But so did the German duo of Francesco Friedrich and Thorsten Margis. That is, over four runs each, the aggregate times of the Canadian and German sleds were exactly the same to the hundredth of a second. Less noted amid the media attention given to the gold medal tie in PyeongChang, but no less extraordinary, was that the bronze medal team from Latvia finished .05 seconds behind. Three sleds over four runs were separated by five hundredths of a second.[1] *Globe and Mail* sportswriter Cathal Kelly pondered the double gold medal, inferring that an actual winner may have been captured by the timers: "Olympic clocks are capable of measuring to the 10,000th of a second, but a hundredth is the accepted maximum in bobsleigh. If the official timekeepers know the truth of it, they are sworn to secrecy."[2]

There are three key truisms of contemporary sport reflected in the above example. First, athlete placing is increasingly determined by infinitesimal differences in performance and timing. The difference between first, second, and third place and beyond routinely comes down to tenths, hundredths, or thousandths of a second. Second, given this, advanced technologies are used to measure and record athletic performance and to assist officials in determining placing. The photo-finish is one such technology and was the determining factor in the Fourcade/Schempp decision. Third and finally, it is a truism that contemporary, professional sport is as much a media event as it is an athletic event. Though the Olympics may be an exaggerated example, it is not an aberration. Contemporary sport is extraordinarily big business and its existence cannot be separated from its symbiotic relationship with media including television, radio, film, photography, social media, and the internet.

Along with these truisms, the opening example raises many interesting questions. Why is the photo-finish used in biathlon but not bobsleigh? Why is biathlon timed to the tenth of a second and bobsleigh to the hundredth? Do Olympic clocks really time performances to the 10,000th of a second? And what about in non-Olympic events? What happens to the decimals beyond the tenth and hundredth? Do officials or other personnel see these more precise numbers? And, perhaps most interestingly, does timing to the 10,000th of a second capture "the truth of it" as suggested by Kelly? This book addresses these and related issues through a critical, historical analysis of the photo-finish and the use of images as evidence in sport. A central premise of the book is that the photo-finish is a complex cultural artefact. It is a collective practice of individuals and groups including athletes, fans, officials, sports technology companies, media corporations, and national and international sports federations. And as the opening example shows, the photo-finish is not universal – it is employed in different ways by different people according to different rules and to meet different goals.

Athletics, horse racing, automobile racing, sailing, swimming, and skiing are among the many sports that routinely employ the camera in ways that either replace or augment the human eye. The resultant photo-finish images have become a mainstay in newspapers, television broadcasts, sports magazines, and other sports-related media outlets, and are often the site of heated debate and discussion. Yet despite their import and ubiquity in contemporary society, such images have received virtually no sustained analysis. I argue that finish-line images used as decision aids in sport have both immediate and far-reaching impacts. In the former case, they serve as proof or evidence in sporting contests and thus have significant financial implications both for individual sports professionals and for the vast industries of sports entertainment and sports gambling. In the latter, the images function across scientific, professional, and lay communities and participate in cultural debates on the limits and capabilities of the human body, the relationship of human and machine vision, and the subjective and objective status of sport and of photography. As such, a critical analysis of the photo-finish is not just warranted but has much to offer academic and non-academic audiences alike.

The photo-finish has its origins in the late nineteenth century. As a concept, it was proposed in the 1870s, and the earliest actual uses of the camera to determine placing date to approximately 1890. During this time, and within the sporting community, the camera was promoted as a tool to correct the fallibility of human vision in the form of dead heats or incorrect calls. This is aptly summarized in an 1892 issue of *Outing* magazine by one of the earliest and most prominent finish-line photographers, John C. Hemment. Writing on his experiments with instantaneous photography, Hemment noted, "some of my pictures showed that what had been considered 'dead heats' were really not *dead* at all. In fact, my photographs proved, what I had long suspected, that there was in reality no such thing as a 'dead heat.'"[3] Hemment's comments, and particularly his belief in the ability of the camera to eradicate the dead heat, mirror popular and professional accounts of horse racing, yacht racing, and athletics of the late nineteenth century that spoke promisingly of this potential for the camera in sport.

The camera was used to determine placing in sport throughout the opening decades of the twentieth century, especially within horse racing. Over this period, the photograph's status as an objective and accurate record of a race was debated and eventually accepted, though not universally. The photograph was used to determine placing in the 1912 Stockholm Olympics and continued to find use in subsequent major track and field competitions. During the 1930s the moving camera was increasingly used in place of still cameras, eventually giving rise to the slit camera and the development of the photo-finish as we know it today. The watchmaker OMEGA provided official stopwatches for the 1932 Olympic Games in Los Angeles and, by the early 1940s, started to establish itself as the dominant finish-line timing and imaging company in the world. Today, finish-line timing and imaging systems capture data at a rate of 5,000 to 10,000 samples per second, with OMEGA boasting that its new equipment subdivides the second into millionths. And yet, as is clear from the PyeongChang Games and hundreds of similar, contemporary cases, athletes continue to "dead heat."

This raises an important set of questions: if two racers, horses, automobiles, sleds, or otherwise are so close at the finish line that a group of officials cannot clearly determine a winner, why not have multiple winners? If timing devices award racers the same time to a tenth or hundredth of a second, why not declare a tie? Why was a tie accepted in the bobsleigh example cited earlier but not in biathlon? Why have we moved from splitting the second into tenths at the turn of the twentieth century to now splitting it into millionths in order to "prove" that one person, animal, or piece of equipment crossed the line ahead of another? And, given this technological advancement, why do we still "dead heat"? Is this an example of Evgeny Morozov's technological solutionism, through which "complex social situations" are transformed into "neatly defined problems with definite, computable solutions?"[4] Does the photo-finish recast the complexity of human competition and physical effort in the form of training and racing into an easily quantifiable, finite, computable product, as in placing? Following Morozov, does the existence of the photo-finish presuppose the dead heat as a problem to be solved? And what is at stake in this process?

I am reluctant to call this a history of the photo-finish because of the gaps in the project. The book focuses almost exclusively on English-language sources and emphasizes Western European and American and Canadian examples. And the chapters focus on different issues and aspects within the larger history of the photo-finish. In this way, and following Thomas King, the book is more accurately described as an account of the photo-finish in sport, albeit an historical one.[5] I follow Ludmilla Jordanova's insistence that historical research on visual material involves "sustained careful looking," including both a qualitative analysis of the visual object combined with a detailed "life history."[6] To this end, the book attends to the material and cultural specificities of images as they are created, distributed, debated, and interpreted within relevant sporting communities.

The approach in the book is informed (and therefore limited) equally by my own disciplinary training and practice and by the uniqueness of the subject of study. I am a humanities-based scholar trained in art history and visual culture studies with research interests in the uses and roles of visual material, especially photographs, in institutional practices. The project draws primarily from the history of photography, science and technology studies, sport studies, and communication and media studies. Methodologically, the project is iterative, following the leads and questions that arise in the research process. Most simply, I began with the questions of "who," "what," "where," "when," "how," and "why" and worked outwards to larger, more abstract

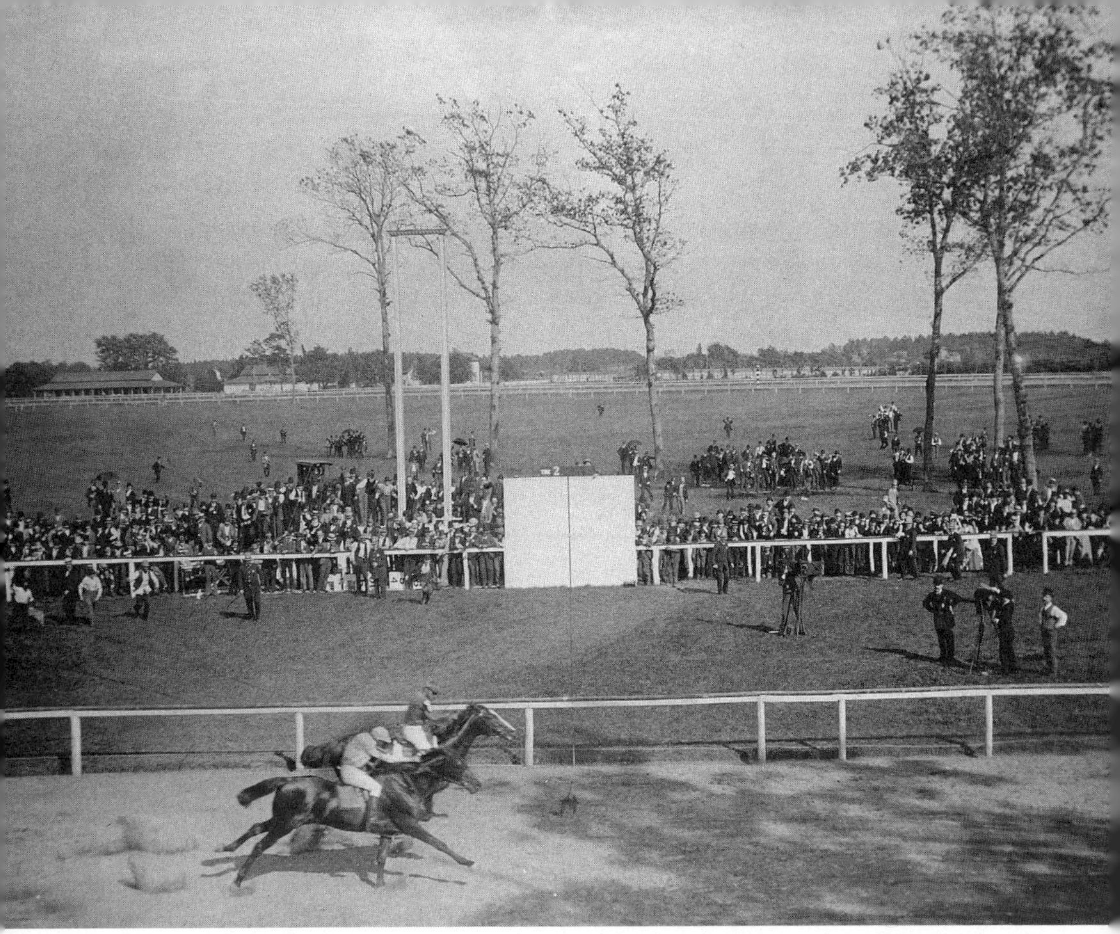

1.1 John C. Hemment, finish of the Salvator v. Tenny Match Race, 1890.

questions around the impact of the photo-finish on sport and on cultural conceptions of truth, evidence, and objectivity. In Jordanova's terms, I followed the material and cultural "lives" of the photo-finish. In this way, the book emphasizes the complexity of the photo-finish as a cultural artefact rather than tracing a single theory, method, actor, narrative, or technology over its use.

The book draws from archival materials at the Olympic Studies Centre in Lausanne, Switzerland, George Eastman House in Rochester, New York, and the Keeneland Library in Lexington, Kentucky, as well as extensive secondary-source materials, both academic and popular. The book is also informed by numerous conversations with sports timing and imaging professionals, fellow non-elite athletes, and one elite-level coach, and by continued participation in online timing and photo-finish communities.

A photo-finish is a fascinating and, I argue, largely misunderstood object. Figures 1.1 and 1.2 help to explain. Figure 1.1, from 1890, is often referred to as one of the first examples of a photo-finish, and as perhaps the earliest

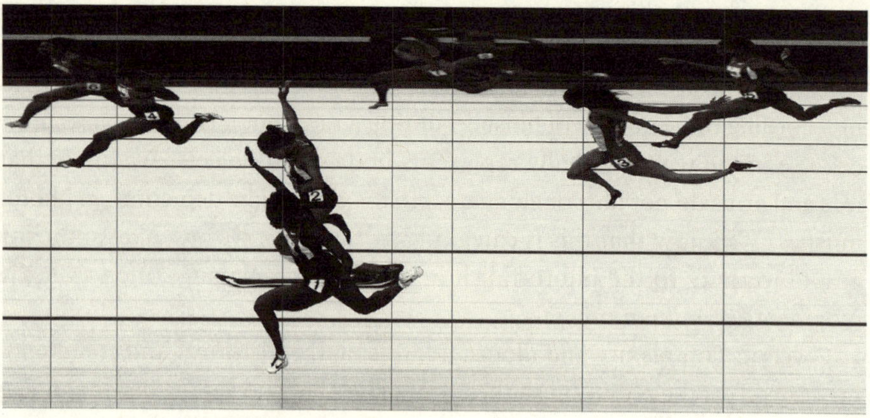

1.2 Inside camera photo-finish of women's 100m, 2012 US Olympic Trials.

surviving example. It was taken by John Hemment and is the finish of the famous Salvator vs Tenny race at Sheepshead Bay racetrack. The image is famous within racing and race photography communities because of the importance of the race as well as the technological innovation of Hemment. However, it is not a photo-finish. Figure 1.2, by contrast, is a photo-finish. It captures the finish of the women's 100m race at the 2012 United States Olympic Trials. This image is also famous because the use of the photo-finish in the determination of placing at the 2012 trials was the site of significant controversy. Nonetheless, and for our immediate purposes, Figure 1.2 is a photo-finish.

The essential difference between the images of Salvator vs Tenny and the 2012 US Trials is that the former is a photograph *of* a finish and the latter is a photo-finish. The difference is not a matter of semantics. Photographs of finishes perform the traditional function of the photograph in that they capture a distinct time in space: Salvator and Tenny just before they pass the finishing post, frozen in time. By contrast, a photo-finish captures a distinct space over time. The 2012 image is a composite of a series of tiny slices of time stitched together in a way that looks similar to a photograph *of* a finish, but it is a fundamentally different visual object. In this way, the photo-finish is on first glance a bit misleading. The image seems to show a series of runners as the first crosses the finish line and the others approach the line. In reality, the image shows all runners crossing the same space at different times. Kris Belden-Adams thus notes that the photo-finish is illogical in that it is both true and false at the same time.[7] That is, it is accurate and reliable in terms of recording the sequence of finishers during a race, but it is clearly inaccurate or false in the way it visually represents bodies and objects. We know that legs and arms do not blur or elongate into the elastic-like depictions in photo-finishes. We know that this is categorically false. Yet we attribute authority and objectivity to the photo-finish in determining placing, often over the judgments of human officials.

Given its complexity and illogic, addressing the historical and contemporary "lives" of the photo-finish therefore moves beyond simply understanding how a technology works or how placing is determined in elite-level sport. Understanding the photo-finish necessarily involves the history of technology, but it is also about the relationship between humans and technology; how we come to see, believe, and contest the veracity of visual material; and how we define, practise, and measure sport and athletic performance. To address this larger field of practice I explore three interrelated issues throughout the book: the problem of representation; objectivity and visual evidence; and the quest for records.

The Problem of Representation

The camera's ability to produce "realistic" or verisimilar images has long been acknowledged as a property unique to the medium. The print historian William Ivins Jr described the photomechanical image as an "exactly repeatable pictorial statement," arguing that there had never been as important an invention in the history of communication.[8] The ontology of the photograph has been most specifically addressed by, and tied to, the semioticians Charles Peirce and Roland Barthes. Under Peirce's three-tiered semiotic system of icons, symbols, and indices, a photograph is best understood as an indexical sign because of its direct relationship with the object being represented.[9] That is, whereas a painting of a dog can be an image of no particular dog (it could be entirely the product of the artist's imagination), a photograph is understood to guarantee that the dog being represented exists. This is because, in order for the photograph to exist, it had to occupy the same time and space as the live animal in order for light to enter the camera's lens and record the animal's likeness. Roland Barthes refers to this as the photograph's unique status of *having-been-there.*[10] Returning to Figures 1.1 and 1.2, we do not question the veracity of these images because of their indexical status – the co-presence of the camera and its subjects in time and space guarantees that these specific horses and these specific runners *have-been-there* and that these events took place.

One result of the indexicality of the photographic image has been to accept photographic and other machine-made visual materials as inherently unmediated, objective, and accurate representations of their subjects. Too often this status is attributed to a nineteenth-century "revolution" through which picture-making suddenly became objective. Work addressing the history of photography has done much to dismantle this understanding of the medium, stressing instead the historically and culturally specific conditions of the medium's truth status. Although Ivins praised the exact repeatability of photomechanical images, he nonetheless positioned the photograph within a millennia-long history of print-making that was largely defined by a desire for information and communication.[11] Similarly, Geoffrey Batchen de-emphasizes photography as a specific type of technology to position it within a larger historical desire of image-making. He writes: "even if we continue to identify photography with certain archaic technologies, such as camera and film, those technologies themselves embody the idea of photography or, more accurately, a persistent economy of photographic desires and concepts."[12] And Joel Snyder traces the development of photography – and particularly its ties to objectivity – to Renaissance theories of vision and to the attempts by post-Renaissance artists to produce a pictorial equivalent to vision.[13]

Where Ivins, Batchen, and Snyder emphasize the broad historical trajectory of image-making, other scholars have taken up the medium's claims to objectivity as they were built in specific social and institutional contexts. Scholars including John Tagg, Allan Sekula, Nicole Rafter, Sander Gilman, and Sarah Bassnett have traced how the camera has been used in areas including criminal anthropology, psychiatry, policing, and urban planning.[14] A central result of this work is to critique the representational status of the photograph, breaking from the notion of the image-as-mimesis – the photograph as a representation *of* a pre-existing subject – to understand the way that its meaning, function, and evidentiary status are built through historically specific contexts of use. This is captured in the polysemic title of Tagg's foundational book, *The Burden of Representation: Essays on Photographies and Histories*. Understood from this perspective, there can be no single explanation for how photography functions in sport, just as there cannot be for its use in other practices such as policing, medicine, physics, biology, or criminology; rather, each has its own unique and multiple trajectories.

I have taken up this aspect of the medium in my history of police photography, and here it is sufficient to note that photography's adoption into various social and institutional practices and its status as a purveyor of truth should be seen as a product of both photography's nature and its culture.[15] In the former, the photomechanical apparatus was and is able to produce highly verisimilar images in ways and quantities that other modes of visual representation (printing, drawing, painting) cannot. In the latter, the gradual accumulation of a discourse of objectivity surrounded the photograph as it was increasingly employed across a range of social institutions and practices from the late nineteenth century. Returning to Figures 1.1 and 1.2, these photographs depict their subject matter in a highly realistic manner, beyond what could be accomplished through other modes of visual representation. However, this verisimilitude does not guarantee their status as objective, accurate, or evidentiary documents. Instead, their status and meaning also depend on historically and culturally specific sets of relations and desires and mutable conceptions of truth, accuracy, objectivity, and evidence.

Such is the case with the photograph for use in sport. The photographic image provided athletes, coaches, fans, and the news-reading public with access to verisimilar images like they had not seen before. And its use as a form of evidence to determine placing was built through decades of work that promoted and challenged the objectivity and accuracy of the photomechanical image. And as the opening example in this chapter shows, its status as a form of evidence is still mutable and deployed differently according to each sporting context. A central task of this book is to illustrate this process and to make visible the public and professional discourse around the use of the photo-finish as a form of evidence in sport.

The problem of representation addressed in relation to the history of photography has been taken up in numerous other disciplines as part of what W.J.T. Mitchell called the "visual turn."[16] Writing in 1994, Mitchell identified a shift in academic work away from the linguistic model that had dominated for decades and towards an interrogation of the role of the visual in their own subject areas as well as its treatment within the historiographies of their disciplines. Led by art history and, later, visual culture studies, disciplines as diverse as biology, criminology, communication studies, anthropology, and geography have experienced this visual turn, with sport history being the most recent addition.[17] Regardless of the specific discipline, much of this work has simply called for scholars to take images more seriously rather than treating them as supplements to an oral or written argument. But the best of this work has interrogated the active roles and uses of images, particularly in making claims to truth and objectivity. Work in science and technology studies (STS) has been particularly strong in this regard.

Bruno Latour and Steve Woolgar's late-1970s ethnographic analysis of the work within an endocrinology laboratory is foundational in addressing representation in the social construction of scientific fact.[18] The authors emphasize the centrality of inscriptions – manifested as diagrams, lists, tables, pictures, and other forms of representation – in laboratory work, and position the inscription as the lifeblood of the sciences. In studying the day-to-day activities of the laboratory, Latour and Woolgar found that inscriptions took on particularly powerful roles and were understood both as direct copies of the object of study and as proof or confirmation of a study's theories, assumptions, or hypotheses. The focus on inscription and representation was the subject of the now-famous 1990 text, *Representation in Scientific Practice*, co-edited by Woolgar and Michael Lynch.[19] Woolgar and Lynch's collection brought together scholars interested in how scientific objects and facts are created, with particular attention to the role of representation and inscription in laboratory and scientific work.

Representation and inscription have remained important topics in STS, with recent work taking specific aim at the problem of representation.[20] To this end, Catelijn Coopmans and Janet Vertesi have partnered with Lynch and Woolgar to revisit the issue of representation as taken up in earlier STS work.[21] Specifically, and in a manner similar to photographic historians, they challenge the notion of representation as it literally suggests a re-presentation of a given object, thereby presupposing a mimetic relationship between representation and the "real" world. On this issue, Lorrain Daston writes, "Images have come into their own as a source for the history of science, even if we are still learning how to interpret them and to emancipate ourselves from text-centered analogies such as 'reading images' and 'visual literacy.'" She goes on to explain, "Perhaps the most tenacious of these word-obsessed metaphors is the idea of representation itself: an image is said to 'represent' something in the world, as a word 'refers' to it." Daston's comment exemplifies Mitchell's notion of the visual turn and takes a position similar to the photographic historians cited previously, one which stresses the co-constitutive relationship of representation and (scientific) practice, positioning them less as discrete entities than as mutually constituting agents.

Other STS scholars have identified a noticeable gap in this scholarship, namely the lack of attention given to users. With a specific nod to feminist studies of science and technology, Nelly Oudshoorn and Trevor Pinch point to "the almost exclusive attention it [STS] gives to experts and producers and for the preference it gives to design and innovation in understanding socio-technical change."[22] They note instead an interest in "how users consume, modify, domesticate, design, reconfigure, and resist technologies."[23] This critique of the production-centric approach of much STS is helpful in illuminating the agency of users, just as photographic historians and visual culture scholars have done in emphasizing the agency of viewers in the meaning-making process.

Specifically within the world of sport, the intersection of producers and users is foregrounded in Rayvon Fouché's excellent book *Game Changer: The Technoscientific Revolution in Sport*. Fouché examines the co-construction of sport and technoscience, addressing topics including prosthetics, bodily modifications, or materials engineering such as the Speedo Lazer LZR swimsuit.[24] He writes, "understanding the place of technoscience within sport goes beyond the tensions between body and machine. Sport is bound together by and through an evolving network of athletes, engineers, designers, publics, and technoscientific artifacts."[25] Fouché refers to these networks as "sporting communities" and a central project of his book is to trace the incorporation and refutation of socio-technological change in such communities. Similarly, I address the "sporting communities" involved in the photo-finish as it brings together fans, athletes, sponsors, corporations, athletic federations, and time-keeping companies, among others, in determining placing in sport.

The field of sport studies is one of the most recent disciplines to make the "visual turn" and is only beginning to tackle the problem of representation. Understood in a more broad sense, representation has been a concern of sport studies scholars since the 1970s, particularly those interested in the mediation of sport – in other words, how sport and its participants are represented in media. Michael Real's 1975 analysis of the SuperBowl and a 1977 special section of the *Journal of Communication* gave rise to the notion of the mediated event being distinct from the live event.[26] The McLuhanesque title of the special section, *Sports: The Medium Is the Stadium*, effectively highlights the way this work drew attention to the medium as much as its message, stressing the structuring properties of media on sport.

The 1970s work was a direct response to the growing symbiosis of media and sport. The late 1950s and early 1960s were a pivotal time in the sports/media relationship: television sets were increasingly common in the household; the introduction of colour television, communication satellites, and videotape meant that sports broadcasting could rise to new levels; the Sports Broadcast Act was passed in the US in 1961, allowing sports leagues to negotiate as a single entity (instead of individually as teams); and broadcast networks negotiated directly with the leagues, ultimately selling air time to advertisers.[27] This ultimately gave rise to what Sut Jhally has called "the sports/media complex," so that, by the mid-1970s, sports and television had developed a fully symbiotic relationship: sports provided broadcasters with content that attracted a large, previously untapped demographic and which therefore attracted increased advertising revenues; and the enhanced ability to negotiate as leagues rather than as teams provided sports with increased revenues as they sold the television rights to their games.[28] Decision-making and placing in sport necessarily increased in both scale and importance within this highly lucrative sport marketplace.

The symbiotic relationship between sports and media, combined with the rapid increase in sports broadcasting during the latter half of the twentieth century, formed the basis for a proliferation of scholarship in the 1980s and 1990s that placed particular emphasis on the role of the media – often visual media – in the production, dissemination, and framing of sports entertainment.[29] Where the 1970s work stressed the difference between live and mediated events, books such as Lawrence Wenner's *Media, Sports, and Society*, as well as his subsequent collection, *MediaSport*, and David Rowe's *Sport, Culture and the Media* emphasized the larger social and cultural implications of mediated sport. Increasingly informed by critical theory and cultural studies, work in the critical study of sport from the 1980s to the present often takes a more theoretical perspective to sport and addresses social constructions of gender,[30] race,[31] and national and regional identity.[32]

Regardless of the specific focus of analysis, this continually expanding body of literature has been and is essential in problematizing and critiquing mediated sport – including its visual mediation in the form of television, film, and photography. Importantly, and as relates to the visual, this work is limited by its treatment of representation as a broad category (such as the representation of men, women, or nations in sports media). In so doing, this work fails to address the problem of representation that has been taken up in the history of photography, visual culture studies, STS, and other areas following the visual turn.

There are a few notable examples of scholarly work dealing with sport that directly address the problem of representation.[33] Douglas Brown has analyzed the central role of photography in the modernization of mountaineering, showing how the medium and the sport were partners in creating a distinct mountaineering aesthetic at the turn of the twentieth century.[34] Similarly, he examines the philosophy and tenets of Pierre de Coubertin's Olympic movement as they were manifested and articulated through publications such as *Olympic Review*.[35] Brown stresses the role of this pictorial and literary work in building a modernist aesthetic alongside the paintings and artwork of cubists, futurists, vorticists, and others. The central role of photography and visual culture is taken up by Robin Veder in her extensive and thorough work on modern dance, physical culture, and posture reform movements of the early twentieth century.[36] Like Brown's work, Veder's shows that the embodied practice of doing sport cannot be seen or properly conceived without attending to the co-constitutive relationship of visual media (including photography) and the sporting body.[37]

The through line in these various approaches to the problem of representation – whether in the history of photography, science and technology studies, sport studies, or communication and media studies – is the positioning of visual material as a constituent part of any given field of practice. It rightly calls for a move away from treating the image as a mimetic representation *of* a pre-existing object to instead understanding the image and its meanings as active and mobile. In terms of the photo-finish, such an approach highlights the discursive networks through which the photographic image and its subjects are created, articulated, deployed, refuted, made and re-made, all under changing historical circumstances. Such is the approach in this book, which might best be summarized as a shift in emphasis from representation to co-construction.

Objectivity and Visual Evidence

The work of photographic historians has done much to illustrate that photography's unique claim to objectivity is largely a cultural construction. Indeed, the medium's adoption into numerous social practices was often treated with great hesitancy, especially when the fields in question were concerned with truth and accuracy. Jennifer Mnookin has traced the adoption of the photograph into the American legal system, noting that the photomechanical image was initially viewed with significant suspicion and was only considered evidence when corroborated by an eye-witness.[38] And Karin E. Becker has identified that, as it was adopted by the news media, the photograph was initially equated with sensationalism and entertainment rather than fact-based reporting, which was the domain of the written word.[39] As these and other authors have shown, mechanical objectivity was not the birthright of the camera but was built in unique and discipline-specific ways.

The most extensive work on objectivity, and the most helpful in understanding the photo-finish, is that by Lorraine Daston and Peter Galison. In their 2010 book *Objectivity*, the authors analyze scientific image-making from the eighteenth to twenty-first centuries. Focusing specifically on the scientific atlas, their work effectively problematizes the notion of objectivity as a universal, trans-historical concept, positioning it instead as something that is historically and culturally specific. They write, "objectivity is one epistemic virtue among several, not the alpha and omega of all epistemology. Objectivity is not synonymous with truth or certainty, precision or accuracy."[40] To this end, Daston and Galison outline three primary ways of seeing and knowing – what they refer to as "epistemic virtues" – in the eighteenth, nineteenth, and twentieth centuries. The inclusion of "virtue" is important and the authors are careful to defend their use of the word: "The term 'epistemic virtues,' with its ethical overtones, is warranted. Ethos was explicitly wedded to epistemology in the quest for truth or objectivity or accuracy. Far from eliminating the self in pursuit of scientific knowledge, each of the epistemic virtues depended on the cultivation of certain character traits."[41] In other words, for Daston and Galison, the changing conceptions of objectivity in picture-making had as much to do with changing conceptions of the scientific self as they did with changing practices of representation.

For Daston and Galison, eighteenth-century atlas-making was dominated by the "truth-to-nature" epistemic virtue. Exemplified in the figure of Carolus Linnaeus, picture-making in this era was about depicting the typical of a given species. Key to this task was the position of the scientist – the atlas-maker – as expert. The atlas was therefore entirely the product of individual expertise, and it took figures such as Linnaeus to discover and represent what was believed to be the inherent truth of the natural world. The scientific image was not the product of nature but of the expert, and it was the visible intervention or mediation of the expert that gave the image its legitimacy. By contrast, the nineteenth-century epistemic virtue of mechanical objectivity can be read in part as a reaction to the dominating presence of the expert in eighteenth-century scientific work. Nineteenth-century work was defined by a "self-denying ethics" and continued self-surveillance through which the scientist strove to remove him/herself from the representational process.[42] Daston and Galison refer to this as "non-interventionist objectivity."[43] Exemplified in Erwin Christeller's images of "tattered tissues," mechanically produced or non-interventionist images were positioned as stencils of the real and as able to speak for themselves, without the interfering bias of the human.

The epistemic virtue that dominated the twentieth century – trained judgment – referenced both earlier epistemes and is visible in the expansive x-ray atlases of Rudolph Grashey. Grashey's atlases bring together the visual accuracy of the mechanically produced image with the expert authority of the trained professional (Grashey), the marriage of which is essential for the scientific validity of the image. As explained by Daston and Galison, "manipulated to build on the natural, but structured to bring out specific features by means of expert understanding, the twentieth-century image embodies professional experience; it is pictorial presentation by (and for) the trained eye."[44] This passage points to a key difference in the notion of expertise in the eighteenth- and twentieth-century epistemic virtues. In the former, expertise was a metaphysical given – it was something one "had" or "didn't have." By contrast, in the latter, expertise is something that is built through continued training and practice.

Daston and Galison's work on objectivity is helpful in addressing the photo-finish as it reveals the mutually constitutive forces of the image and its producers and users in the production of visual evidence. Like similar work in science and technology studies, it emphasizes an engagement with visual material before it becomes "black-boxed" and awarded the authority of objectivity and evidence. It is also important in showing objectivity to be a dynamic, contested concept that is built and re-built in historically and culturally specific conditions. This is precisely the strategy of this book – to trace the ways in which the photo-finish is created, discussed, challenged, defined, and used as a form of evidence in sporting contests. And as per Daston and Galison, addressing this process sheds light on the underlying epistemic virtues of image producers and users.

The Quest for Records: Modernity, Technology, and Sport Performance

The photo-finish is a constituent part of modern sport and is inextricably bound to modernist goals of rationalization, standardization, and bureaucratization. And, as exemplified in the Olympic motto, "Faster, Higher, Stronger," sport shares modernity's often teleological view of progress. While sport predated the modern era, it went through a profound transformation in the late eighteenth and nineteenth centuries. During this time, and within a context of an increasingly industrializing, urbanizing, and colonizing environment, relatively free forms of play were replaced with tightly structured and regulated games. Developments in transportation, particularly railways and bicycles, and communication in the form of telegraph and telephone provided the necessary infrastructure for this transformation, and emerging capitalist markets provided financial backing and incentive.[45] Richard Gruneau addresses much of this in his recent book on sport and modernity.[46] He acknowledges the ties between games and contests from antiquity and medieval Europe to the modern era, but stresses the distinctly modern aspect of sport as it developed in the eighteenth and nineteenth centuries. For Gruneau, "the emergence of modern sport in Europe and North America involved the remaking of this jumble of diverse gaming and sporting practices ... into a more unified, regulated, and purposeful social and cultural *field* of practice."[47] And so, "by the beginning of World War I, one can discern the clear outlines of a distinctive, and self-consciously modern, field of sporting practice, dominated by western nations."[48]

The modernization of sport is most famously taken up in Allen Guttmann's influential text, *From Ritual to Record: The Nature of Modern Sports*. As the title implies, Guttmann contrasts the ritualized (often religious) nature of primitive and ancient sports with the secularized and standardized nature of their modern successors. A central feature of Guttmann's analysis is that modern sport is defined by a continued quest for achievement in the form of records, underlain by programs of specialization, rationalization, organization, and quantification. On the never-ending quest for records and the move away from ritual in sport, he writes, "when qualitative distinctions fade and lose their force, we turn to quantitative ones. When we can no longer distinguish the sacred from the profane or even the good from the bad, we content ourselves with minute discriminations between the batting average of the .308 hitter and the .307 hitter."[49]

Like Guttman, Lewis Mumford argues that the emphasis on minutiae is a defining feature of modernism. Mumford uses the example of sport and the quest for records to make his case:

> to cut a fifth of a second off the time of running a race, to swim the English channel twenty minutes faster than another swimmer, to stay up in the air an hour longer than one's rival did – these interests come into the competition and turn it from a purely human contest to one in which the real opponent is the previous record: time takes the place of a visible rival.[50]

Thus for both Guttmann and Mumford the quest for records is two-fold: it is a quest for setting records, as in sporting performance; and it is a quest for making records, as in the production and accumulation of documents and information. And both scholars point to the abstracting properties of this quest, and the ways it reconfigures sport from an emphasis on the human to an emphasis on the record.

The modernization of sport and its quest for records took concrete shape through the formation of sports-regulating bodies in the form of associations and federations. These groups ensured the standardization, regulation, monitoring, and records-keeping functions of sports that remain today. Between 1863 and 1906, thirty official associations and federations developed in the United States, France, England, Switzerland, and Germany. These covered football, swimming, cycling, rowing, athletics, and tennis.[51] In Canada, the Montreal Amateur Athletic Association formed in 1881, followed shortly by the Toronto Athletic Club.[52] As it did in other institutions and practices of the time, the camera contributed to this quest for standardization, regulation, and records, as it provided an efficient means for measuring, monitoring, and recording the newly modernized sports.

Photography is also an inherently modern practice. While Batchen and Snyder have rightly identified pre-modern desires for image-making as a precursor to photography, the particular combination of camera and film in the late nineteenth century was intertwined with a larger modernist project that emphasized measurement, standardization, efficiency, and documentation. Between the mid-to-late nineteenth and early twentieth centuries, the camera was increasingly employed by hospitals, schools, factories, prisons, and police stations, and by anthropologists, sociologists, and criminologists, all of which used the camera to record and document their subjects. Early experiments in using photographs as evidence in sport therefore have fascinating parallels with Alphonse Bertillon's use of the camera in creating the criminal identification record, the time and motion studies of Frank and Lillian Gilbreth, Frederick Taylor's work on scientific management, and anthropological uses of the image such as with Robert Flaherty's *Nanook of the North*. In this way, the quest for records that is essential to modern and contemporary sport is as much about the accumulation and articulation of information as it is about recording dominant sporting performances. Photographs of race finishes and photo-finishes serve this dual function: they provide visual evidence of a record performance and they also provide records (documents) of and for sport.

The role of technology in sport's quest for records is hard to overstate. The increasing professionalization and commercialization of sport – the ultimate product of sport's modernization – has been paralleled by an increasing array of technologies to enhance the sporting body, to measure and record its performance, and to communicate and mediate that performance publicly from niche markets to the spectacle of the Olympics.[53] The symbiotic relationship of media and sport as first outlined by Jhally could easily be extended out from media and communication technologies to consider technology more broadly, from baseball bats and ski wax to hyperbaric chambers and blood-boosting. The centrality of technology to sport and to the sporting body has increased exponentially in the era of "smart" technologies and in the contemporary pursuit of "marginal gains" – that is, the drive to achieve ever finer physiological and mental gains in sporting performance.

This pursuit is visible everywhere in contemporary sport, perhaps nowhere more so than in Nike's Breaking2.[54] The project was an attempt in 2016 to break the two-hour marathon, for which Nike brought together physiologists, psychologists, materials engineers, biomechanicists, and others to research and put forward the best possible athlete, gear, and course for the attempt. Three runners were chosen – Eliud Kipchoge, Lelisa Desisa, and Zersenay Tadese – and followed an intricate training, nutrition, and health regimen designed to coax every last bit of effort from their bodies. Nike sought to control every possible variable for the attempt, spending millions of dollars on the effort. They chose an F1 racetrack in Monza, Italy, as the venue, after carefully researching numerous locations that would provide the most conducive conditions of temperature, humidity, wind, and elevation. A team of pacers would run in V-formation to shield the three runners from wind, and a pacing car, complete with large digital clock, drove a consistent pace around the track to finish in exactly 1:59:59. A laser mounted to the car projected a horizontal band across the track, indicating the pace needed to break two hours. Numerous advances in materials engineering were employed, including Nike's AeroBlade tape-strips which were attached to the runners' lower legs in order to reduce wind-drag, and the Vapour Fly Elite shoe which was said to provide a 4 percent increase in efficiency. Runners even received training on how to smile during hard efforts, as research has shown a positive correlation between performance and running relaxed and "happy."

Breaking2 didn't achieve the purported goal of breaking the record: Kipchoge ran an extraordinary 2:00:25 with Desisa and Tadese slowing earlier in the attempt. Yet it did yield extensive merchandising opportunities for Nike. National Geographic partnered with Nike to make a documentary of the attempt and the famed shoe was made available to the public, albeit in slightly modified versions (and at a considerable cost). And the project yielded an extensive set of records: massive quantities of data and information on bodily performance and materials engineering that Nike can use in future product development. What Breaking2 did more than anything else was make publicly visible the extensive use – including research and development – of technology to enhance sport performance in the quest for records. True to Mumford's example, in Breaking2, "time takes the place of a visible rival."[55]

This contemporary drive for performance enhancement is taken up in a growing body of literature, both academic and popular. Tara Magdalinski's *Sport, Technology and the Body: The Nature of Performance* and Rayvon Fouché's *Game Changer: The Technoscientific Revolution in Sports* are particularly noteworthy and important for my own project on the photo-finish.[56] In differing ways, these authors identify binaries and false narratives that constitute modern and contemporary sport. For Magdalinski the binary of nature/artifice is particularly important, and for Fouché it is the mythical notions of pure performance and fair competition. Both authors point to an underlying belief in pure performance as animating continued technological advancements in sport which seek to maximize athlete performance but do so in natural, acceptable (and legal) ways. Magdalinski's and Fouché's books are filled with examples of attempts throughout history to boost athlete performance, particularly in contemporary sport as athletes and coaches strive to shave hundredths of a second from their time or to alter their distance by millimetres. The unrelenting, often insidious, and sometimes lethal nature of this drive is made more clear in the bestselling popular accounts of David Epstein (*The Sports Gene*), Mark McLusky (*Faster, Higher, Stronger*), Bryan Fogel (*Icarus*), and Alex Hutchinson (*Endure*).[57]

What emerges from both the academic and popular accounts of the topic is recognition of a "win-at-all-costs" sporting culture within which technology/technoscience plays an increasing role in athletic performance. Within this environment, contemporary sports media continually ponder whether we are approaching the limits of human performance. Fouché takes this up as a recurring theme in his work and posits something of a technoscience arms race in sport. He writes, "we are, for all intents and purposes, at a precipice where the differences between the bodily abilities of athletes in a sporting domain may become so infinitesimal that athletic performance may cease to determine the outcomes of sport competitions."[58] Fouché wonders whether competition in sport will move off the field and into the lab so that "a sporting body becomes another medium through which to display the latest scientific knowledge or technological innovation."[59]

Despite the idiosyncracies of their accounts, the works by Magdalinski, Fouché, Epstein, McClusky, Fogel, and Hutchinson as well as similar work by contemporary sports scholars and journalists focus on the performance side of athletic competition, specifically how athletes' bodies are poked, prodded, tweaked, or otherwise manipulated (legally and illegally) in the pursuit of marginal gains. Like these authors, I am interested in the narratives that animate sport and the relationship between sport and technoscience; however, I am interested less in performance than in how that performance is measured and awarded. In other words, and as taken up in this book, is the history of the photo-finish underlain by beliefs in a win-at-all-costs attitude and in a teleological quest for "pure" and "perfect" measurement whereby timing and imaging systems are held to produce definitive, infallible measurements of athlete performance?

Structure of the Book

The three interrelated issues – the problem of representation, objectivity and visual evidence, and the quest for records – underlie the book but are not treated sequentially or uniformly throughout. Instead, they serve a heuristic function, helping to shape and give form to the particular history – or account – of the photo-finish I am presenting. This account emphasizes the co-construction of technology and sport, broadly conceived, with specific attention given to issues of human and machine vision, photographic truth and objectivity, and decision-making in sport. The photo-finish is not simply a tool used to determine placing; it is a complex cultural artefact and collective practice, an analysis of which reveals as much about the "nature" of sport and human performance as it does about technological invention.

The book is organized chronologically, though each chapter takes up distinct issues and concerns within the use of visual evidence in sport. Chapter 2 examines the historical origins of using photography to determine placing in sport. The practice of "instantaneous photography" developed in the mid-to-late nineteenth century and, concerned as it was with the photographing of movement, several instantaneous photographers took to photographing sport. Chapter 2 focuses on one such photographer: John C. Hemment, one of the earliest and most prolific photographers to call for the image's use in determining placing in sport contests. The chapter traces the emergence of a paradox that has underlined the photo-finish from its origins to the present: namely, the issue of human fallibility. Hemment and his contemporaries lauded the capabilities of the camera to capture objects and events in the visual field that the eye could not see, such as one horse crossing the finish line ahead of another. However, Hemment's work in creating a photo-finish was ultimately unsuccessful because of a different type of human error. Hemment's finish-line photography relied on his own ability to trigger the shutter release at the precise moment horses crossed the line, something he was rarely able to do.

Chapter 3 takes up the distinction between photographs *of* finishes and photo-finishes. Instantaneous photographers of the late nineteenth and early twentieth centuries were able to capture photographs of finishes; however, by the middle decades of the twentieth century, true photo-finishes were being produced. This period saw the development of the still camera, the moving camera, and the slit camera ultimately necessary for the photo-finish. The chapter traces this technological development from the horse-racing track to athletics, with a focus on the Olympic Games. Material advances in imaging were paralleled by a professional and public discourse that sought to find balance between the human eye (the official) and the electric eye (the machine) so that their relationship was complementary and not adversarial.

By the 1940s the photo-finish had become a reasonably well-known practice and, following World War II, a competitive marketplace for photo-finish services began to emerge. Chapter 4 addresses the development of the photo-finish from the 1940s to the twenty-first century, noting the ascendancy of an "automation-as-accuracy" discourse which actively promoted machine-based measurement of athlete performance. However, and in contrast to the previous chapters, the focus of chapter 4 is less on particular technologies than on the larger institutional context of their use. Specifically, the chapter examines the rise to prominence of OMEGA within the sports timing and photo-finish marketplace, with specific attention paid to the Olympic Games. OMEGA presents a productive case study as it has garnered near-monopoly status as the timing provider for the Olympic Games and is a world leader in timing and photo-finish services more broadly. The chapter addresses correspondence and contracts between OMEGA, its predecessors and affiliates, the International Olympic Committee, and other Olympic partners to illustrate the complex and competitive institutional context of the photo-finish.

Chapter 5 moves from the institutional to the individual, providing a detailed examination of a single use of the photo-finish. The women's 100m at the 2012 US Olympic Trials represents a "perfect storm" in photo-finish history. Third place in the event was at first announced as being awarded to Jeneba Tarmoh, but that decision was quickly rescinded and third place declared a dead heat between Tarmoh and Allyson Felix. At the centre of this decision and the ensuing and largely public controversy was the interpretation of a photo-finish image. Chapter 5 analyzes the Tarmoh/Felix dead heat to illustrate the numerous actors and influences involved in creating and interpreting a photo-finish. The chapter then addresses the differential application of the photo-finish across different sports. Individual sports federations have different policies for the use of timing and photo-finish systems to determine placing, including whether placing is determined based on timing to the tenth, hundredth, or thousandth of a second. Examining the idiosyncracies in the application of timing and the photo-finish in sport, the chapter argues that there are distinct limitations to timing and the photo-finish as they are applied in the natural environment.

The book concludes with two discussions, looking "beyond the finish line." The first is a response to the limitations of the photo-finish addressed throughout the book, and calls on sports federations to make clear the rationale for timing to the tenth, hundredth, or thousandth of a second in their respective sports. Such statements should make clear that there are distinct limitations to the accuracy of timing and photo-finish equipment as it is used in the live environment. The second positions the photo-finish within a larger and mythical quest for pure performance and its pure measurement. The development of the photo-finish reads as a history of increasingly precise measurement and, true to its modernist underpinnings, as a teleological drive for perfect measurement. In this way, the photo-finish mirrors a similar drive in sport performance which seeks to extract every ounce of energy from the athlete's body. Such drives for pure measurement and pure performance threaten to rid sport of its fundamental human-ness through the eradication of perceived human errors and inefficiencies.

CHAPTER TWO

Instantaneous Photography: Nineteenth-Century Origins of the Photo-Finish

The concept of using a camera to determine placing in sporting contests was identified as early as 1879 in the newspaper *The Spirit of the Times*.[1] Eadweard Muybridge claims to have "proposed" using a camera to determine a horse race in 1877.[2] An 1884 issue of *Photo News* references the use of a camera to aid race judges.[3] And the editors of the *British Journal of Photography* cited this potential use of the camera in 1888.[4] But it is difficult to identify with any precision the first actual example of the use of the photograph to determine placing in sport. Tom R. Underwood's *Thoroughbred Racing and Breeding* and John Hervey's *Racing in America 1922–1936* both cite an 1886 race in Connecticut as the first use of a photo-finish, but provide no further details.[5] An 1889 article in *Outing* magazine mentions that the photographer Ernest Marx "has been successful in determining the winner in close or 'dead heats' of racing contests" but again no details are provided.[6] Jerome O'Neill also attributes the origins of the practice to Marx,[7] as does J.P. Bovay of Swiss Timing, writing that "it was in 1888 that Ernest Max [Marx] accomplished the first photographic finish of a sports event – a horse race."[8] An 1891 essay in *Outing* references an 1888 rowing race in which an amateur photographer used an image to show race officials who had won.[9] Also in *Outing* the photographer John Hemment is cited in an 1892 article saying "I took up photography seven years ago [1885] as a means to determine the real winner in all close athletic contests."[10] And horse-racing historian Philip Von Borries identifies an 1890 photo by John Hemment as likely the first photo-finish image, writing that "many consider it to be the progenitor of photo-finish photography."[11] Despite this lack of a precise starting point, it is clear that the use of the photograph to determine race results began in the mid-to-late 1880s and was used as evidence in sporting contests by the early 1890s. Thus, within a very short few years, the photograph as evidence in sport went from concept to practical reality.

From the 1850s, scientists, artists, and photographic enthusiasts began to explore ways to capture movement in photographs. In the history of photography the work of Eadweard Muybridge and Étienne-Jules Marey is synonymous with this period. The images by these photographers and their contemporaries significantly transformed how people understood and represented human and animal movement. Less well-known is the contemporary development of "instantaneous photography," of which both Muybridge and Marey were a part. Instantaneous photographers of the late nineteenth century specifically explored the use of the camera to document sport and leisure activities. The practice emerged in a confluence of activity that included the development of dry-plates for cameras, experiments on human reaction time, and attempts to photograph depth and motion in the neurosciences. Tracing the development of instantaneous photography in the closing decades of the nineteenth century reveals the ways in which the photographic image was explored as a form of evidence in sport. In the pages of sources including the *British Journal of Photography*, *Outing Magazine*, *The Thoroughbred Record*, *The American Annual of Photography*, and *The Sporting Life*, editors, writers, and photographers were exploring the possibilities of the photograph to document sporting events, gradually calling for its use to determine race results.

Photographing Movement

Jules Janssen, Muybridge, and Marey are key figures in early experiments to photograph human and animal movement and, as such, their work can be identified as part of the foundation for the photo-finish. Janssen's key contribution to the practice of photography was his construction and use of a photographic apparatus to study the 1874 transit of Venus. Specifically, Janssen built a photographic revolver controlled by a clock that was able to record 84 daguerreotypes on a circular plate over 70 seconds.[12] In her excellent book, *A Tenth of a Second: A History*, Jimena Canales attributes Janssen's work with the photographic revolver as helping to shift attitudes in the scientific community towards the validity of photographic evidence. She writes, "the photographic revolver was an essential part of a new, emerging, and highly contested evidentiary regime that, through chronophotography and its 'inverse,' sought to eliminate individual differences in the observation of moving phenomena by capturing tenth-of-a-second moments."[13] In this way Janssen's work offered up a new photographic apparatus to capture movement but also played an important role in the growing discourse on photography, vision, and objectivity.

Eadweard Muybridge is best known for his 1887–88 *Animal Locomotion*, a series of nearly 800 plates produced from tens of thousands of images he made documenting human and animal movement. *Animal Locomotion* was the product of Muybridge's work at the University of Pennsylvania, begun in 1884 at the invitation of then provost William Pepper and with the help of the painter Thomas Eakins. By this time Muybridge's fame as a photographer was well known. He developed a reputation as a talented landscape photographer in the 1860s, but his work in the early 1870s with Leland Stanford, a former governor of California, brought him heightened fame. Among his many pursuits, Stanford owned a horse-breeding farm in Palo Alto, California. He hired Muybridge to photograph his horses in motion, most specifically his prize horse, Occident, in order to better understand their movement with the ultimate goal of more productive and successful treatment and training of the horses.

After several years and attempts to capture an accurate sequence of images of the horse in motion, Muybridge had success through a method he patented in 1879 in which he created a type of outdoor studio with a track for the horse to run on, set against a flat backdrop to eliminate extraneous visual information (see Figure 2.1). Across from the backdrop, twelve cameras were placed at equal horizontal intervals with a cord running from each camera's shutter across the track, perpendicular to the horse's movement. As the horse ran through the space, it tripped the cords, releasing the shutters of the cameras and producing twelve sequential images at 1/1,000th of a second.[14] Muybridge went on to a prolific but also troubled career that has been well documented within and outside the history of photography. More than Janssen and Marey, Muybridge's work is referenced as being a key influence on the development of the photo-finish and on the instantaneous photographers of the late nineteenth century who explored the use of the camera in sport. Central to this was Muybridge's innovation of having the horses rather than the photographers trip the shutter release, something

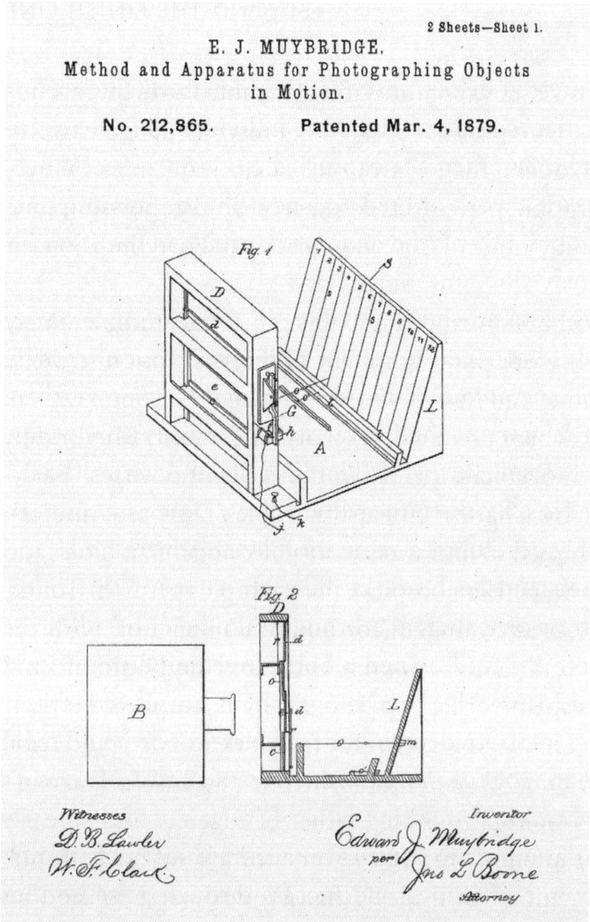

2.1 Muybridge's method for photographing horses in motion, 1879.

that would prove to be a significant problem for early uses of the photograph in sport.

Étienne-Jules Marey was a French physiologist who adopted the camera for use in his studies of human and animal movement. Marey's use of the camera was influenced by Muybridge; however, Marey developed a technique distinct from his contemporary. Where Muybridge produced a series of discrete images produced by discrete cameras, Marey photographed movement onto a single plate (and later film) by using a shutter that captured a slit of space rather than a complete frame. The result was that Marey captured movement within a single photographic frame rather than across a series of frames. Marey referred to this work as "chronophotography." In his early efforts with the camera, Marey borrowed from Jules Janssen and built a "*fusil photographique*" or photographic gun, which exposed the plates through a rotating disc-like apparatus that resembled a revolver. Thus in contrast to Muybridge, who produced a series of discrete images (twelve images produced by twelve cameras), Marey recorded a sequence of movement on a single photographic plate. Marey's success in compressing time and movement onto a single frame of film was an essential precondition for the photo-finish.

There were of course other contributors to this effort, most immediately Ottomar Anschütz, whose work photographing animals in motion strongly paralleled that of Muybridge and Marey. Outside this specific context, there were attempts – many of which predated the work of Janssen, Muybridge, and Marey – to capture movement for use in the medical sciences. Early-nineteenth-century work by Charles Wheatstone, Jules Duboscq, and Jan Evangelista Purkinje attempted to find ways to visually document biological states. And at the famous Salpêtrière hospital, photographers Adrien Tournachon and Albert Londe created images for and in conjunction with the neurological studies of Guillaume-Benjamin Duchenne de Boulogne and Jean-Martin Charcot respectively.[15] Charles Darwin employed Oscar Rejlander to photograph facial expressions for his work in *The Expression of the Emotions in Man and Animals*, published in 1872. And Darwin's polymath cousin, Francis Galton, founding father of eugenics and an early adopter and experimenter in photography, even created a hand-held, "rapid-view instrument for momentary attitudes" that allowed users to see (but not record) motion in a way similar to that found in Muybridge's images.[16]

The camera's use in these and other initiatives within the then-burgeoning development of the natural and social sciences is well known. Summarizing the work of Janssen, Muybridge, Marey, and their contemporaries who were seeking ways to photograph movement, Marta Braun writes: "the photography of movement challenged the generally held belief that the camera can only reproduce what is visible to us (if only we knew how to look). Instantaneous photography of moving objects established a world that is unavailable to our vision – a world beyond the reach of our senses."[17] The ability to capture and represent human and animal movement not only transformed how people represented movement (as in artists and scientists being able to more accurately illustrate their subjects) but also caused something of an epistemological shift. It did so by undermining or at least questioning the authority of the human eye. Long-held beliefs in how humans and animals move, based on what the eye could see, were not just called into question but proven to be emphatically incorrect. The clearest example of this came with Muybridge's work photographing horses, which disproved the long-held belief that horses ran in a way similar to a rocking horse, with front and back legs stretched out simultaneously.

Importantly, though, the camera did not replace the human eye. True to Daston and Galison's arguments on the history of objectivity, there was no abrupt shift in authority from human to machine; rather, the discourse within and outside the photographic community at the time shows that the capabilities and limitations of the human and camera were subject to ongoing and uneasy negotiations.[18] An 1890 article in the journal *Science* effectively illustrates this position. The article is mainly composed of photographs – twelve reproductions of Anschütz's images of a man throwing a javelin – while the limited text marvels at the capabilities of the medium: "It is only by means of photographic apparatus that any single and separate phase of motion can be seized and rendered visible to the eye. Thus it becomes apparent that photography enlarges the power of vision to an extent which is truly wonderful."[19] The first sentence clearly separates the technology of the camera from the capabilities of the human – "only by means" of the camera can we seize motion. But the second sentence rescues the role of the human, positioning the technology as an extension rather than a replacement of the eye. This debate and discussion about the relationship between the human eye and the camera eye (a trope that was often used to humanize the camera) is present throughout photographic literature at the time and is an essential component in the development of the photo-finish. The uneasy relationship between these two types of eyes was of key concern in the development of instantaneous photography.

Instantaneous Photography

The phrase "instantaneous photography" served as a generic descriptor for photographers from the 1850s through the time of Muybridge and beyond who sought to capture motion in their images. Instantaneous photography is not a particularly well-known or acknowledged practice within the history of photography. In one of the rare studies of the topic, Philip Prodger refers to it as a movement, but not in "the classic art historical sense." Instead, he describes it as "founded and orchestrated by a loosely affiliated community of like-minded people. It was what might be described as a *vernacular* movement – a grassroots upheaval, organized around a singular wish: to freeze motion in time."[20] Prodger shows how photographers including Gustave Le Gray, Henry Peach Robinson, Charles Nègre, Oscar Rejlander, George Washington Wilson, David Octavius Hill, Robert Adamson, and André-Adolphe-Eugène Disdéri worked as early as the 1850s to capture scenes of motion in their pictures. These early instantaneous efforts focused primarily on coastal (beach) and city scenes, capturing the movement of ocean waves or busy city centres.

Prodger's writing on instantaneous photography is tied to the larger project of his text, which is an examination of Muybridge's work at Stanford and at the University of Pennsylvania. As such, he discusses early instantaneous experiments to identify the larger photographic context within which Muybridge worked. His discussion ends with the rise of Muybridge, Marey, Anschütz, Eakins, and the other chronophotographers that came to dominate this type of imagery in the late nineteenth century. For Prodger, the instantaneous movement largely ended with the 1888 release of the Kodak camera. By this time, the technical specifications required to capture movement in an image that posed a challenge to photographers of the 1850s, '60s, and '70s had been overcome. For Prodger, this brought a close to the instantaneous movement.

By contrast, my own research on the topic shows that instantaneous photography remained very much alive during the 1880s and 1890s and even into the early twentieth century. Instantaneous photography is continually referenced throughout the 1880s and 1890s in many of the major journals at the time, including *The British Journal of Photography*, *The Photographic Times*, *Outing*, and *The Royal Photographic Society Journal*. And it was equally prevalent in major newspapers. The 1891 American Photographic Conference had a section on "Instantaneous Photography as an Aid to Science, History and Art."[21] A comprehensive instruction manual on instantaneous photography was published in 1896 by Captain Abney.[22] And three years earlier, in his book on amateur photography, W.I. Lincoln Adams describes instantaneous photography as relatively new, writing, "instantaneous photography is but a few years old. The introduction of gelatine dry plates about ten years ago made it possible."[23] Therefore, while it is true that major figures within the history of photography such as Muybridge and

Marey may have moved on from instantaneous work in the closing years of the nineteenth century, the movement did not end with them or the Kodak. The technical issues of capturing instantaneous images – which had been the subject of much of the early discussion – had largely been solved with the introduction of the dry-plate process and the creation of ever-faster shutters and better lenses. This did not end the instantaneous movement; instead, it enabled more photographers to take up instantaneous work and to expand the subject matter of their practice. And it is within this context that instantaneous photographers turned their cameras on sport.

Instantaneous photography and its application to sport was taken up sporadically and infrequently throughout photography and sports and leisure journals of the late nineteenth century. The vast majority of the discussion promoted the camera as a leisure pursuit in itself and/or as a tool to record other leisure pursuits, including sport. Images from this time period document sporting events including "action" shots and posed images of horses, athletes and other people and accoutrements from the sporting scene. Figure 2.2 is a case in point. From 1888 and titled "Winning the High Jump," the image is intended to document a sporting activity and to serve as illustration to the text of the article. It is worth noting that most images of this time, including the high jumper, were referred to as "illustrations from pictures" or "illustrations from instantaneous photographs" in the tables of contents of the magazines and journals (if they were referenced at all). Effective and efficient means of reproducing photographs alongside text, such as with the half-tone process, were not widely adopted until the close of the century. Instead illustrators would copy images directly from photographic prints. This is one reason why the precise origins of the photo-finish are difficult to discern – because photographic negatives or prints of the earliest uses have not yet been found.

The evidentiary use of the photograph in sport was first acknowledged in published form at the start of the 1880s and was occasionally referenced throughout the decade. Muybridge was one of the first, possibly the first, to acknowledge the potential use of the photograph as evidence in sport. His entry in an 1882 issue of *Nature* is therefore worth citing in its entirety:

> Telegrams from Paris on Monday state that the "Prix du Jockey Club" had resulted in what is usually called a "dead heat." It is unnecessary

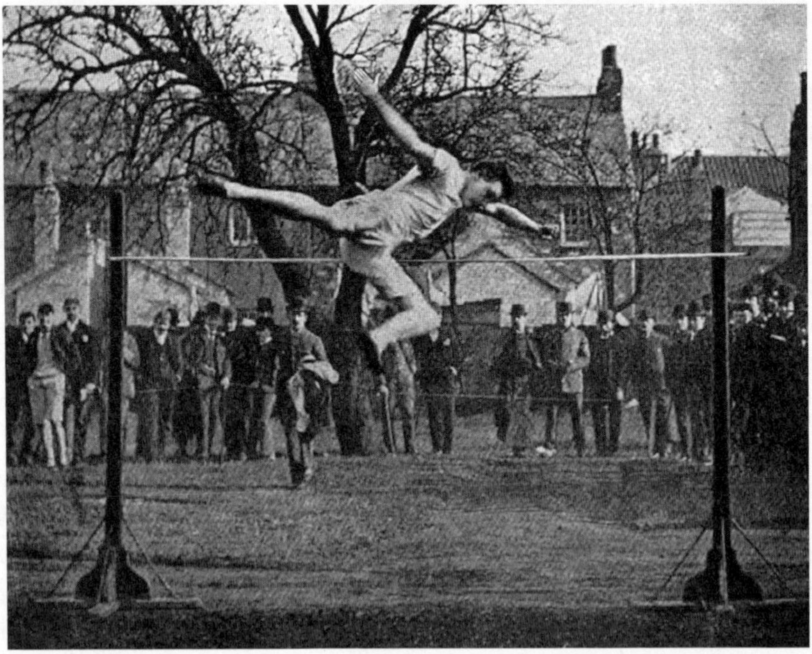

2.2 "Winning the high jump" in *Outing*, 1890.

for me to inform you, that there can be no such thing as a "dead heat." It is called so, I suppose, in consequence of a disagreement among the judges as to which horse first thrusts his nose beyond the winning-post. Are living judges any longer necessary to determine the results of a race? Five years ago I proposed to prove by indisputable evidence the winner of a trotting match which, in consequence of a dispute among the judges, had to be trotted over again. By means of a single thread stretched across the track, and invisible to either horses or their riders, twenty photographic cameras have been made to synchronously record positions impossible for the eye to recognise. With the aid of photography, the astronomer, the pathologist, the chemist, and the anatomist are enabled to pursue the most complex investigations with absolute confidence in the truth it reveals; why should those interested in the trials of speed not avail themselves of the same resource? I venture to predict, in the near future that no race of any importance will be undertaken without the assistance of photography to determine the winner of what might otherwise be a so-called "dead heat."[24]

Beyond Muybridge's words in 1882 there is no record of his use of the camera to determine race results. Even his words suggest that this was simply a proposal rather than an actual use of the camera. Nonetheless, he very clearly outlines the use of the camera as a tool to determine placing in sporting contests. The same prospect was imagined by the editors of the *British Journal of Photography* in 1888, perhaps unaware of Muybridge's claim six years earlier. Under the title "The Camera on the Racecourse," the editors note, "When standing near the judge's box on Epsom racecourse one day recently, we thought of the inestimable service that was capable of being rendered by photography to determine, with unerring accuracy, whether the chestnut passed the winning-post two inches ahead of his rival, and whether in this case the *vox populi* was not the *vox vari.*"[25]

Though the intersection of photography and sport was taken up tangentially in numerous periodicals, the topic received its most significant and sustained discussion in *Outing* magazine, a periodical that ran from 1882 to 1923. The New York–based magazine covered a wide range of sports and leisure activities, including amateur photography. Discussions of photography as a medium and particularly the tensions between its subjectivity and objectivity featured prominently in the first two decades of the magazine, mainly in the form of discussions on how to take a good picture, what types of plates, shutters, and developing solution to use, and favourable subject matter. In this way, the discussion in *Outing* mirrored that in other photographic journals of the time. But as *Outing* was a magazine devoted to outdoor and leisure pursuits, it was not long before writers were singling out sport as a subject worthy of instantaneous work.

W.I. Lincoln Adams was a primary figure in advancing the relationship between sport and photography, writing a series of articles on the topic in *Outing* and elsewhere between 1889 and 1892. Adams was a prominent figure in the world of photography at the time; he was a frequent contributor to several journals including *Outing*, *The Photographic Times*, and *The American Annual of Photography*, and served as the editor of the latter two for several years. He also published an instruction manual, *Amateur Photography: A Practical Guide for the Beginner*, in 1893, which was based on a collection of his previously published journal articles. And an unauthored article on the work of Anschütz in an 1890 edition of the journal *Science* was almost certainly the work of Adams, as significant portions of the text match an essay of his in an 1891 issue of *Outing*.[26] More than any other individual figure of the time, Adams identified and advocated for the specific benefits and capabilities of the camera for use in sport.

In an 1889–90 two-part series, "Instantaneous Photography," Adams mentioned Muybridge's work, noting that his plates were "very valuable acquisitions to science; but considered as pictures they are scarcely satisfactory."[27] For Adams and for many others writing in *Outing*, photographs were to be technically proficient (accurate and objective) but also artistic in the sense that they were supposed to convey a sense of beauty or wonderment. This is what Adams means when saying that Muybridge's work is "scarcely satisfactory" when considered as a "picture." This dual characteristic of being accurate and artistic is something that animated the use of the photograph in sport for decades, further illustrating the uneasy relationship of the presumed objectivity of the photomechanical image and the subjectivity of human operators.

In the same article Adams makes specific mention of the dead heat – which is one of the earliest discussions of the phenomenon as it relates to the camera:

> Ernest Marx, a young photographer of Plainfield, N.J. has been successful in determining the winner in close or "dead heats" of racing contests. According to his photographs there is no such thing as a "dead" heat – one contestant must always be at least an infinitesimal distance ahead of the others; and by his camera, stationed immediately under the wire and automatically exposed by electricity at the right moment, the actual winner may always be known.[28]

The bulk of Adams's article is taken up with discussion of the technical apparatus needed to make instantaneous pictures, including a tripod and finder to be attached to the camera. The second essay in this series goes into further detail on the technical specifications for making instantaneous pictures, including a list of the best dry-plate makers and those companies producing celluloid film. There is little discussion of sport in this article, though Adams notes that athletics makes a particularly good subject for instantaneous photographers and cites the work of Ernest Marx as being especially noteworthy. The essay includes several pictures depicting instantaneous work, including a horse being exercised, a man riding a bicycle down a staircase, and a man returning a tennis ball (Figure 2.3).

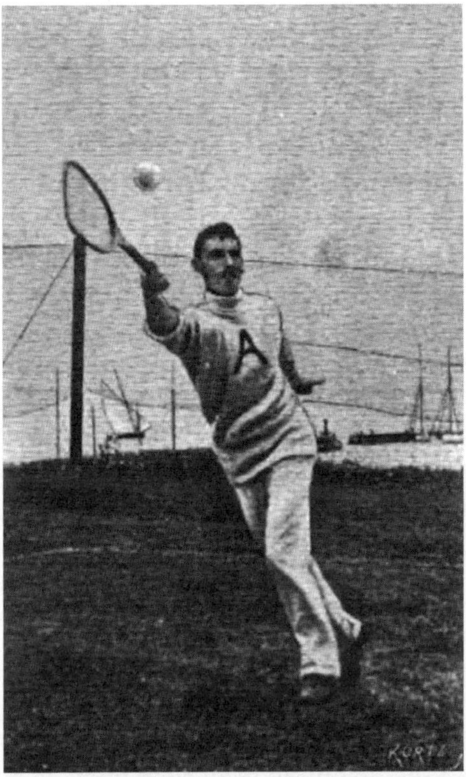

2.3 "Returning a ball" in *Outing*, 1890.

Marx is identified by both Jerome O'Neill and J.P. Bovay as being the first photo-finish photographer, or at least having produced the first photo-finish image. Unfortunately, there is very little documentation of Marx or his work and I have not been able to locate any of his images. The existing sources refer to his work in 1888 (without relevant citation), after which he largely disappears from the historical record, particularly as it relates to photographing races. An 1889 story in the *Seattle Post Intelligencer* includes an interview with Marx where he describes his process of taking instantaneous pictures of horse races. As part of the interview he shows the reporter his image of a June 27, 1888 race at Sheepshead Bay where Eolian finished two lengths ahead of Fitzroy.[29] The image is not reproduced as part of the story, but it is enough to note that the winning horse finished ahead by two lengths, meaning that placing would easily have been determined by eyesight and that Marx's photograph would have been unnecessary. In contrast to Marx's general absence from the historical record, his contemporary, John

C. Hemment, has an active presence in professional and popular presses of the time. Hemment was the leading practitioner of finish-line photography at the time and many of his images were printed in newspapers and sports periodicals. In addition, Hemment's images exist across a few disparate locations, with the Keeneland Library in Lexington, Kentucky, housing the largest collection with several thousand of his photographs (only some of which are finish-line images).

John C. Hemment and Photographing Finishes

Hemment was born in Cambridgeshire, England, in 1862 and moved to the United States in 1879. He was an accomplished athlete in England, particularly in ice skating, and continued this trend in the United States setting the 200-yard record in 1895.[30] Hemment took up photography in 1884–85, as he recollected in newspaper and magazine articles of the 1890s.[31] And given his athletic interests it is unsurprising that he often turned his camera on sport. He was hired as the official photographer for several horse-racing tracks in the United States and his images were published in *Collier's Weekly*, *The Illustrated Sporting News*, the *New York Journal*, and *Harper's Weekly.* He became a successful and recognized photographer relatively quickly to the extent that in 1898 he was hired by the United States government to photograph the Spanish-American War, specifically the wreck of the USS *Maine* in Cuba. This resulted in his 1898 book on the topic, *Cannon and Camera: Sea and Land Battles of the Spanish-American War in Cuba, Camp Life, and the Return of the Soldiers*. And it is interesting to note that Adams wrote the introduction to the book, once again citing Hemment's talent in photographing athletics: "Mr. Hemment has been a recognised leader for a number of years among the most skillful photographers in the country, especially in instantaneous work, having successfully photographed … the most difficult athletic events. An athlete, also, himself, he was peculiarly well fitted to undertake the hazardous enterprise of photographing the scenes and deeds of the recent war with Spain."[32] While the book is primarily a collection of images, Hemment's own writing is instructive in understanding the positioning of the photographer and his images. In an Appendix titled "Hints to Amateur and Professional Photographers," Hemment stresses that while good equipment is a must, it is ultimately the skill of the photographer that produces good pictures. He uses a military metaphor to explain: "the camera is like the gun of the war ship: while the gun can do the deadly execution, while shot and shell are brought to a state of perfection by our skilled artisans, the man must be behind the gun. So it is with the camera."[33]

Hemment continued his war photography at the beginning of the First World War as the official photographer for the American Red Cross.[34] He is cited as a distinguished figure in the field of big-game hunting,[35] and he also worked as an official photographer and motion photographer on expeditions to Africa and the Arctic.[36] In this last capacity he even wrote an article for *Motion Picture Magazine* on his "search for the missing link," a "half-man, half-monkey" that he intended to photograph.[37] There is reference to Hemment attempting to motion-record an entire cycling race of the Kings County Wheelmen, of which Hemment was a member, so that it could be played back to members for their entertainment.[38] Hemment married and had children, and while there are records of the deaths of his wife and two sons, no such record exists for Hemment. A 1933 notice in the *Los Angeles Times* states that Hemment and his son Harold had gone missing (and were presumed to be in Los Angeles) but no update was given. His son's death notice is evidence that the son was found, but there is no indication of Hemment's whereabouts or death post-1933.[39]

Returning to Adams and *Outing*, in a subsequent article, "Some Modern Achievements of the Camera," Adams shifted attention to Hemment, whom he would go on to work with for years. His discussion of Hemment underscores his favourable view of the photographer:

> Mr. John C. Hemment, of Brooklyn, has made the camera an indispensable adjunct to the judges of all close finishes. He is the official photographer of the Coney Island Racing Association, the Monmouth Park Association, the Saratoga Association and many other of the leading racing associations. All close finishes are photographed by him. He photographs in less than the one-thousandth part of a second, and thus succeeds in securing pictures of the fleetest horses or runners perfectly "sharp" in every particular.[40]

Adams takes up the photographing of sport in significant detail in a second two-part series in 1892, "Photography and Athletics." And here he continues to highlight Hemment, whom he refers to as "the leading photographer of athletic pictures in this country, if not in the world."[41] Most importantly, Adams specifically highlights Hemment's work on using the camera to determine placing in sporting races. On Hemment he writes,

> it was through his love of athletics and all manly out-of-door sport that Mr. Hemment first became interested in photography. He had often been struck with the difficulty which judges encountered in trying to determine the winner in particularly close heats. It occurred to him that an instantaneous photograph of the finish would, in all cases, be reliable means for determining just who the winner really was, and accordingly he began to experiment with a camera to attain this desired end.[42]

Adams then quotes Hemment, who continues this origin story: "I took up photography seven years ago [1885] as a means to determine the real winner in all close athletic contests."[43] Hemment describes how his pictures attracted the attention of the press, enabling him to charge for their use. He then speaks directly to the authority of instantaneous photographs: "some of my pictures showed that what had been considered 'dead heats' were really not *dead* at all. In fact, my photographs proved, what I had long suspected, that there was in reality no such thing as a 'dead heat;' and having been so successful in catching distinct pictures of close finishes, my photographs naturally came to be looked upon as valuable in deciding the result of all close contests."[44]

The second article in this series continues the discussion of Hemment's work but is a precise description of his developing process, specifically his work in the darkroom. Adams quotes Hemment noting that the use of photography to determine placing in athletic events is in its infancy but on the rise quickly, with Hemment predicting that "the time is not distant when an official photographer will be attached to every racing association and athletic club in the country as an indispensable official."[45] He continues by stressing the evidentiary authority of the image in something of a call to arms to amateur photographers. On the use of the camera to determine placing, he notes, "Photography has a great mission to fill in this direction. It alone can establish beyond doubt the existence of truths that have been heretofore regarded as mere hypotheses. Let us all unite," he concludes, "in assisting our beautiful art to the fulfillment of the greatest expectations which have been cherished in its behalf."[46] Adams closes the piece by noting that many of Hemment's predictions are coming true and that "the instantaneous photographer is also a familiar figure now on the occasion of any athletic performance of importance. His value as an impartial judge is being more widely recognized every day."[47]

The relationship and work of Adams and Hemment must be seen as foundational to the photo-finish. Notwithstanding the celebratory tone of their writing and comments, the two brought early, public, and dedicated attention to the use of the camera to determine placing in sport. Where Adams was the lead promoter of the photograph as an evidentiary tool in sport, Hemment was its chief practitioner, and both were well-established and well-regarded members of the photographic community at the time. Together with their contemporaries, Adams and Hemment formed, through their conversations and writings, a small but growing network of athletes, photographers, and writers that began to outline the possibilities of using a camera to determine placing in sport.

Both Adams and Hemment are almost entirely absent from the literature on the history of photography. Hemment is a particularly interesting omission in that he was a highly prolific photographer. He photographed sports for several decades, documenting the people, places, and scenes of various sporting contests. And though this type of documentary work dominated his practice, he was also specifically interested in using the camera to determine placing. This latter interest was noted by several reporters and writers of the time but was also explicitly identified by Hemment in one of his infrequent publications. In an 1891 essay, "Photography Applied to Sports," in the *American Annual of Photography*, he speaks directly to the evidentiary use of the camera: "Photographing the finishes of races, as an aid to the judges, and to prevent the possibility of a wrong decision is, I believe, the latest phase of its existence, as I am not aware this was ever done until my appointment as Official Photographer to the Coney Island Jockey Club at the beginning of the Spring Meeting."[48] He continues to identify concerns about wrong decisions in sporting contests and positions the camera as a technological solution to the fallibility of the human official: "There has been at different times a good deal of dissatisfaction expressed at the decision of the judges in close races. Handicapped as the human eye is by a certain slowness and persistence of vision, it is not safe to trust at all times to its evidence. The photographic eye has no such limits."[49] And finally he positions his own work with the camera as a solution to the increasing problem of decision-making in sport: "Therefore there arose a demand for a more infallible arbiter than the most accurate judge who ever awarded a race. Nor has this demand remained unjustified, for on several occasions the judges have awaited the development of my plates before posting the winning numbers."[50] This last claim is further supported in a follow-up article by Hemment in 1892 where he notes, "I have worked three hours to bring up four plates of rapid exposures made when it was raining, but it was necessary to have them to know the positions of racing horses at the finish, and I got them."[51]

Hemment's comments in the *American Annual of Photography* are interesting for many reasons, not least of which is how they speak to the process of decision-making in sports at the time. Up to the mid-1880s the winners of sports contests were determined by a human judge (or judges). In terms of horse racing, judges stood in a booth at the finish line quite literally looking for the winner. Figure 2.4 of the "Judges Stand" by Hemment effectively shows this organization. Yet there was growing concern or dissatisfaction – found in newspapers of the era – around judging, specifically the potential for error in close races. And so it is within this context that Hemment took up work at various racetracks and actively promoted his role (and the role of his images) as infallible judge.

Hemment's comments also point to the dual role of his images. Images of race finishes could be used as an aid to judges after the fact to confirm or refute a decision that had already been made. Or, more importantly and innovatively, they could be used to make the decision. The images would of course still have to be read by judges, but the distinction is important: in the former, the determination is made based on viewing a live event; whereas in the latter, the determination is made based on viewing a photograph of a live event. This latter use is especially noteworthy given the relatively rudimentary technology available at the time. Where Hemment's pictures in the 1890s took as long as three hours to develop, in twenty-first-century sport, decisions are made and results are posted on stadia scoreboards almost instantaneously.

Finally, Hemment's comments are interesting in that they reflect the then-developing episteme of mechanical objectivity as taken up by Daston and Galison. Hemment and his contemporaries actively worked to position the

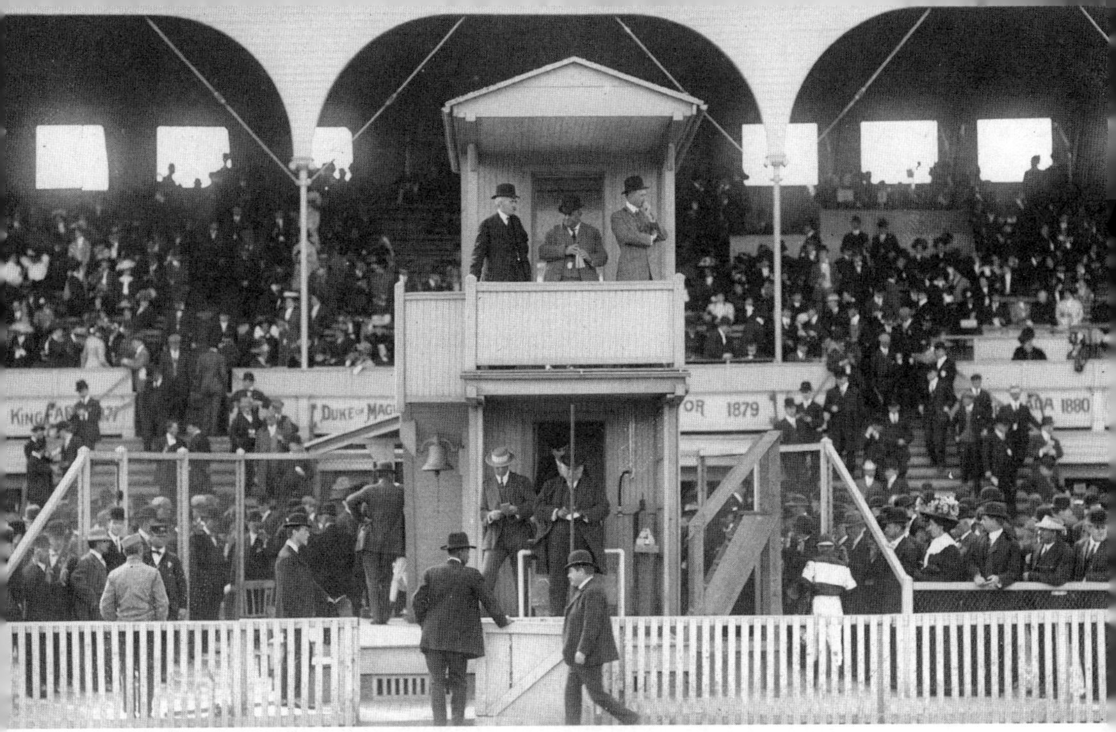

2.4 John C. Hemment, "Judges Stand at Pimlico Race Course," 1909.

camera as an objective tool of representation, especially as measured against what was perceived as the inherent subjectivity of human officials. Hemment refers to the human eye as "handicapped" and "not safe to trust" and positions the camera eye as a "more infallible arbiter." This infallibility was directly tied to the mechanistic nature of the camera. In this way, Hemment's pictures and the comments by him, Adams, and others benefited from and contributed to a growing discourse of mechanical objectivity. Within such a space, the camera's claims to infallibility were co-constructed alongside and in opposition to the fallibility of the human eye.

Hemment further outlined the process for taking finish-line images in an 1891 interview published in the *Brooklyn Eagle*.[52] He used a camera with two achromatic lenses so that he could produce two images in rapid succession "without moving the plate or the camera or changing my position." He also employed a separate lens mounted to the top of the camera as a finder, so that he could track the horses as they raced and release the shutter at the precise moment the horses crossed the finish line. He was stationed directly perpendicular to the finish with his camera "on a line with the wire [finish line]." And to create a strong contrast against the horses' heads, Hemment had "a white background, with a line representing the wire ... directly opposite on the other side of the track." He also noted that at the

Saratoga track he had a darkroom adjacent to his photographing station so that he could develop prints immediately. Finally, there is a much later reference, in 1939, that Hemment's setup also included a line that ran across the track, connecting the line of his camera with the line on the whiteboard and finishing post, though I have not found much evidence of this in Hemment's images.[53]

From Theory to Practice: Hemment's Finish-Line Photographs

The idealized setup described by Hemment is most clearly seen in an image he included with his 1891 essay in the *American Annual of Photography* (Figure 2.5). The image shows that Hemment was at close to ground level, perpendicular to the finish, and the winning horse is photographed at the precise moment it crosses the line and set against a contrasting white backdrop. In this way, "Taragon v. St. Luke" could well have been necessary in the decision-making process, as the two horses are incredibly close at the line. Nonetheless, Hemment makes no mention in the article of the role this image played in the race. A second image included in the article shows a similar but less ideal setup (Figure 2.6). The image shows La Tosca crossing the finish line first but Hemment's positioning renders the white backdrop useless. And the clear separation between the horses means that the image would not have been necessary to determine placing.

A similar configuration is present in what is one of Hemment's most famous images, at least within the horse-racing community. This is the image documenting the finish of the Salvator v. Tenny race from 1890 (Figure 2.7). The racing historian Philip von Borries refers to this as likely the first photo-finish image, a claim backed by Maarten Vanvolsem in his book on strip photography.[54] The image generally conforms to the idealized configuration described by Hemment. He is perpendicular to the finish line and is clearly positioned in or near the judging booth, as there are no judges or booth visible on the other side of the track. There is a white backdrop with a black vertical line flush with the finishing post and there appears to be a line running across and above the track to Hemment's position. This particular configuration would help in determining placing. Nonetheless, there is a major flaw in the configuration in that Hemment's elevated position renders the white backdrop useless. Presumably the race judges were in the lower

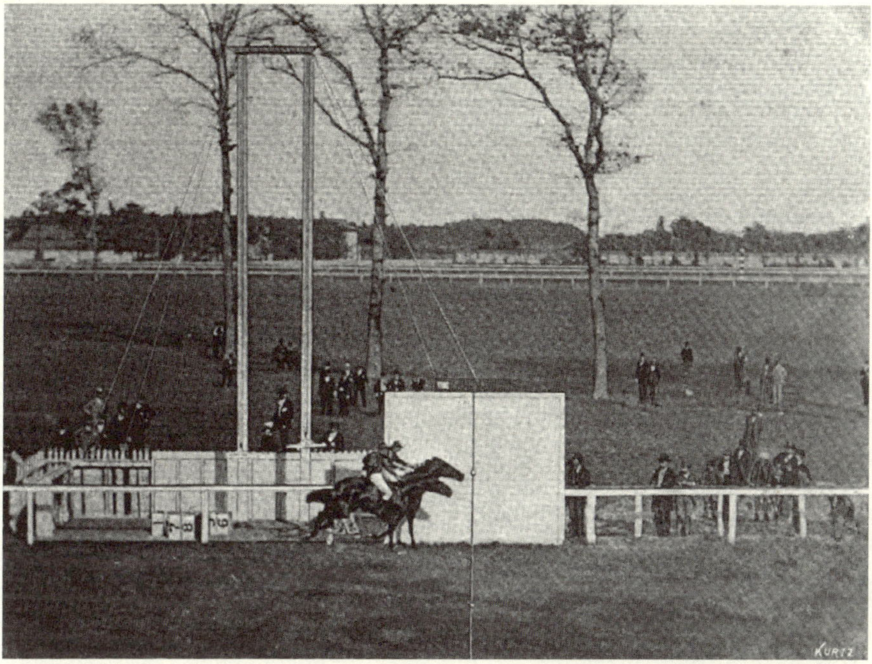

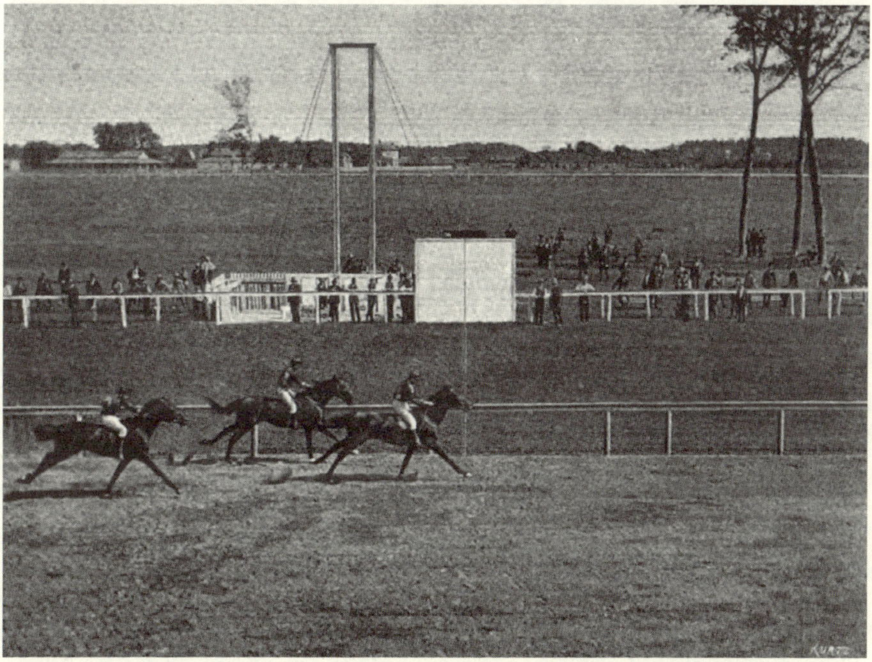

2.5 *Top* John C. Hemment, "Finish Between Taragon and St. Luke," 1891.

2.6 *Bottom* John C. Hemment, "La Tosca – 19 ½ yards per second," 1891.

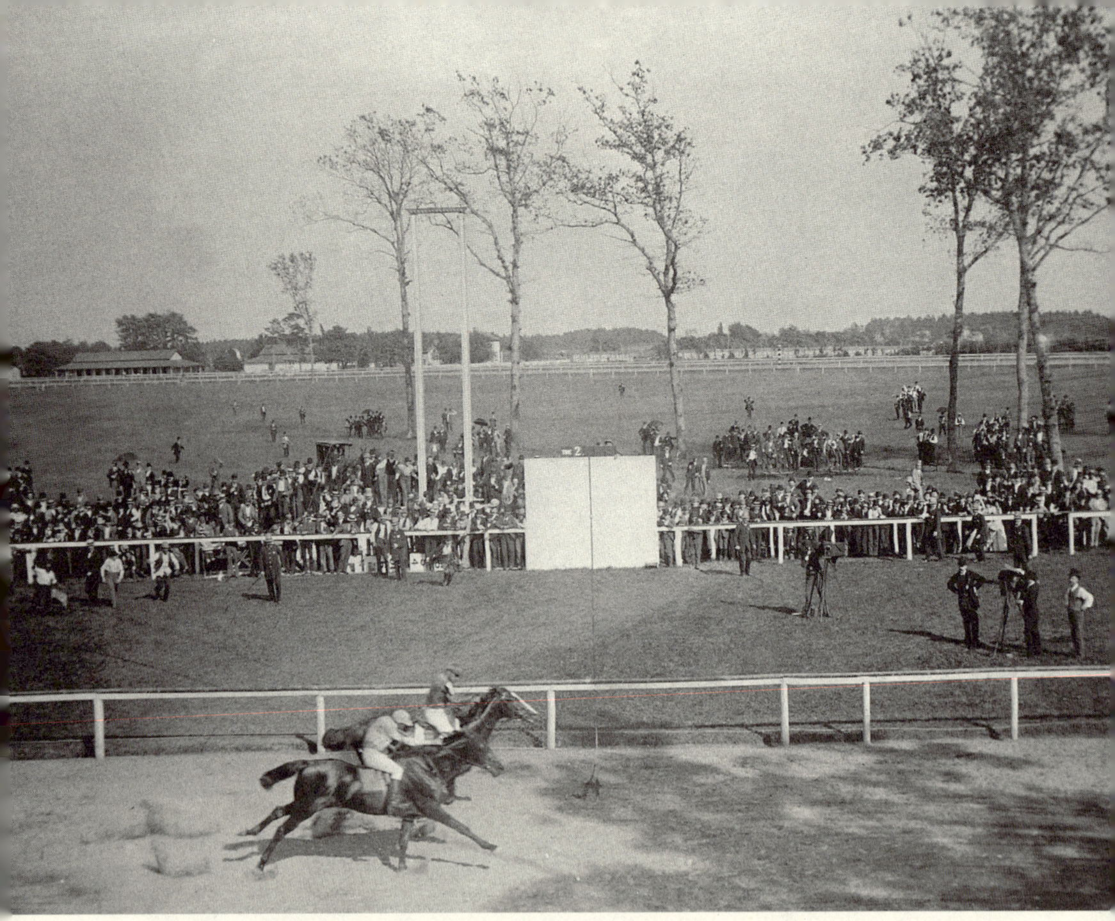

2.7 John C. Hemment, finish of the Salvator v. Tenny Match Race, 1890.

portion of the booth and could use the backdrop for their own determination. The image is also problematic as a photo-finish for another reason. The horses are not photographed at the moment they cross the finish line but slightly before. Therefore, while it may be reasonable to assume that the horse on the inside of the track won the race, the result could not be argued to be conclusive based on the image. As a result, and in contrast to Von Borries and Vanvolsem, I argue that the Salvator v. Tenny image could only have been useful as a supplement to the judge's decision; it could not have been used to make the decision. It is a photograph of a finish, but it is not a photo-finish.

Importantly, this seeming anomaly in Hemment's configuration is actually found repeatedly in his horse-racing images. In fact the idealized configuration described by Hemment is the exception rather than the rule: many of his surviving finish-line images (from a sampling of surviving photographic prints) veer significantly from the idealized configuration described in his writing. Figures 2.8 through 2.13 exemplify the point and are indicative of Hemment's finish-line images. Hemment tended to be positioned at an oblique angle, slightly elevated, and located separately from the judges. Figures 2.12 and 2.13 show the white backdrop similar to the Salvator v. Tenny race, Figures 2.10 and 2.11 show a black background with contrasting white line, and Figures 2.8 and 2.9 have no backdrop (2.8 does not even include a finish line). None of the images show a line running over the track connecting the backdrop to the finishing post. These inconsistencies, especially when viewed against the more idealized version in the Taragon v. St Luke image, suggest that these images function more as a record of the races in question than as decision aids used in determining placing.

There is another inconsistency in Hemment's finish-line images that is particularly important and follows that in the famous Salvator v. Tenny image. In the images that do show a finish line, and particularly those where a backdrop is present (exemplified in Figures 2.10 through 2.13), the horses are recorded not at the moment of crossing the finish line but at moments before or after. This is due to a key limitation of race finish photography at this time. Despite the advanced technology available in the form of dry-plates and celluloid film, fast shutters and electromagnetic shutter releases, a human operator was still needed to trip the shutter release. Hemment's setup allowed him to follow the horses around the track through the use of a finder, but capturing the precise moment of finishing required equally precise and consistent reaction times. As Hemment noted, "A lightning perception is absolutely necessary. When the impression is taken in such a small fraction of a second's time one dare not anticipate. He must see the horse's nose plumb with the wire before he touches the spring."[55]

The inconsistencies in Hemment's images are due to the novelty of the practice and because the particular configuration used by Hemment differed by racetrack. Nonetheless, there are two important conclusions that can be drawn. First is that Hemment's images could not be used to determine placing. Without being perpendicular to the finish line, set against the white or black backdrop, and taken close to the action, these images could not be used to break a tie or a dead heat. What then was their purpose, and what of Hemment's role as official race photographer at numerous racetracks? The most likely explanation is that Hemment's work as a track photographer was primarily that of documenting the racing scene. Indeed the vast majority of Hemment's racing images in the Keeneland Library are scenes

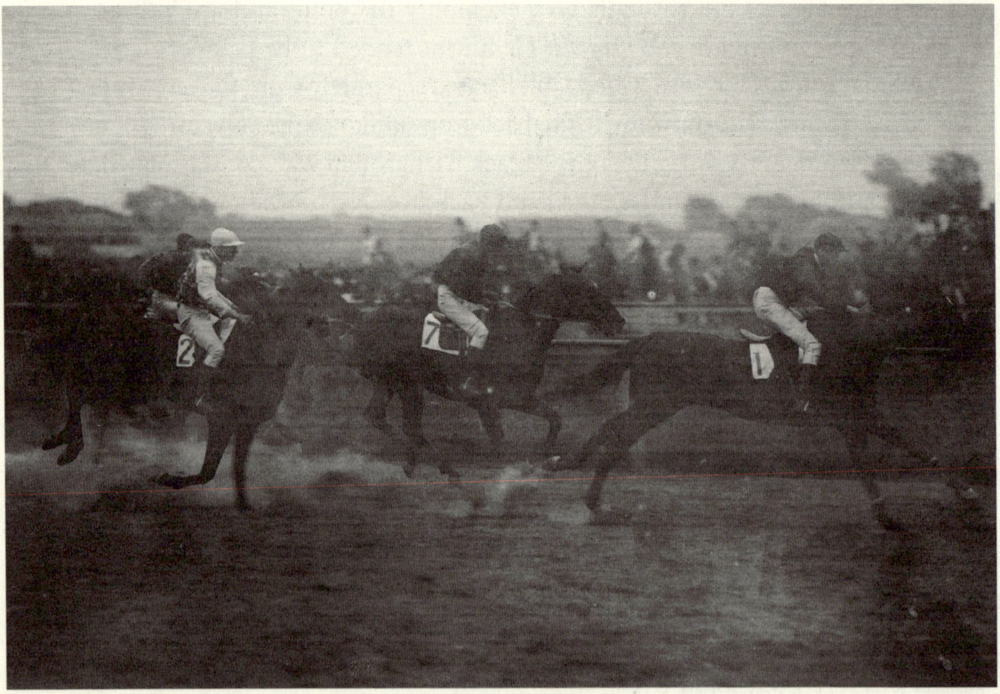

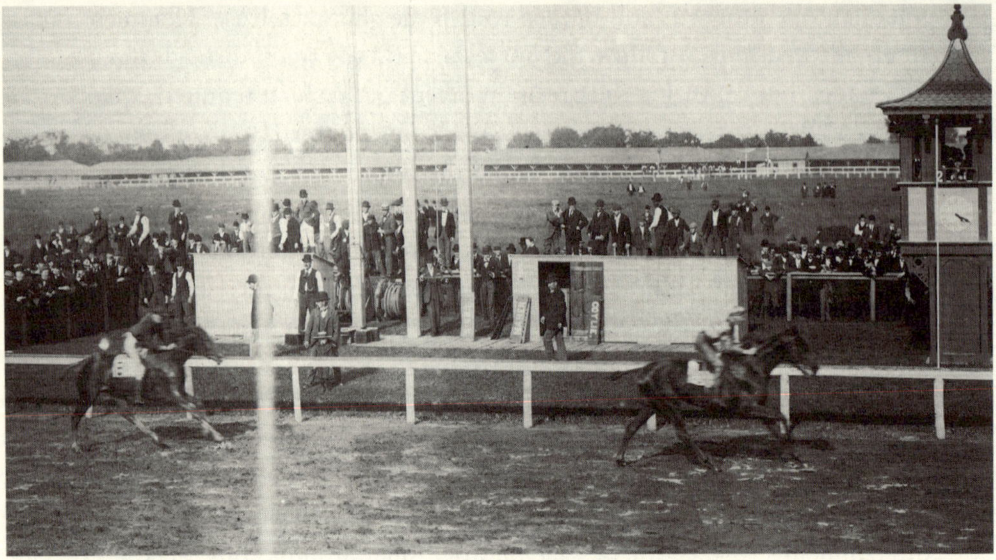

2.8 *Top* John C. Hemment, finish of the Suburban Handicap at Sheepshead Bay Race Track, 1896.

2.9 *Bottom* John C. Hemment, finish of the Brooklyn Handicap at Gravesend Race Track, 1897.

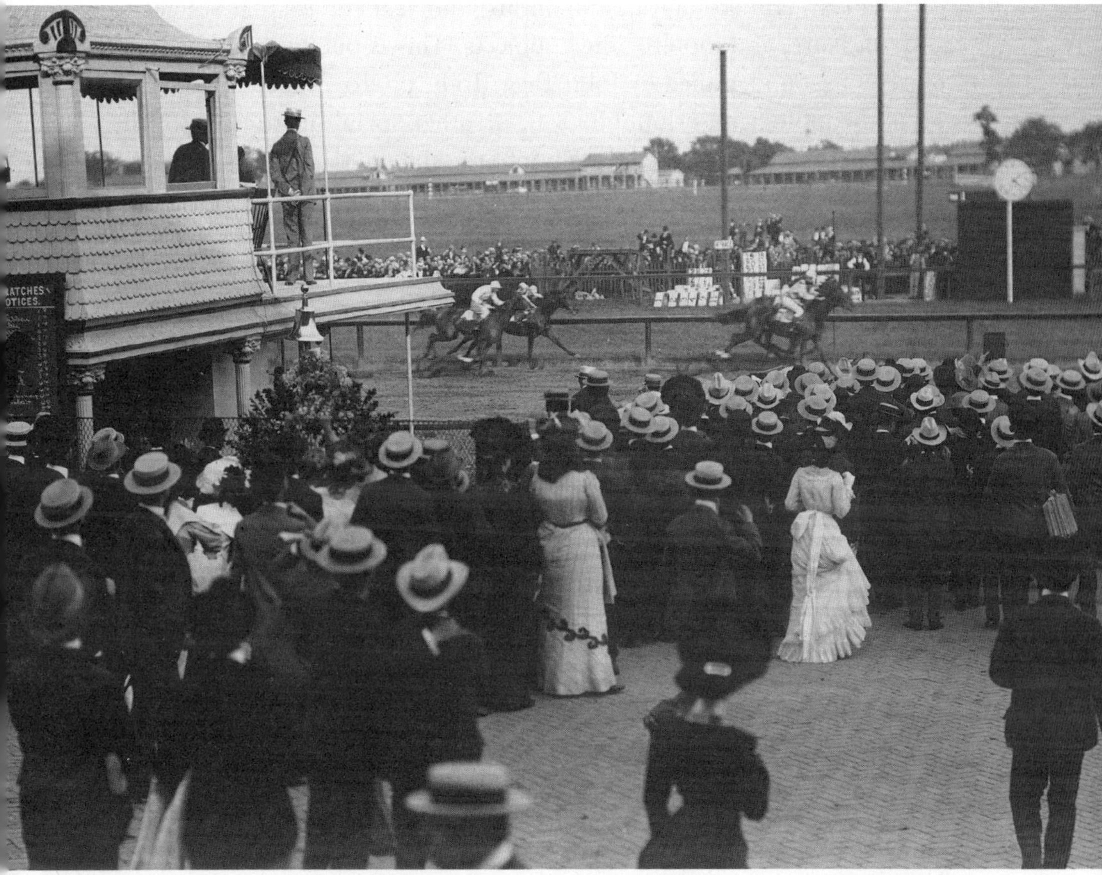

2.10 John C. Hemment, finish of the 1902 Futurity at Sheepshead Bay Race Track, 1902.

of patrons, jockeys, horses, the racetrack, and other accoutrements of the racing community. Even the bulk of his finish-line images embody this documentary rather than evidentiary function. In this way Hemment's images function as part of modern sport's quest for records by documenting the expanding, increasingly regulated horse-racing industry.

The second, related, conclusion follows directly from the first. Hemment's work, and particularly the ideal configuration positioning him perpendicular to the finish and with the horses set against a white backdrop, exemplifies the modernist push to rationalize and standardize the live sporting environment. The horses set against the white or black backdrop recall not only the clear precedents in the work of Marey and Muybridge but also those in larger medical, criminological, and anthropological studies that sought to record, measure, and monitor their subjects. This is one of the "burdens" of representation identified by John Tagg. To be photographed by medical, legal, anthropological, criminological, or other social institutions of the nineteenth century was to be brought into the state in the form of a record. Alan Sekula refers to this as the "bureaucratic-clerical-statistical system" of the archive.[56] And despite its specific use in hospitals, prisons, schools, or other social institutions, the underlying goal was the same: to systematically record the subject, compiling increasing numbers of records and information. In a similar way, Hemment's experiments with finish-line photography contributed to the modernizing tendencies of horse racing and other sporting communities as they sought to document and, ultimately, control and regulate their practices. Hemment's photographs are thus key early examples of Guttmann's quest for records and of the camera's role in abstracting the live sporting environment into a set of static documents, in this case photographic records of the horse-racing scene.

The Commercial Market for Sport Photography

Before leaving Hemment and instantaneous photographs of sport, it is important to note that there is also evidence at this time of a developing commercial market for finish-line work, in terms of both pictures and the equipment necessary to take them. Instantaneous photographs of sport (not just of finishes) found a welcome home in the rapidly expanding newspaper business. The desire for this type of imagery was identified by several writers and photographers at the time, including Hemment, who wrote in 1891, "the day is not far distant when an official photographer will be attached as an indispensable officer to every racing club and athletic association in the country. More than that, the great daily papers will keep a photographer on their staffs, for illustrated articles are an important feature of latter-day journalism."[57] As with his prediction that instantaneous photographers would serve as infallible judges at all important sporting events, his prediction about their role as journalists is equally exaggerated. Nonetheless, photographs of sport did play an important role in the burgeoning news market.

Figures 2.14 and 2.15 point to this market for images and are fascinating objects in relation to the photo-finish. Figure 2.14 shows a dramatic scene

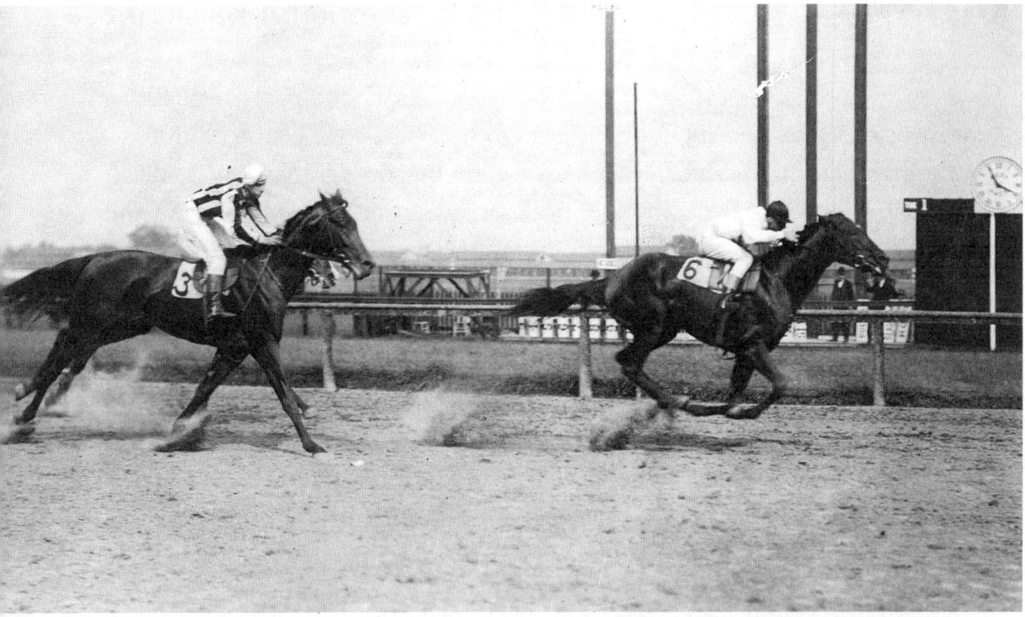

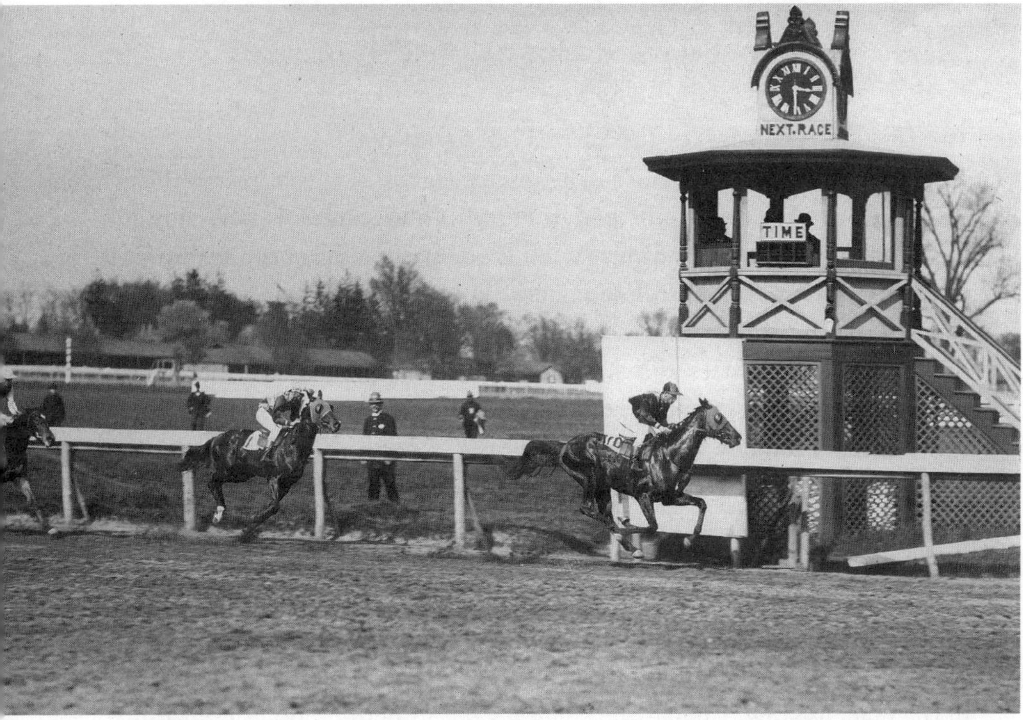

2.11 *Top* John C. Hemment, Goldsmith winning the Equality Stakes at Sheepshead Bay Track, 1903.

2.12 *Bottom* John C. Hemment, Song and Wine winning the Laureate Stakes at Morris Park Race Course, 1904.

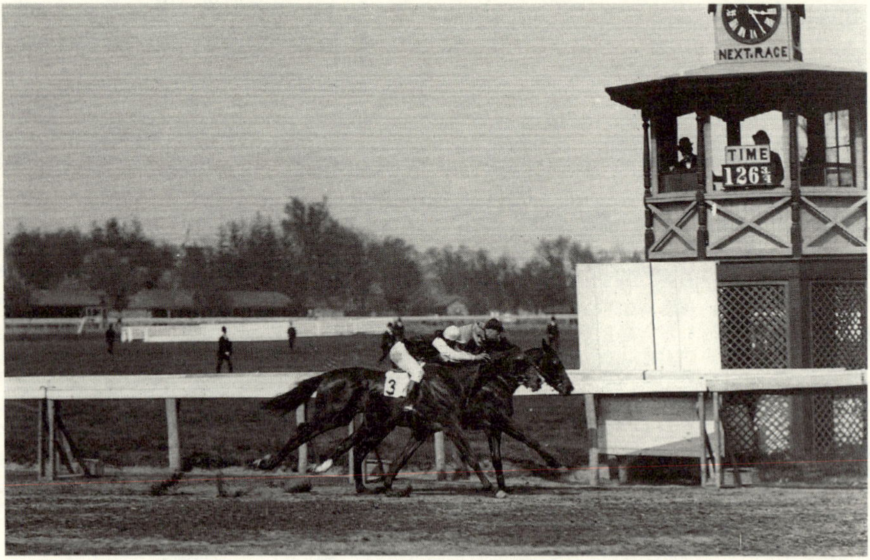

2.13 John C. Hemment, Dolly Spanker winning the New Rochelle Handicap at Morris Park Race Course, 1904.

with horses racing to the finish. The inset image is an illustration of Hemment's photograph of the Brooklyn Handicap (Figure 2.9), showing his finish-line image configuration. Figure 2.15 shows a series of illustrations based on Hemment's finish-line images taken from the 1890 Spring Meet at the Sheepshead Bay racetrack. What is most interesting is that the illustrations show the horses at the precise moment of crossing the line. Yet we know from Hemment's surviving photographs that he rarely was able to capture this moment, typically getting the exposure before or after the horses crossed the line. It is therefore highly likely that the illustrations have been manipulated to further heighten their drama for the reading public. Yet, in the articulation of these illustrations as having been produced from Hemment's finish-line photographs, the images borrow the camera's claims to objectivity to suggest (falsely) that the illustrations accurately represent the race finishes. In doing so, these images further promote the objectivity of the machine-made image and suggest yet another function of finish-line photography, that of content for sports journalism and sports media. In this latter sense, Hemment's images serve as precursors to the sport/media complex of the mid-to-late twentieth century.

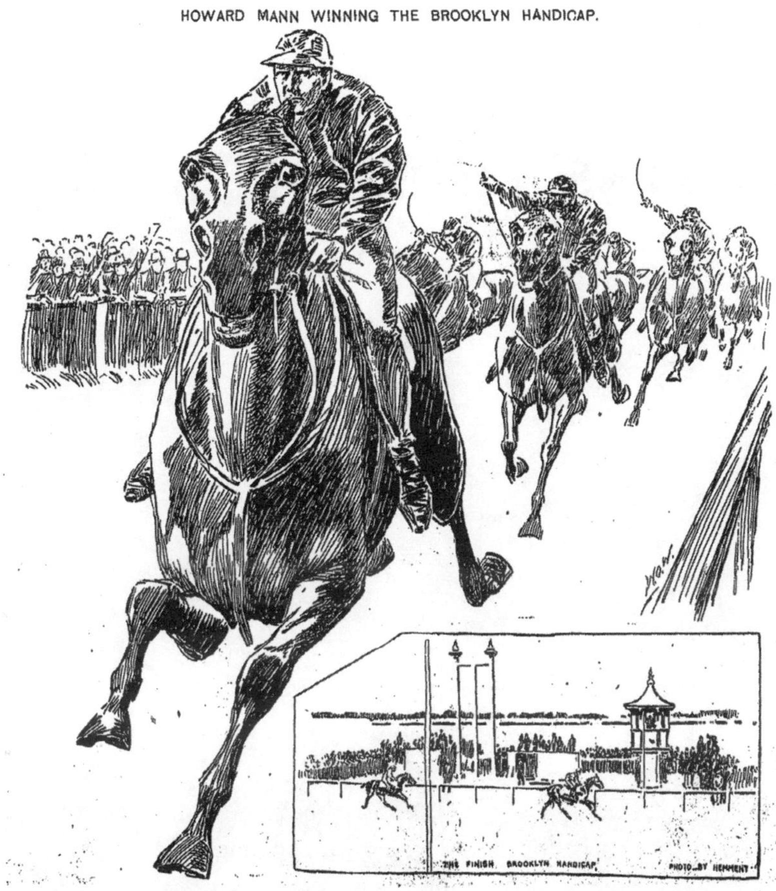

2.14 Illustrations based on Hemment's photographs. From *The World* (New York), 1897. The inset image is a reproduction of Hemment's photograph of the finish of the Brooklyn Handicap, shown as Figure 2.9.

In addition to this market within the news industry, there was also recognition of the value of the camera for the racing and gambling industries. In fact the origins of the photo-finish cannot be separated from the financial interests of determining placing, especially in horse racing. An editorial in an 1888 issue of the *British Journal of Photography* spoke directly to the commercial potential of the photo-finish. Concluding the article titled "The Camera on the Racecourse," the editors offer the following:

> We submit, for the benefit of enterprising professional photographers, the hint that a well taken photograph of this class would prove a veritable gold mine to the possessor of the negative, as not only every

CLOSE FINISHES AT

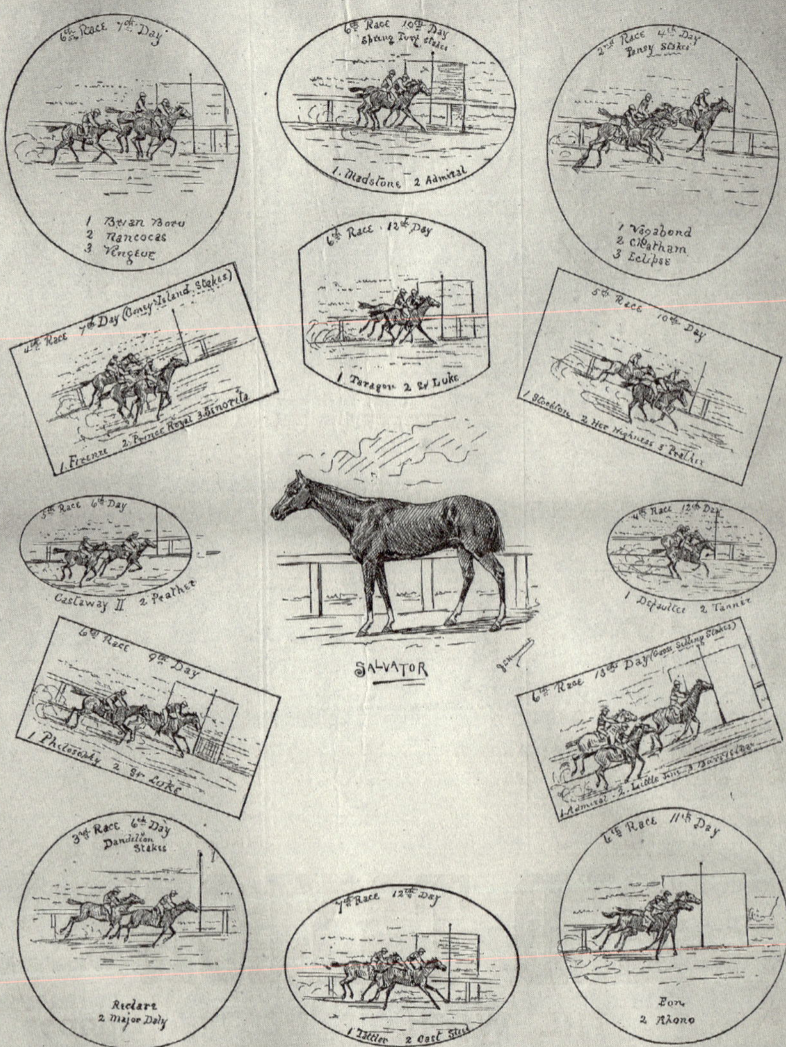

INSTANTANEOUS PHOTOGRAPHS OF THE CLOSEST FINISHES AT THE SPRING MEETING OF 1890 OF THE CONEY ISLAND JOCKEY CLUB.

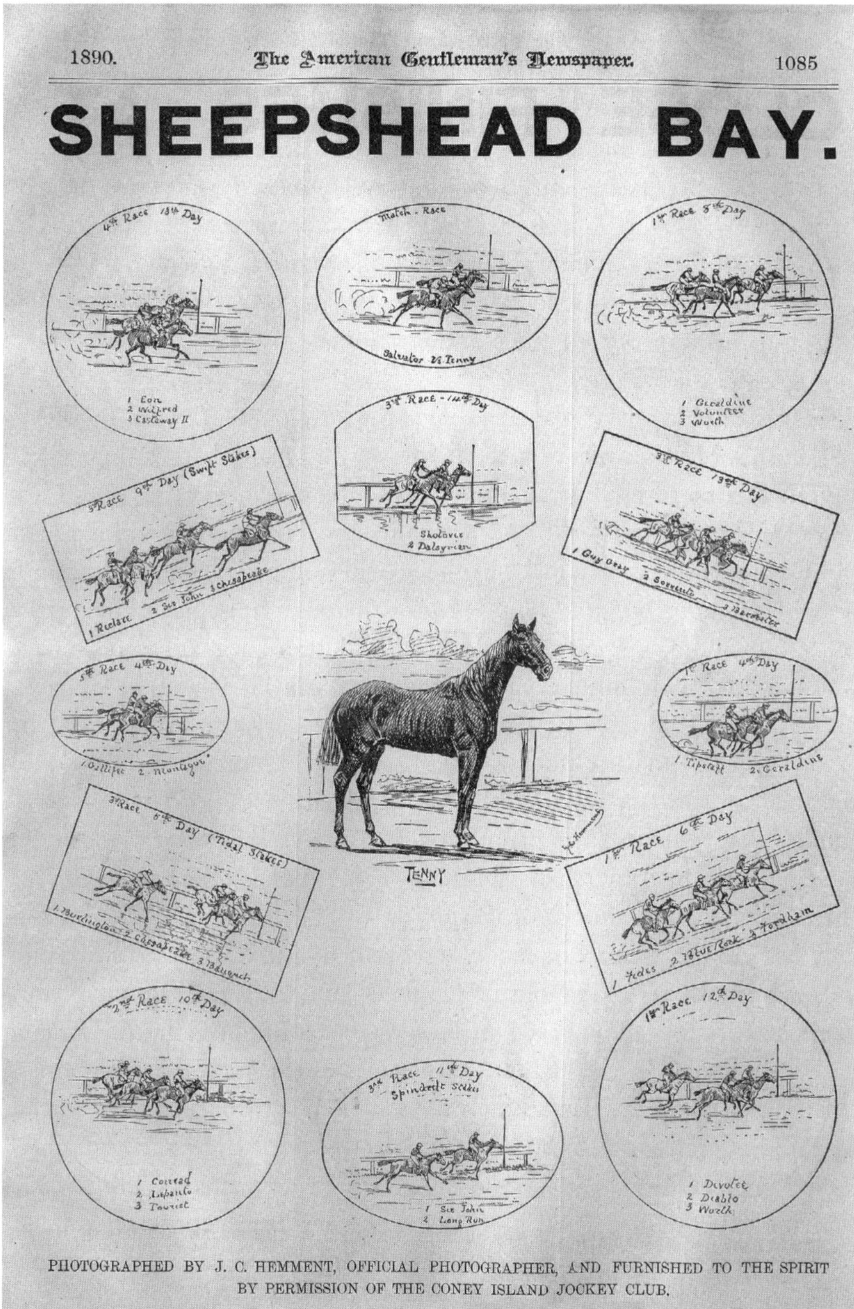

2.15 Illustrations based on Hemment's 1890 work at Sheepshead Bay. From the *Spirit of the Times*, 1890.

> devotee of the turf and every owner of a racehorse would become a patron, but also the large majority of the betting fraternity and sutlers of the course in obscure parts of the world.[58]

An 1891 essay on Hemment's work in the *Brooklyn Eagle* states the case more directly: "Hence it seems reasonable to suppose that people who risk large sums of money in important races will sooner or later demand proof of the judge's decisions, when the finishes are in doubt, in the shape of an instantaneous impression, taken and developed on the spot by the official photographer of the track."[59]

Adams and Hemment played a role in the development of this market as well. Both specifically mentioned the type of equipment that was best for instantaneous pictures. For example, Prosch shutters were favoured and publicized in the writings of both Adams and Hemment, and Hemment spoke of a custom camera made by the Scovill Company. In an 1892 edition of the *American Annual of Photography*, there is a full-page ad for Prosch shutters, including one called the "Athlete" Shutter. The text for this specific shutter reads: "Our 'athlete' shutter has all the movements of the 'Triplex,' but has been produced with special reference to very rapid movement, for use on Athletic and Race-track work. It is a decided success. The 'king' photographer of sporting events, John C. Hemment, uses it exclusively."[60] A similar ad appears in 1898 promoting the Athlete Shutter at 1/300th of a second and the Special Athlete Shutter at 1/600th of a second (Figure 2.16). The *American Annual of Photography* was published by the Scovill Company and Adams was a frequent contributor to and editor of the journal.

This is not to say that Adams, Hemment, and others conspired to commercialize photographing race finishes, or that journalists did the same in relation to sports entertainment. Rather it is to highlight that even at this early stage, a commercial market for the practice was being explored, further expanding the network of bodies and objects – the "sporting community" in Fouché's terms – in the collective practice of race-finish photography. Just as Hemment, Adams, sports journalists, and enthusiasts promoted the infallibility of the camera to make sports decisions, so too did companies such as Prosch and Scovill.

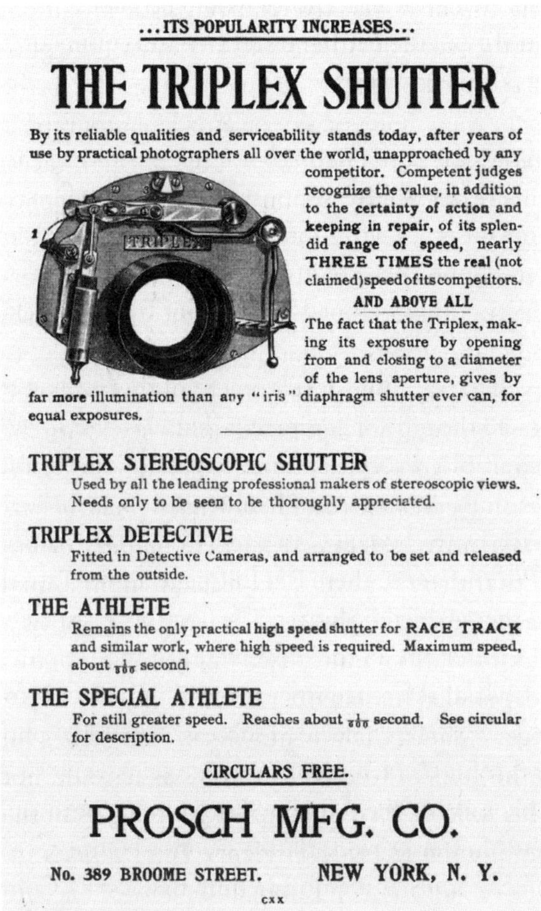

2.16 Prosch advertisement for the Triplex Shutter, 1898.

Conclusion

By the closing two decades of the nineteenth century, instantaneous photographers were increasingly exploring sport as part of their subject matter. Dry-plate and then celluloid film and advancements in shutter speed and lens quality – not to mention the portability of cameras exemplified by Kodak – enabled photographers to capture scenes of sport that had not been possible in the preceding years and that were also readily consumed by an interested public. Although the practice of photographing sport was commonplace by the end of the century, the notion of using a camera to determine placing in sport was only taken up sporadically. Beginning in the early 1880s with

Muybridge, the idea of the photo-finish received relatively little attention. However, and largely through the work of Adams and Hemment, the photograph as evidence in sport received brief but dedicated attention in the years straddling 1890. Hemment was employed as a racetrack photographer at several tracks and was exploring ways to photograph the finish of races, and his work was actively being promoted by Adams and others in the photographic community.

The discourse that emerged around the use of photography in sport during the 1880s and 1890s is central in the development of the photo-finish, most notably as it foregrounded the necessary but uneasy relationship between humans and technology. Janssen, Muybridge, and Marey had all used the camera to reveal objects and movements that could not be seen with the naked eye. Their uses of the camera exposed what were believed to be truths of the natural world and in some cases corrected previously held beliefs about how humans and animals moved. Hemment's work similarly promised to reveal a hidden truth: that there is always "at least an infinitesimal distance" between horses in a race and that there can be no such thing as a dead heat.[61] To reveal such hidden truths required two things: an apparatus to make the unseen seen; and a skilled human operator.

The writings by Muybridge, Adams, Hemment, Marx, and others all ceded tremendous power to the camera to capture nature as it could not be seen by the human eye. This followed a dominant understanding of the camera at the time, as exemplified in the title of Henry Fox Talbot's influential 1840s text, *The Pencil of Nature*. For Talbot and many of his contemporaries and successors, the photograph was understood to be a direct representation, if not the product, of nature itself. In a similar way, the early proponents of the evidentiary use of the photograph in sport regarded the camera as something that could reveal hidden, natural truths that are invisible to the naked eye (one horse, boat, bike, or runner must always be in front of another). Recall the 1890 article in *Science* that noted it was "only by means" of the camera that we could see distinct phases of motion in a javelin throw.[62] This deployment of the camera reflected the modernist drive – in sport and elsewhere – to mechanize and automate. Positioning the camera as the "pencil of nature" performed and reinforced notions of mechanical objectivity, whereby the authority of the image is guaranteed through the automation and mechanization of the image production process, letting nature speak for itself.

However, the early use of the camera in sport was not purely an act of Daston and Galison's noninterventionist image-making. Alongside the power attributed to the camera, photographers, writers, and reporters of the time also constructed the instantaneous photographer as a uniquely talented and qualified professional. Hemment made the comparison to firing a gun – the best technology is only good in the hands of a skilled operator. Adams speaks of Hemment's unique abilities in this capacity not just as one of the technically best instantaneous photographers of the day but as an athlete and artist. The Prosch company described Hemment as the "king" of sport photography. And Hemment and other instantaneous photographers of the time regularly spoke of the artistry needed to take proper instantaneous pictures; the camera alone was not enough. In this way the accuracy and objectivity of the finish-line image was necessarily tied to the unique skills of the photographer. As with the figure of Linnaeus in Daston and Galison's "truth to nature" episteme, it was the expertise of the finish-line photographer that helped to guarantee the accuracy of the image. The end result is a somewhat paradoxical co-construction of the fallibility of the human eye and the infallibility of the machine eye, but only when the latter is operated by the former.

This paradox also meant that the images of instantaneous photographers in sport were not necessarily accepted as accurate. A central challenge was that, despite the development of celluloid film, shorter exposure times, and better hardware, cameras still had to be tripped by a human operator. For all of Hemment's advances in taking photographs of finishes, the success of a given image was still entirely dependent on him. As Hemment noted, "A lightning perception is absolutely necessary. When the impression is taken in such a small fraction of a second's time one dare not anticipate. He must see the horse's nose plumb with the wire before he touches the spring. The man who photographs finishes must be able to keep cool and to work with great rapidity and precision."[63] And yet if we look at Hemment's finish-line work (Figures 2.6 through 2.11), it is clear that his images lacked the consistency and precision necessary to determine placing. They could only function as a supplementary record of the decision made by race officials.

Hemment faced specific opposition in relation to work he did photographing athletics in 1890. In one particularly telling example, finish-line pictures he made were said to attest to a new quarter-mile record by W.C. Downs.[64] Harry Cornish of the Boston Athletic Association questioned the result and sought to prove or disprove Hemment's picture, suggesting that the photographer may have altered the image. Hemment claimed to be at a specific location when the picture was taken, and so Cornish proposed to re-enact the finish and have Hemment make the same pictures to prove he had not altered the initial results. A 29 November 1890 story in *Sporting Life* describes the case: "Their [Cornish and the BAA's] offer to M. Hemment, however, was made in good faith, and they thought he would be pleased to accept, upon reasonable terms, to vindicate himself and his pictures, as hard names have been applied to him, and he has even been charged with having 'doctored' the negative." The article then outlines the proposed setup for the re-enactment:

> Downs will be allowed to place himself, or the photographer will, so that Hemment's picture will be duplicated. Measurements will be taken, so that it will be known exactly where Hemment stood. He claims that he stood about fifteen feet from the finish. It is believed that in his excitement he moved up much nearer. Other photographs will be taken to cover every point of the dispute. There is no doubt that Downs will gladly accept this opportunity, and an immediate answer is expected of him. The trial will probably be made the latter part of the week.[65]

Ultimately, the re-enactment did not take place and Hemment was spared the task of proving himself. As noted in a December 6 issue of *Sporting Life* in the same year, "contrary to expectation, nothing was done in the Downes [*sic*] record case. Mr. Curtis, who has the matter in charge, reported against admitting new photographs as evidence. Mr. Hemment's picture will not be considered in the matter."[66] Nonetheless, the proposal to re-enact a race in order to re-photograph its finish is an extraordinary example of the tenuous position of the photograph and photographer in sport at the time. Hemment's expertise was being called into question and the proposed solution was to be found in the camera. Here again is the fraught relationship of the human eye and machine eye that is indicative of modernist uses of the camera.

This concern about the reliability and efficacy of finish-line images had been voiced publicly on more than one occasion. A 15 July 1888 edition of the *New York Press* identifies the Coney Island Jockey Club's potential adoption of the camera as a decision aid but ultimately defers to the expertise of the human official: "The positions of the horses as they cross the finish line, no matter how close they may be together, ought certainly to be apparent to the men in the judges' stand." Nonetheless the piece continues to endorse the use of the photograph to document finishes, just not for evidentiary purposes but because it would be "an immense satisfaction to the betting public to see a photograph of every close finish."[67] Eight years later, in 1895, a notice in the *Thoroughbred Record* issues a much stronger condemnation of the photo-finish and specifically its human operator:

> The people who pretend to photograph dead heats and other kinds of heats are now treated with scant courtesy by track managers, because they have no faith in the correctness of the snap shots. The operator of the camera is just as liable to shoot at the wrong time as at the precise fraction of an instant required by accuracy, and the knowledge of this fact has discredited his work. The experiment of photographing finishes has been repeatedly tried, and we know of no first-class track that relies upon the camera. The snapshot judge is a discarded member.[68]

As it was used in other contexts at the time, such as in policing, the natural sciences, anthropology, law, and medicine, the photograph's status as an objective, accurate form of representation was not simply accepted. A central challenge to the photograph as evidence in sport was, paradoxically, the same thing it was said to fix: human fallibility. Instantaneous photographs in sport were promoted as bringing heightened accuracy and objectivity to judging, which was increasingly being called into question. However, to have their images serve as a form of evidence, instantaneous photographers required perfect, precise, and consistent reaction time. Hemment's work in capturing horses before, at, or after the line, from differing vantage points, and with various levels of clarity reveals the limits of instantaneous photography in sport during the 1880s and 1890s. As advanced as they were and as interesting as they are, these images are not photo-finishes but photographs of finishes, the evidentiary value of which was not given but was built and contested according to the unique parameters governing each context of use.

CHAPTER THREE

Electric Eyes, Eyes in the Sky, and Two Eyes: From Photographs of Finishes to Photo-Finishes

Despite continued technological advancements in photographic image-making in the closing decades of the nineteenth century, the predictions of Muybridge, Adams, Hemment, and others that instantaneous photography would forever eradicate the dead heat in sport did not come to pass. Hemment and his contemporaries were correct that photographs of sport would be popular with sporting and camera enthusiasts and in the burgeoning news industry; however, their use as evidentiary documents in sport stalled significantly over the turn of the twentieth century. As sport was increasingly regulated and standardized, the use of the photograph as evidence faced two primary problems. First, it was dogged by the issue of human reaction time and the inconsistency of photographers trying to capture horses or athletes at the precise moment they crossed the finish line. A second key limitation, but not one explicitly addressed in the professional or public discourse, was the incompleteness of the photographic record. Images from the instantaneous photographers only captured a single image of the finish and so could only show who won the race. With the growing modernization and professionalization of sport and the attendant emphasis on regulation, standardization, and records-keeping, images such as those by Hemment were quite limited.

Both of these limitations were actively addressed during the first several decades of the twentieth century. The period from roughly 1900 to 1940 is marked by a drive towards greater precision and accuracy in sports timing and imaging. And automation was central to this drive. Materially, this took form in the move from human-operated stopwatches to more automated, electronic timing systems. More abstractly, "electric eyes" and "camera eyes" were positioned as more infallible than their human counterparts. The opening decades of the twentieth century are marked by the emergence of a discourse surrounding the automation and mechanization of sports decision-making.

Photographing Time

Two patents taken out contemporaneous with the work of Hemment and the other instantaneous photographers proposed substantial improvements to finish-line imaging.[1] The first, patented in 1894 by William C. Petri, was an "Apparatus for Photographically Recording Time, Position, and Speed" (Figure 3.1). Petri's invention offered two novel aspects to the finish-line image. First, in addition to photographing the finish of a race, Petri also required that a picture be taken at the start of the race. Petri also called for the placement of a clock within the photographic frame so that times could be captured along with placing. In this way, Petri promoted his device as being able to determine not just the placing but also the time of each racer (horse or human) as well as their speed and the distance between the contestants.

The second patent, submitted in 1896 and approved in 1899, offered further enhancements to the process (Figure 3.2). William Ephraim Barber's "apparatus for making racing-records" connected the start and finish of the race with a clock through an integrated electrical circuit. Triggering the circuit opened the starting gate, started the clock, and released the camera shutter to record an image of the start. Similarly, triggering the circuit again at the finish photographed the horses (or other racers) at the line while simultaneously stopping the clock. What is most interesting in Barber's process is the inclusion of vast amounts of information in the finish-line photograph. Like Petri, he had a clock put in place at the start/finish line which would appear in the photographic image. However, he also added new information: a board would display the race number as well as the specific portion of the race (start, finish, quarter, etc.) and a separate board showed the names and numbers of the jockeys. In conjunction with this numbering scheme, Barber required that jockeys be fixed with a number via an armband on their jerseys.[2] The end result, shown within Barber's patent as Figure 2, is a finish-line image that is rich with information.

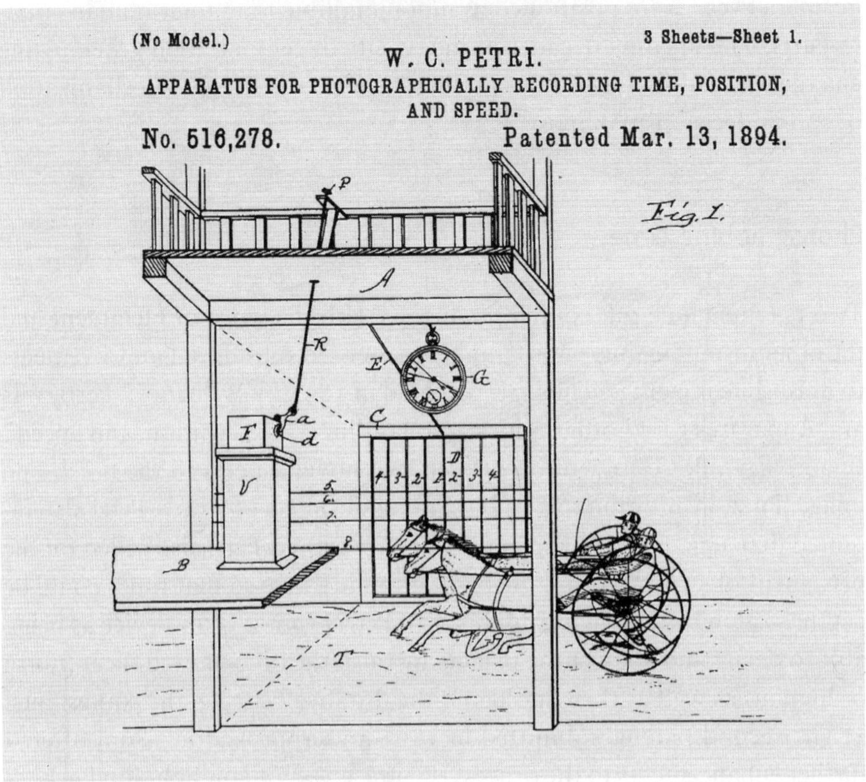

Where Hemment's images captured horses within close proximity of the finish, Petri's and Barber's proposed apparatuses are considerably more systematized and standardized. They combine a visual record of horses or humans crossing a finish line with a time stamp and other identifying information. As such, the apparatuses proposed by Petri and Barber exemplify the modernist drive for record-keeping – Sekula's "bureaucratic-clerical-statistical system" and the use of the camera within this effort.[3] The patents by Petri and Barber point to another central drive in the modernization of sport: automation. Marx and Hemment utilized an electromagnet to release their camera shutters in an attempt to negate some of the idiosyncracies and/or deficiencies of human reaction time and more laborious forms of shutter release. Barber's patent in particular proposed a solution in the form of a complete electrical circuit that united the start, finish, camera, and clock. Human operators were still required to trip the circuit, but his apparatus

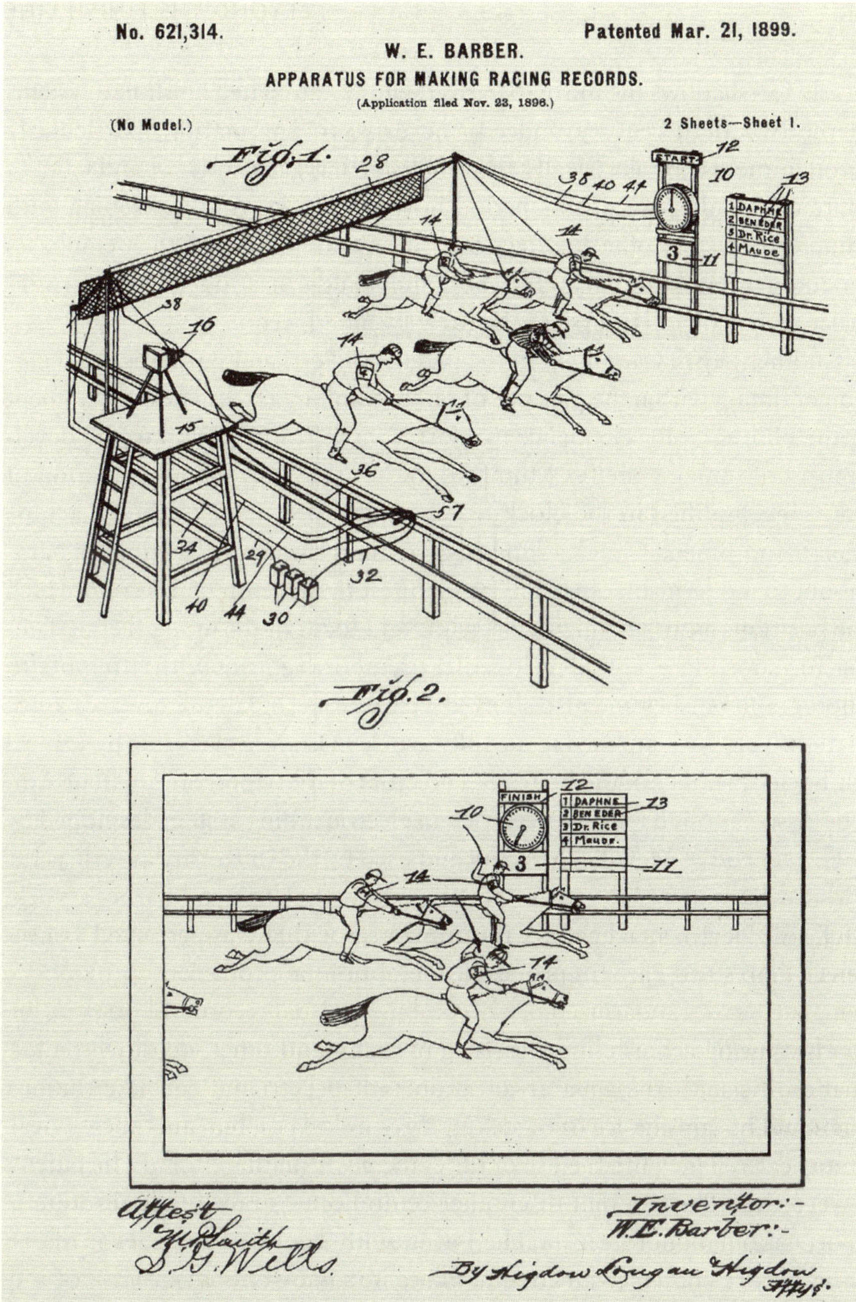

3.1 *Opposite* William C. Petri, "Apparatus for Photographically Recording Time, Position, and Speed." Patent, 1894.

3.2 *Above* William Ephraim Barber, "Apparatus for Making Racing-Records." Patent, 1896.

clearly foreshadows the move towards the fully automated finish-line systems of the twentieth century. Indeed, the drive to automation, particularly through the use of electrically triggered starting gates, clocks, and camera shutters, is indicative of this period in sport history. And in keeping with Mumford's history of technology, machine metaphors – with their emphases on automation, electricity, efficiency, and standardization – rise to prominence in sporting discourse of the early twentieth century.

Another key development in the patents of Petri and Barber is the inclusion of timing within the practice of photographing races. The development of the photograph as evidence in sport is inextricably bound to the development of timing systems. Mumford locates the control and regulation of time – exemplified in the clock – as a central precursor to the "machine age."[4] And Jimena Canales similarly identifies the control of time as paramount to modernism, especially as manifest in the tenth of a second which she positions as an organizing principle and focus of the modern era.[5] Timing for sporting events developed contemporaneously with attempts to photograph finishes and also showed a clear drive and desire towards automation. This is exemplified in an 1887 article in *Outing* magazine by Samuel M. Baylis, member of the Board of Directors of the Montreal Amateur Athletic Association. Baylis wrote about an electric timing system developed by C.H. McLeod of McGill University and used by the University as well as the Montreal Amateur Athletic Association. As with Petri's and Barber's work, McLeod's device sought to fix the human error that was perceived as negatively impacting race timing. Baylis describes the problem:

> The time of a race being, therefore, of such significance, it follows that the official time-keeper is an important personage, and lest there should be any chance of mistakes, *three* are appointed, and in case of any discrepancy between their times the *average* is taken and officially recorded. The fact that discrepancies do occur is proof that absolute accuracy has not been reached even with the finest watches in the hands of experienced men, and while it may be only a question of a *fifth of a second*, this may be enough to make a "record," that laurel wreath of modern Olympic games [emphasis in original].[6]

McLeod's device is a closed circuit which unites a starting gun with a string pulled across the finish line. These are connected to a chronograph which in turn activates a pen that records the time on a rotating disc. A key feature of the apparatus was that it was tripped at the finish line by the athlete, as opposed to an official operating a stopwatch or triggering a shutter release as is the case in the Petri and Barber systems. In this way it followed Muybridge's work with racetrack cameras in documenting a horse's gallop. Like earlier systems, McLeod's device could only record the time of the first person to cross the line; however, unlike earlier systems, it did so according to the athlete's body. McLeod's timing apparatus was praised for its accuracy and objectivity. Baylis notes that it was used in 1883 and 1884 by both McGill and the MAAA and again in 1886 for a cycling race, "proving an unqualified success and compelling admission from the most skeptical that means had at last been found of placing "time-keeping" on a scientific basis and insuring accuracy beyond question."[7]

As already noted, the use of the photograph as evidence in sport entered a period of relative stasis over the opening decades of the twentieth century. O'Neill defines this roughly thirty-year period from 1900 to 1930 as "a hiatus, during which photo finish seems to have fallen into disrepute, probably because of the lack of adequate triggering devices."[8] While the problem of triggering devices is true, it only partially accounts for the stall in development. The development and deployment of advanced imaging and timing technologies are also necessarily tied to the economic health of the sporting world and the larger society at a given time. In her history of thoroughbred racing in America, Mary Simon chronicles the dramatic ebbs and flows that characterized the racing industry in the opening decades of the twentieth century.[9] The exponential growth of horse racing, and gambling, at the turn of the twentieth century led to a series of anti-wagering laws starting in 1907 that nearly devastated the industry. The racing industry weathered World War I but purses remained quite low, rising again in the 20s only to be cut down by the stock market crash of 1929 and the Great Depression that followed. As the world emerged from the Depression, the anti-wagering laws of the early 1900s were eventually relaxed in the 1930s, so that by the 1940s horse racing was again a highly lucrative industry, netting $13 million in gambling revenues to New York State alone in 1940 (which is roughly $213 million in 2018 dollars).[10] And so while triggering devices were of concern within the sporting community, it is wrong to suggest that photographing race finishes was on hiatus over these years. Instead, the pace in development of the photo-finish has more to do with the tumultuous political and economic environment of the twentieth century. Regardless of pace, the opening decades of the twentieth century were pivotal in establishing the objective authority of the image in sport.

In what follows I address this period of sport history – approximately 1900 to 1940 – through two related but disjointed practices. First, this chapter addresses the continued use of the camera in horse racing, with particular attention paid to the 1930s. By the mid-1930s, the objectivity and accuracy of finish-line photography as well as its relationship with human vision were actively being debated in the horse-racing community. Second, this chapter looks at the adoption of the camera in athletics, with a focus on the Olympic Games. Though the French employed chronophotography in physiological studies of athletes at the 1900 Paris Games, the first formal use of a photograph to determine placing at the Olympics happened at the 1912 Stockholm Games. These two practices merge in the 1930s with the adoption of movie cameras to record races and determine placing, ultimately culminating in a key invention by Lorenzo del Riccio, an optical engineer then working for Paramount Studios. Del Riccio invented the slit camera to record the finishes of races and in so doing announced an essential inversion in the imaging process which I define as marking the difference between photographs *of* finishes and photo-finishes. Where in the early 1900s the camera captured a distinct time across space, by the late 1930s it was used to capture a distinct space across time.

The Electric Eye and the Eye in the Sky

The process for photographing finishes of horse races remained relatively consistent over the first three decades of the twentieth century, with a few notable advances. Faster film and shutter speeds enabled photographers to quickly and relatively easily capture intervals up to 1/1,000th of a second. The Speed Graphic, developed in 1912, was one such camera and was prominent in the news industry at the time, including use for capturing sporting events. Developing times were also reduced from several minutes to roughly thirty seconds, depending on the particular track and camera configuration, thus making the use of photographs of finishes at live events considerably more viable. Track photographers began taking pictures from high above the track rather than from the slightly elevated judges' stand: a direct response to the problem of a judge's view being obscured by another horse or jockey. To raise the camera to a higher vantage point, separate towers were built or the camera was fastened to an existing piece of track architecture such as the judging booth. These devices came to be known as the "eye in the sky," owing to their raised position. Finally, during the 1920s, the development of photoelectric cells led to the proliferation of camera systems and uses that ranged from television sets to automated security systems. In relation to the latter, photoelectric cells enabled cameras and other devices to be automatically tripped when an object crossed through a beam of light. News media in the 1920s and 1930s are filled with stories of such "electric eyes" across a wide array of uses including automated traffic signals, bank and home security systems, automated factory labour, and fire sprinkler systems.[11] Within the horse-racing industry, photoelectric cells were used at the finish of races with cameras and timers being tripped as horses broke a beam of light running across the line. Noting the advances in starting gates and the introduction of the photo-finish in American horse racing, Mary Simon describes the 1930s as a period of "remarkable innovation and growth."[12]

Rather than trace these developments in detail it is sufficient to note that the overall process of photographing horse race finishes remained the same until the gradual adoption of movie cameras in the 1930s. The 1930s saw a proliferation of camera systems developed to record races and specifically to determine placing. John Hervey speaks to this transformation in his 1937 chronicle, *Racing in America 1922–1936*.[13] He refers to the processes employed by Hemment and others in the late 1800s as "crude" and their results "uncertain."[14] But he notes that "the progress made in motion-photography that has occurred in response to the extravagant success of the 'movies' has made possible what we have today – cameras capable of taking 200 progressive exposures in one second, which record the progress of the horses from a position well above the wire until it has been passed."[15] He then identifies the colloquial name for the cameras as well as their status as objective and accurate: "the popular designation of these new contrivances is the eye in the sky, as they are operated from a position high in the air upon the grandstand roof or even above it. As the modern man is camera-minded he accepts their findings without question or dissent, barring a few confirmed pessimists who stubbornly refuse to accord them entire confidence."[16]

Hervey introduces his brief discussion of the "eye in the sky" with a passage that underscores the drive to modernize and mechanize imaging and timing in horse racing. He writes:

> What has been termed the mechanization of racing has, in conformance with the spirit of the Machine Age in which we live, proceeded to the regret of those sportsmen who cleave to the old ideals and would preserve the turf from too much modernization, but to the satisfaction of those who, on the other hand, are sticklers for precision, quick action and standardization. The introduction of the stall-gates has already been chronicled. In their wake, as a mechanical mode of starting a race, has been introduced another mechanical mode of deciding its finish. In all cases where the positions of the contending horses are in any doubt when they pass beneath the wire, the camera, and not the placing judges, is now the arbiter, with the proviso that the judges interpret the photograph.[17]

Hervey's writing on the topic perfectly encapsulates the modernist discourse in sport at the time. He describes the "Machine Age" using the terms "precision," "quick action," and "standardization," and notes that "modern man is camera-minded" and unfailingly accepts the veracity of the photographic image. By contrast, a "few confirmed pessimists" "cleave to the old ideals" and want to shield horse racing from too much modernization. The passage speaks to the larger cultural fascination with the industrializing and mechanizing aspects of the modern era. It is therefore no surprise that the discourse to emerge from 1900 to 1940 is infused with references to electricity and the machinic eye. The use of the photo in sport and the development of imaging and timing systems were as much about exploring the relationships of human and machine vision as they were about determining placing in sporting contests.

In his chronicle, Hervey also identifies a surprising irony of the "eye in the sky," what he calls a "striking effect" of this transfer of authority from the human eye to the machine eye: a dramatic increase in the number of dead heats. For the period Hervey covers, 1922 to 1936, there was only one dead heat up to 1933. Following the continued adoption of more automated systems and the "eye in the sky," the number of dead heats grew exponentially, so that in 1936 there were 115.[18] Hervey does not offer an explanation for this effect but it is most probably because the camera revealed that races were considerably closer than judges initially thought. In other words, prior to the 1930s judges were confident in their decision-making capabilities and their ability to objectively determine which horse crossed the line first. Following the adoption of the "eye in the sky," and cameras capturing 200 or more images per second, judges' certainty began to wane. And the increasing professionalization of horse racing with the attendant financial stakes in betting revenues, media attention, sponsorship, and advertising would have added pressure to the drive for accurate and objective vision.

Hervey's assertion that, by the mid-1930s, the camera had supplanted the judge as the arbiter of truth in horse racing simplifies a convoluted and often messy transformation. Numerous, competing systems were developed and employed at different tracks. These were variously and inconsistently referred to as "electric eyes," "camera eyes," or "eyes in the sky," repeating the same trope that instantaneous photographers had used decades earlier. Santa Anita used a system developed by Harry Day of Electrical Research Products, which was also adopted by Washington Park in 1936. In Day's system, the camera was placed 120 feet from the track and 60 feet off the ground to provide for clear, unobstructed images.[19] The Waite camera at Tropical Park (Florida) was replaced by a system designed by Earl and Aaron Harvey in 1937[20] and a camera designed by James J. Jones was in operation at Hialeah Park (Florida) and fourteen other tracks in Chicago, New York, and Maryland.[21] A particular selling feature of the Jones camera – and one that became a selling feature of movie camera–based systems – was that it also allowed for the public projection of slow-motion finishes of races.[22] As described in a 1938 article in *The Blood-Horse*:

> On a screen perhaps two feet square is projected a still picture of the finish, one of these projectors being under the grandstand, another on the totalizator board back of the club house. Beneath the still pictures is a second screen, about a foot high, two feet long. On this is projected a continual slow motion picture of the finish of the race, so that the curious may see whether the winner was coming out, dropping back, or merely holding on.[23]

It is interesting and perhaps unsurprising to note that the development and use of movie cameras to determine placing in sport thus served a double role as a form of evidence and entertainment.

Movie-camera systems were considerably more expensive than traditional still cameras. The Day system used at Santa Anita and Washington Park cost between $26,500 and $46,000 (roughly $475,000 to $825,000 in 2018 dollars).[24] One very interesting solution to this – and one which directly takes up the challenges of the earlier still camera systems – was developed in 1935 by Marshall Cassidy for Hialeah Park in Florida. Cassidy used a Speed Graphic camera mounted to the roof of the grandstand, capturing images to 1/1,000th of a second and taking three minutes to develop the finish-line photograph. Cassidy had a "carpet thread" run across the finish that would trip an electromagnetic shutter release on the camera. What was interesting about Cassidy's system was that he placed the thread 5 feet 2 inches ahead of the finish line. This distance was settled on through trial and error and was an attempt to remedy the problem of reaction time. Cassidy found that tripping the shutter release at 5 feet 2 inches from the finish yielded the best odds of catching the lead horse at the finishing line. However, and as with earlier efforts, Cassidy's system could not consistently catch the horses exactly at the line, and, as it used a traditional still camera, it was only useful in documenting the first-place finisher and any other horse in the immediate vicinity.[25]

The proliferation in camera systems in horse racing during the 1930s was paralleled by public and professional discourse that debated the merits of these systems. Articles in newspapers of the time as well as in prominent horse-racing magazines such as *The Thoroughbred Record* and *The Blood-Horse* effectively illuminate the concerns. The bulk of the debate centred on the issue of human versus machine officiating, and it is worth noting that some of the discussion was quite nuanced in its understanding of the issues at play. A June 20, 1936 article in *The Blood-Horse* addressed the growing public concern over race-finish photography, beginning with a key criticism that "writers on the subject have lumped all finish photography together under the very poorly chosen name of 'camera eye' or 'electric eye.' This has obscured, to many interested persons, the fact that the cameras used at various tracks are of several different types."[26] The article concludes by noting that,

> before anything can be said of the accuracy of the method, one must know exactly what type of camera is being used. If it is one which stops the leader or leaders exactly at the finish line, then it is extremely accurate – far more accurate than the most highly trained human eye. If it is one which misses the actual finish by some inches, it may still be of considerable assistance to placing judges, but it is not absolute and should not be treated as such.[27]

One of the central technological concerns of the critics of race-finish photography was the issue of parallax: that the camera distorts objects closer to the lens and magnifies objects further away, meaning that the outside horse would have an advantage in finish-line photography where the camera is positioned on the inside of the track. F.R. Becker wrote an impassioned defense of the human judge in 1936, citing the issue of parallax and even suggesting that horses with small heads or short necks were at a disadvantage in race-finish photography.[28] And the camera system of Earl and Aaron Harvey for Tropical Park was praised because it "virtually eliminates the magnification of the outside horse."[29] The issue was significant enough that the Bureau of Standards within the United States Department of Commerce issued a report on the subject. After a careful examination of the camera system at Saratoga, the Bureau concluded that, if the camera is properly stationed perpendicular to the finish line, there is no problem of parallax.[30] Finally, in an attempt to bring an end to the debate, the editors of *The Blood-Horse* wrote, in 1941, "As far as the Blood-Horse is concerned, arguments about the accuracy of finish cameras are foolishness ... But many persons still continue to judge the camera's accuracy by their own eyes, which is really on par with attempting absolutely accurate measurement by pacing off a distance."[31]

Importantly, while proponents of race-finish photography such as the editors of *The Blood-Horse* called for an end to debates about the merits of these systems, they did nonetheless recognize their inherent limitations. A 1939 article on an update to the Jones camera system notes that it can capture 360 frames per second so that were a horse running a pace of 1:35 per mile, the camera would record a photo for every 1.8 inches of movement.[32] Here and in other articles of the time there is direct acknowledgment that even high-speed cameras have their limits. At 360 frames per second, Jones's camera could still technically fail to capture the horse at the precise moment the horse crossed the finish line or could fail to decisively show which horse crossed the line first in a particularly close race. The definitive moment might exist in the 1.8 inches between photographic stills.

By the close of the 1930s the use of cameras to determine placing in horse racing was generally, though sometimes begrudgingly, taken to be an acceptable and accurate practice. Yet, and as cited above, there was within the racing community a reasonably nuanced understanding of the limitations of the movie-camera systems. Even at 360 frames per second, there were distinct moments of the finish that were not captured by the cameras. While this distance of 1.8 inches may seem inconsequential, race-finish images at the time were being viewed with tremendous scrutiny. Consider the following description of a "photo-finish" published in a 1941 edition of *The Thoroughbred Record*. The article includes an image of a recent finish and text which explains the race official's reading of the picture: "At first glance it looks as if Whirlaway's nose is not touching the white line either. But look more closely, and it is seen that his nose IS touching the line. His widely extended right nostril blends into the color of the track itself. A magnifying glass, which the Saratoga judges used before posting their decision, shows that the 'dark' spot touching the wire is Whirlaway's nostril, not a hoof-hole in the track."[33] That the judges analyze the image with a magnifying glass and that a piece of the horse's nostril is what ultimately wins the race is evidence that highly precise measurement mattered. And the passage also underscores the necessary presence of the official. The photomechanical image is taken as authoritative but it must first be closely read by an official, ironically with another technological tool (the magnifying glass) to "correct" human vision.

The seemingly small "spaces" between photographic frames served as the basis for the photo-finish system developed by Lorenzo del Riccio in 1937. Before turning to del Riccio, however, it is first necessary to return to the early 1900s and the adoption of the camera for use in athletics. Though Hemment and others proposed and used the camera to determine placing in track, cycling, and yacht racing, the early history of race-finish photography is very much dominated by its use in horse racing. The camera was sparingly deployed in athletics in the early decades of the twentieth century; nonetheless, this period offers valuable insight into the camera's use as evidence in sport.

Photographing the Olympic Games

The first, formal use of a photograph to determine placing in the Olympics came in the 1912 Stockholm Games. Prior to this, Games in Athens (1896), Paris (1900), St Louis (1904), and London (1908) relied entirely on the judgment of human officials and photographs were primarily employed for press or public-relations purposes. One notable exception is the extensive use of chronophotography at the 1900 Paris Games. Chronophotography was officially employed in the "analysis of muscular actions" across nine sports: hurdles, sprints, long-distance running, shot put, discus, long jump, standing high jump, running high jump, and rowing.[34] The Olympic Report describes the process and rationale:

> this method translates, using a series of successive instantaneous images, all the movements of the athletes; the method measures the exact area according to a metric scale or according to the dimensions of an object of a known length represented in the images. It indicates the time that passed between two successive movements of the athlete according to the movement of a needle that makes one revolution per second on the face of the chronograph. We can now know the form, area, and speed of each movement. Is it even necessary to mention that even the most trained eye could not attain such precision [translated from the original].[35]

There is a dedicated section of the 1900 Olympic Report that discusses the results of the work with chronophotography at the Games. The work was done under the Physiology Commission of Sports and much of the discussion takes up the inadequacy of the method, particularly in achieving clear pictures in difficult, outdoor environments. However, where the images were successful, such as with those documenting hurdles, the Commission used the images to study the different positions and movements of the athletes so as to better understand winning performances. Figures 3.3 and 3.4 from the Olympic Report illustrate the case. The first image, titled "Use of chronophotography in inconsistent conditions," shows how the Commission changed the location of their photographic apparatus to get better lighting. The two columns on the left, depicting a running high jump (far left) and sprint (second from the left), point to the problems of dark conditions and shadows. By contrast, the two columns on the right, depicting a hurdle race, are offered to show a more effective use of the camera in brightly lit conditions and against a neutral background.

Figure 3.4 depicts a series of sketches made from the instantaneous pictures made in Figure 3.3 of the French hurdler Pontié. Because the successive instantaneous pictures would have to be displayed across a broad horizontal axis (placing separate photographs beside each other), the Commission instead projected the chronophotographs onto a screen, and then produced a series of sketches overlaying one another. Concluding their work, the Commission offered: "the use of chronophotography offered us detail of the muscular actions and movements they produced and allowed us to measure speed, to understand the mechanics and, when comparing the diverse subjects, to discover some of the secrets to their superiority."[36] The use of chronophotography in this way is unsurprising given Marey's important place in the development of both physiology and photography in turn-of-the-century France. It is nonetheless fascinating, especially as it prefigures twenty-first-century sport imaging technologies such as Dartfish, which show the body in motion in ways that directly parallel the sketch in Figure 3.4.

And so, while the camera was used extensively in Paris, it was not used to determine placing. The Paris Games included several ties and dead heats where, presumably, a camera could have been used to determine placing. The 1904 St Louis Games included a dead heat for first place in a semifinal for the men's 60m dash. As noted in the Official Report, "both men were permitted to run in the final heat by the referee."[37] The 1908 Games in London paid significant attention to the question of officiating, including acknowledging the difficulty of objectively judging sports where "form" was to be considered, such as diving, fencing, and gymnastics. Numerous ties and dead heats were reported, including a four-way tie in the three-mile men's team race in 15 minutes, 5 and 3/5th seconds.[38] It is important to note that in cases of ties neither timing data nor images were used to make a decision. If the tie took place in a preliminary heat the athletes would either advance to the next round or face off again in a subsequent race. If the tie took place in the final, the athletes would receive the same time and, depending on placing, matching medals.

Unsurprisingly, there is a clear upward trajectory in the importance placed on rules, regulations, and officiating throughout these early Olympic

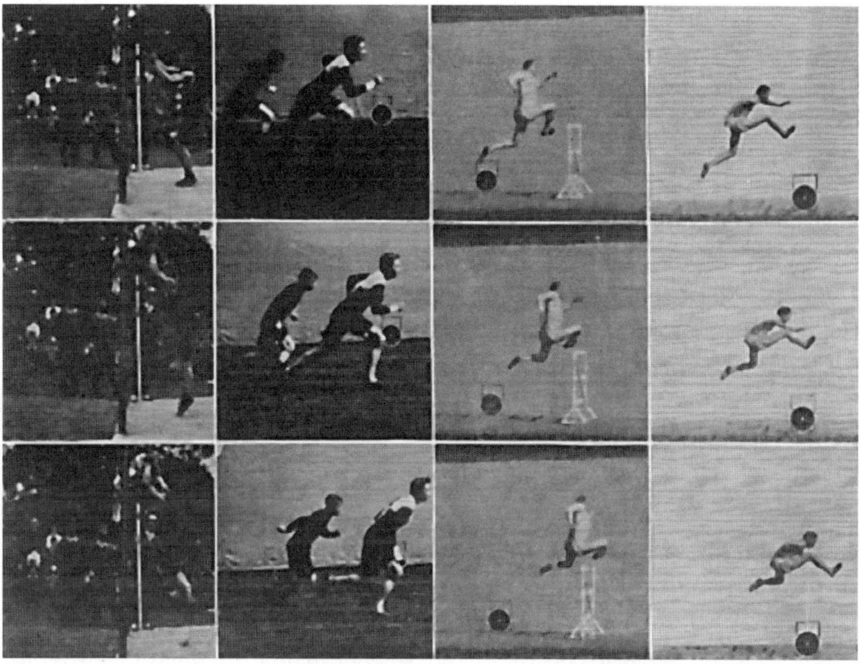

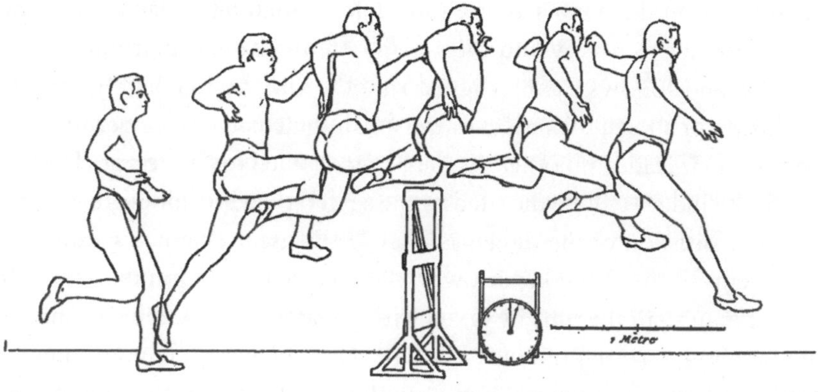

3.3 *Top* “Use of Chronophotography in Inconsistent Conditions.” Official Report of the 1900 Olympic Games, Paris.

3.4 *Bottom* “Sketch of the Frenchman Pontié’s Jump over the Hurdle.” Official Report of the 1900 Olympic Games, Paris.

Games. As Guttmann has outlined, a central component of the modernization of sport was the proliferation of official sports associations and federations at the close of the nineteenth century with their attendant rules and regulations.[39] Numerous national-level associations were developed from the 1860s through the 1890s with international associations following after. The Olympic Games deferred authority to the individual sport federations so long as there was a relevant international body. Where no relevant organizational body existed, the National Olympic Organizing Committee would create and publish rules for the sports in question. This is exemplified in the 1908 London Games, which published an extensive set of rules for sports not governed by an international federation. The 1912 Stockholm Games followed suit and provided detailed procedures for timing and officiating. To exemplify, the regulations for track events give the breakdown for number, role, and position of officials: "1 leader or manager, 1 starter, 6 judges at the finish, of whom one shall be the chief judge, 3 judges of the course, 3 or more timekeepers, 1 secretary, 1 orderly, 2 men at the result-board, 2 men at the start-board, 1 extra man at the finish."[40] This is followed by an extensive description of the placement, roles, and regulations of the judges and time-keepers.

Figure 3.5 shows the judges' stand from the Stockholm Games. As per the regulations provided by the Stockholm Olympic Committee, three judges are to focus on the winner of the race. Each remaining judge is assigned a specific runner to follow and must also note the runner that immediately precedes and follows their assigned runner. And, "immediately after the conclusion of a race, the judges at the finish shall assemble under the presidency of their leader, no other person being allowed to be present. The decision of the judges will be dictated to the secretary, who will make a minute of it. The decision of the judges is final."[41] Figure 3.6 shows a similar arrangement for the time-keepers, with the specific instruction that "only for the first man shall the time be taken with 3 watches." The regulations then stipulate how the final time is to be calculated between the 3 watches and at the conclusion of the race, and as with the race judges, the time-keepers "shall hold a meeting for the purpose of comparing the times shown by the watches, and of having the times officially fixed ... The times are then communicated to the secretary, who shall enter the report in the minutes in due course."[42] The timing instructions clearly show the emphasis placed on the

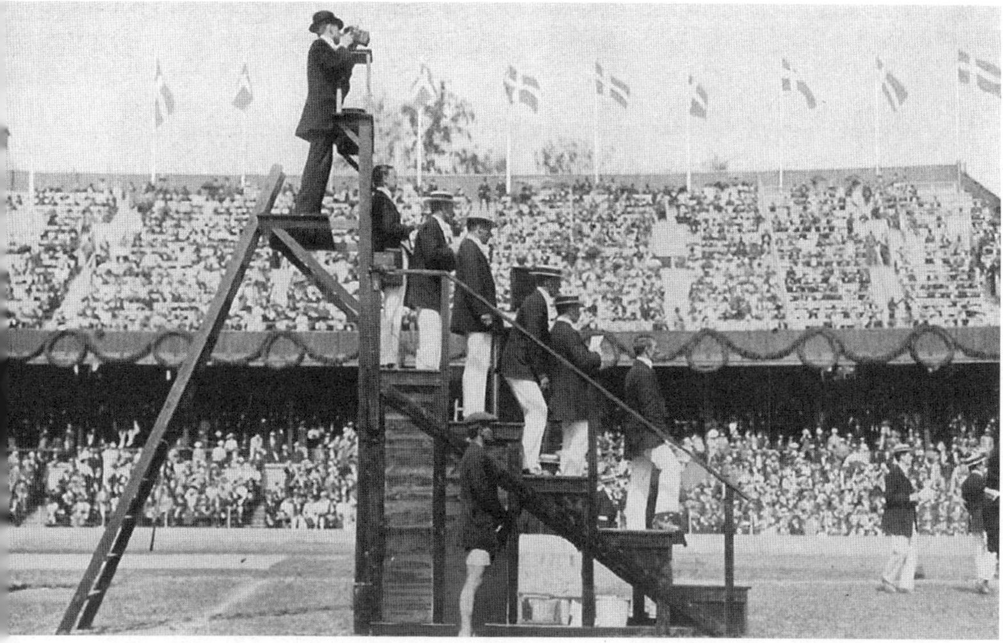

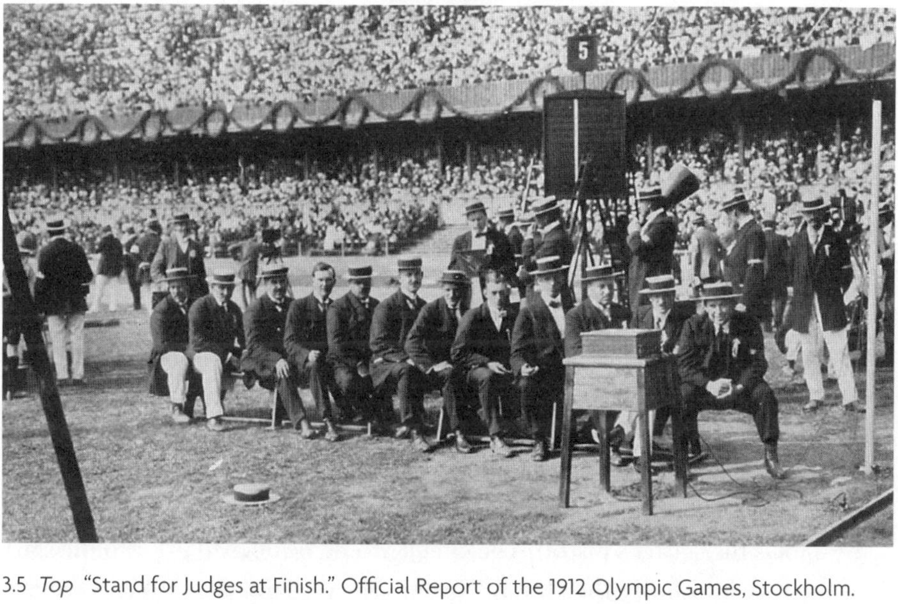

3.5 *Top* "Stand for Judges at Finish." Official Report of the 1912 Olympic Games, Stockholm.

3.6 *Bottom* "Group of Timekeepers, and the Electric Apparatus for Timetaking." Official Report of the 1912 Olympic Games, Stockholm.

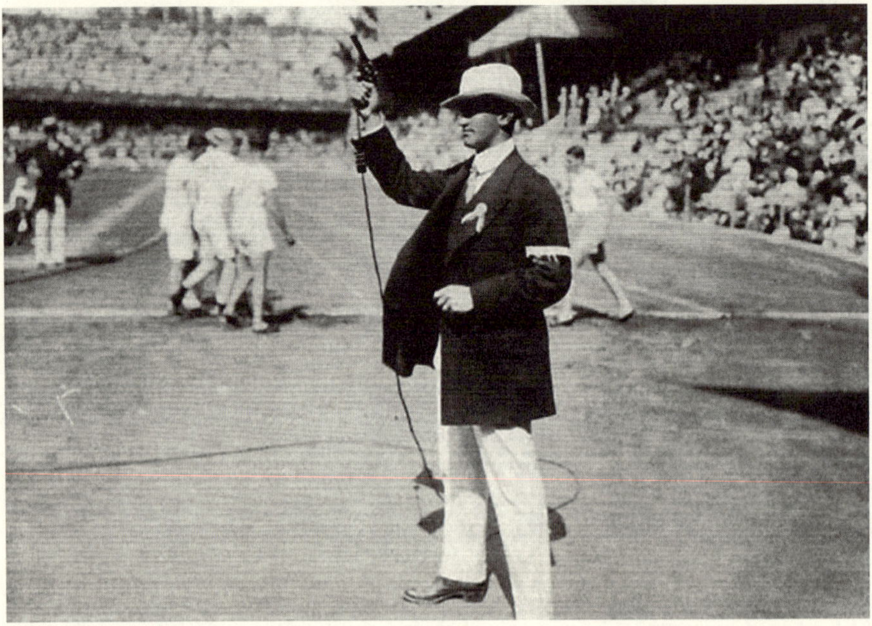

3.7 "Lieutenant G. Uggla, Starter in Flat Racing, Olympic Games." Official Report of the 1912 Olympic Games, Stockholm.

human official and the focus on capturing the time of the race winner rather than those of all participants.

Most importantly, the Stockholm Games also employed an "Automatic Timing and Judging Apparatus." The device was created by Ragnar Carlstedt, C.E., specifically for the Olympic Games and has close parallels in Barber's apparatus for racing records.[43] Carlstedt was a Swedish inventor with a significant history of patents for automatic clocks. His invention for the Games created a circuit that united a starting judge with starter's pistol, the judges at the finish, chronometers, and a photographic camera (Figure 3.7 shows the starter's pistol). The circuit would be opened prior to the start of the race and firing the starter's pistol closed the circuit, simultaneously starting the chronographs. At the same time, the lead finish-line judge would re-open the circuit in order to gain control over the timing and photographic apparatus. There were several chronometers at the finish, each with its own distinct tie to the main circuit. When a runner crossed the finish line, the finish-line judge responsible for tracking that runner (as per above) closed the circuit via contact with his chronometer and a time was recorded. In this way, each runner received a unique, seemingly automatic time, though the chronometer still had to be activated by a human official.

The timing and judging apparatus at Stockholm also included a photographic camera, though this was limited to a single exposure rather than the multiple data points captured by the chronometers. As outlined in the Stockholm Olympic Report,

> in series with the separate contact wire for the chief judge's watch, there was coupled-in a little relay, arranged on a photographic apparatus placed on the winning line. The closing of the circuit released a pawl or ratchet connected with the shutter of the photographic apparatus, an instantaneous photograph being thus obtained of the runner at the exact moment given by the principal judge's watch. By pressing the contacts, the principal judge was consequently able to determine the exact time and obtain a corresponding instantaneous photograph of the first man, and of the second and third men, too, in the event of the result promising to be so close that such precautionary measures were needed.[44]

The timing and judging apparatus used in Stockholm and its description and regulation through the Stockholm Olympic Committee represents one of the first concrete attempts to formalize the use of images as a decision-making tool in sport. The inclusion of the camera in Carlstedt's apparatus was formally required as per the Olympic Committee's regulations. Further, and as cited above, the image was included at least in part for its decision-making capabilities. The Official Olympic Report for the 1912 Games praised the apparatus, noting that it was used for all events on the track and "gave perfect satisfaction" and that "the photographs obtained, gave perfectly distinct pictures of the finish."[45] And though the decision-making capability of the image was not widely discussed or used, it did play a formal role in one race: the men's 1,500 metres.

Figure 3.8 shows the finish of the men's 1,500-metre race, which was won by Arnold Jackson of Great Britain in a then–Olympic record of 3:56.8. The image is not the one used by the judges in determining placing, which I was not able to find, but is taken from the Official Report of the 1912 Games. The second- and third-place finishers each received a time of 3:56.9 with the

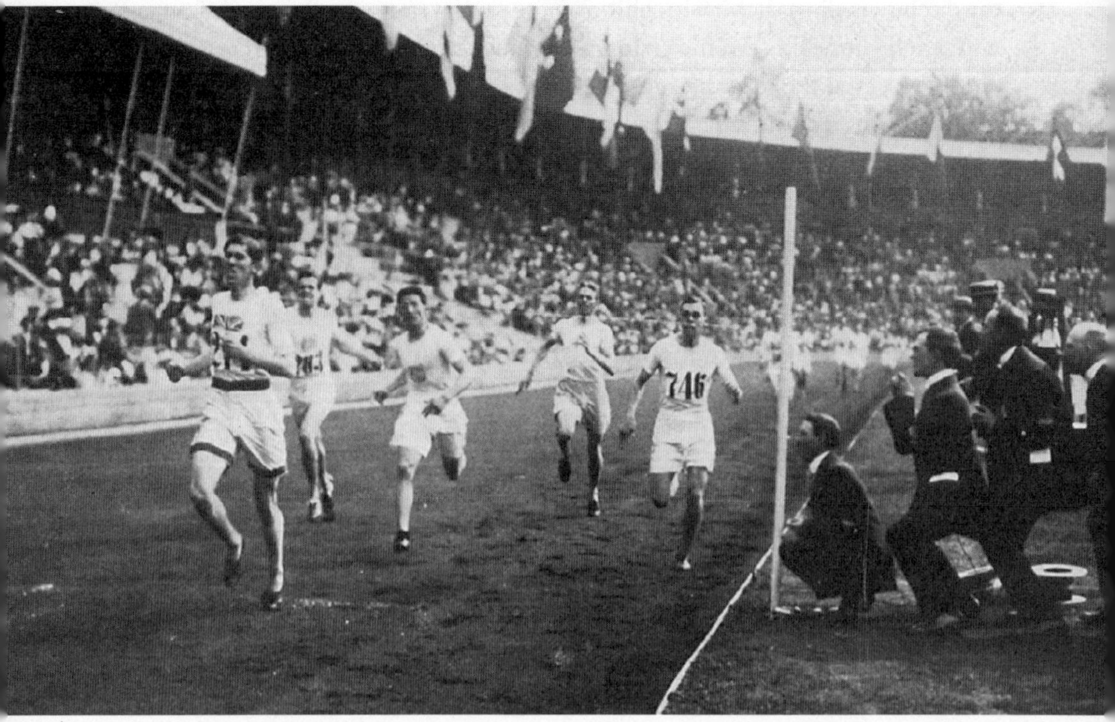

3.8 "1500 M. Flat, Final. The Finish." Official Report of the 1912 Olympic Games, Stockholm.

silver medal being awarded to Abel Kiviat and the bronze to Norman Taber, both of the United States. The placing of Kiviat and Taber was decided through interpretation of a photograph of the finish. The account is documented in the official Olympic Report of the Games: "There was so little between Kiviat and Taber that the judges would not permit the result to be published before the photograph taken of the finish had been developed, the plate showing that Kiviat was a shade in front of his countryman."[46]

The Kiviat/Taber finish was reported on in major as well as local papers, but the use of the photo to determine placing was mentioned only infrequently. The *Topeka Daily State Journal* went to press before the decision had been made, with their account reading: "In the 1,500 meters race the judges were unable to decide who was second. Jackson of England won but Abel R. Kiviat, Irish-American, and Norman S. Taber, Brown university, came in practically together and the judges are waiting the development of a photograph taken of the finish of the race before giving their decision as to which was second and which third."[47] The *Lake County Times* (Indiana) noted, "so close was the race for second place between Kivit and Taber the judges reserved their decision until a photo of the finish was developed before announcing the second and third men."[48] The *New York Tribune* similarly reported that "the judges could not separate Kiviat and Taber for second place, and waited to see a picture of the finish."[49] And slightly more detail was provided by the *San Francisco Call*: "The judges could not decide whether Taber or Kiviat was entitled to the second place until a photograph, taken automatically in connection with the electric timing device, was developed. On examining the photo negative the judges found Kiviat was a shade ahead of Taber."[50]

The Kiviat/Taber decision is instructive in several ways. First and perhaps most significantly, it represents the first formal use of the photograph as a form of evidence to determine placing in the Olympics. However, and also importantly, this use was only possible due to the close proximity of Kiviat and Taber to Jackson, the winner. Carlstedt's design for the "automatic timing and judging apparatus" included provisions for a photograph, but only a single exposure was made and it was triggered according to the first-place finisher of the race. Therefore, while the photograph was useful for determining second and third place in this particular race, as a form of evidence in sport more broadly, it was still tied to capturing the first runner, horse, or other athlete as they crossed the line. Multiple chronometers were used to record the times of multiple athletes, but only one image was taken. To do otherwise would have required several individual cameras arranged at the finish line, each attached to an official, in order to trigger the release at the appropriate time. The heavy dependence on manual labour of this "automated" imaging and timing is perfectly illustrated by the teams of judges and timers depicted in Figures 3.5 and 3.6.[51]

Two Eyes: From Still to Moving Images

Following Stockholm there is little mention or documentation of timing and imaging systems in Official Olympic Reports until the adoption of movie-camera systems in the 1930s. The next Olympic Games took place in Antwerp in 1920 but the Olympic Committee went bankrupt during the Games and so an Official Report was produced retroactively in 1957 by the

Belgium Olympic Committee.[52] It is unsurprising that the report is brief and contains no mention of the imaging and timing systems at the Games. The Reports of the Paris Games of 1924 and the accompanying Chamonix Winter Games identify the people involved in time-keeping but there is no discussion beyond this. The Report does indicate that bobsleigh was timed to the 1/100th of a second in order to avoid complaints or appeals.[53] And the 1928 Games in Amsterdam has a lengthy Report, documenting every heat and race at the Games, but includes no mention of the timing or imaging systems employed.[54]

The use of movie cameras in determining placing, and the shift from still to moving images, took form through two significant developments in the 1930s. The first was an apparatus developed by Gustavus T. Kirby, a long-serving member of the United States Olympic Committee and member of the advisory board of the Intercollegiate Association of Amateur Athletes of America (ICAAAA).[55] Kirby's invention was known colloquially as "two eyes." It was called this because it employed a camera, capturing 128 images per second, but with two lenses: one focused on the athletes, and the other on a chronometer. Kirby collaborated with individuals from Electrical Research Products and adopted work done by the Bell Telephone company on precision timing for his device.[56] The result, shown in Figure 3.9, is a unique and fascinating image in the history of sport. As it recorded all athletes on a continuously moving strip of film, the Kirby system provided a more comprehensive record than previous uses of the still camera. And the inclusion of the chronometer meant that times could be easily and effectively awarded to all race participants, adding even more information to the racing record. Kirby's work united earlier and disparate efforts to combine timing and imaging in the production of a comprehensive racing record. And thanks in part to collaborations with Electrical Research Products and Bell Telephone, Kirby's system also enabled the recording of time to the 1/1,000th of a second, adding more precision to previous practices which recorded to the fifth or tenth.

Kirby's "two eyes" device was purposely developed for use by the ICAAAA and for the 1932 Olympic Games in Los Angeles. Prior to development it was agreed that the device would record times to the hundredth of a second, as this was deemed sufficient precision for determining track events.[57] The device was first used on 14 May 1932 in a Columbia-Syracuse track meet

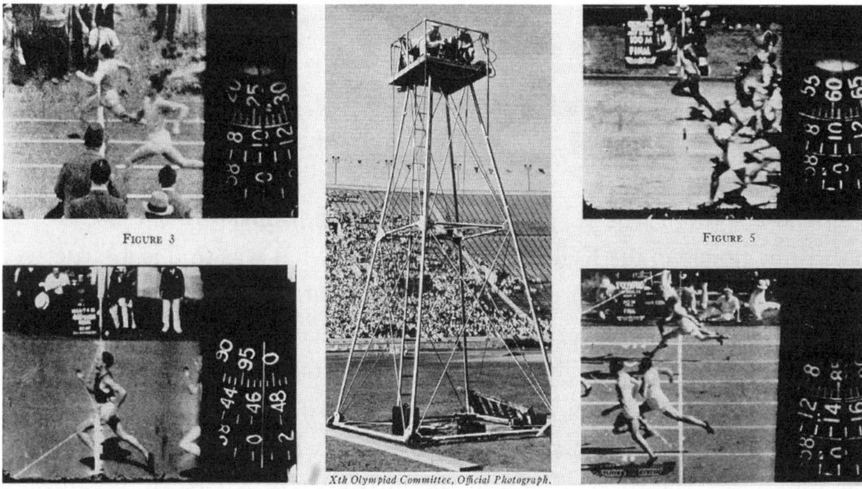

3.9 Page of images from *Bell Telephone Quarterly* showing Kirby's "two eyes" camera in use at pre-Olympic and Olympic events, 1932.

at Baker Field, New York, and its first application at that meet is shown in the top left image in Figure 3.9. Reading from the bottom up, the three rows of the chronometer capture the winning runner's time at 0 minutes, 10 seconds, and 26 hundredths (0:10.26). The device was used for subsequent ICAAAA meets and was shown to the United States Olympic Committee on July 16, 1932 before being employed for the duration of the Los Angeles Games from 31 July to 7 August of that year.[58] At the Games, the camera was positioned sixty feet back from the finish line atop a twenty-five-foot steel tower, following the general model of the "eye in the sky" at contemporary horse-racing tracks.[59]

Kirby was a member of the National Olympic Committee for the Games and also served as a judge for athletics and equestrian events.[60] He was also listed as a US official for the 1928 Amsterdam Games.[61] The Official Report of the 1932 Games is richly illustrated with photographs, including still portraits of the athletes and dozens of finish-line images, particularly those depicting shorter-distance races. However, there is surprisingly little mention of Kirby's apparatus in publications at the time, including news media and official Olympic documents. This is likely because the Kirby system was employed in the Olympics on experimental terms and served only as a back-up to human officials. The system was nonetheless in operation at the Games and was even used to overturn the finish judges' decision in a semifinal of the women's 100m and the men's 110m hurdles finals. For the latter, judges gave American Jack Keller third place but, after consulting the Kirby images, reversed the decision, awarding the bronze medal to Donald Finlay of Great Britain.

Although there was very little media attention given to the use of the finish-line image in the Keller/Finlay decision, what was said is instructive. The *New York Times* referenced that the "camera's eye" had corrected the judge's decision and referred to Kirby's device as a "camera clock."[62] The *Toronto Star* gave slightly more attention to the result and waded into the issue of human vs non-human officiating. The *Star*'s sports editor, Lou Marsh, expressed what a shock it was to see a judge's decision reversed. He noted that the reversal was at the insistence of Kirby as "he and his jury had reviewed the slow motion pictures of the finish of the race." Marsh goes on to note that Kirby was not considered in high regard within Canadian sport due to his "autocratic" ways and controversial decisions at the 1928 Amsterdam Games but that his performance at the Los Angeles Games showed that he was a "square shooter."[63]

On Kirby's camera, Marsh writes, "it makes you wonder how many injustices have been done in former years by the error of the human eye." He further emphasizes the fallibility of human officials, particularly and peculiarly due to their age. He writes, "to pick out the positions of men finishing sprint races ... requires the keen eye of youth," adding the pun, "there are too many old timers on that placing stand." As a solution to this problem Marsh falls back on the notion of the infallibility of the machine, writing, "what we really need is a machine which will take slow motion pictures of the finishes and develop them for reproduction almost instantaneously." And for Marsh this is not simply about the accuracy of judging, but to appease public needs. "The public hates to see the official verdict held up," he writes; "delay creates doubt."[64] Marsh's remarks in 1932 show clear parallels to those of the photographers, writers, and sports enthusiasts of the 1880s and 1890s who saw potential in the camera eye to replace the human eye in sports officiating. And they are paralleled in the discourse of 1930s horse racing as it too adopted the movie camera as a form of evidence. Indeed this same narrative continues to animate discussions of sport and officiating nearly a hundred years after Kirby's "two eyes."

The Official Report of the 1932 Games makes clear that Kirby's system was only used as a back-up to the human officials. After lauding the exacting measurements taken by the Sports Technical Department, the Report notes, "coupled with the accuracy of the course measurements was the certainty of correct timing. Not only had the stop watches used in timing all Olympic events been specially examined and certified by a qualified observatory, but a double check by two electrical timing devices, one operated by hand and the other by a camera, made correct timing an assured fact."[65] A later discussion on the use of timing in athletics events gives a more clear indication of the Kirby system being used:

> The official time for all Track events was that obtained by the timers, appointed by the International Athletic Federation, by means of certified stop watches. Two auxiliary electrical timing devices were used for experimental purposes. Both of these were started by an attachment on the starter's gun. One was stopped by hand at the time the runners hit the tape. The other was provided with a motion picture camera which photographed the runner at the tape and the dial of the time indicator simultaneously.[66]

As further indication of its experimental use, there is a particularly interesting section in the Los Angeles 1932 Olympic Report which offers a comparison of the times taken by the human officials and those recorded by Kirby's system. The data shows differences as large as 17 hundredths of a second, and as small as zero. Though the data do show differences, it is hard to reach any conclusion from the information. This is because human officials used stopwatches timing to the tenth of a second, whereas Kirby's camera recorded to the hundredth. And it is also because the differences in time are not consistent. In some cases Kirby's camera timed the athlete as taking longer, sometimes an equal time, and sometimes quicker. Nonetheless, the data do signal some substantial differences in results depending on the type of timing and imaging apparatus used. And the inclusion of this data in the Official Report shows that advancements in imaging and timing were of concern in elite sport. Indeed, after assessing the 1932 Olympic Games, the International Amateur Athletic Federation called for hundredth-of-a-second timing to become the world standard.[67]

The Kirby "two eyes" camera was not employed in Olympic Games beyond Los Angeles, though a modified version was used for the 1936 Games in Berlin. For the 1936 Games and with the assistance of the "Physikalisch-Technische Reichsanstalt" (Reich Institution for Physical and Technical

Research), a version of the Kirby apparatus was made that functioned like a stereoscopic camera, recording an image immediately before and immediately after the finish. Unfortunately, the images tended to be blurry and the stereoscopic version of the Kirby system was not used again. But as with the 1932 Games, the 1936 Olympics employed the photograph as a form of evidence in determining placing. While there is no record of judges' decisions being overturned by recourse to the photo – as was the case in 1932 – there is increased mention of the use of the image in determining placing. The Official Report of the Games identifies that in the 1,500m men's race "7th to 12th places [were] decided by time camera."[68] The "time camera" was also used to determine 7th to 10th places in the 5,000m men's race[69] and the 3,000m men's steeplechase.[70]

The modified Kirby apparatus was also used to determine podium placing in at least two events. As there was no "separation of the competitors" visible to the naked eye in the men's 100km cycling race, "to decide definitely upon the correct order in which the riders had passed the finishing line, photography had to be resorted to. The time was taken with an electric timing apparatus."[71] The 80m women's hurdles also resorted to the photograph as evidence: "the 80 metre hurdle race ended almost in a tie, Valla (Italy), Taylor (Canada) and Steuer (Germany) reaching the tape practically simultaneously. The judges could not determine who was the victor but the timing camera indicated that Valla was a fraction of an inch ahead of the others and that Steuer crossed the line before Taylor. The time for all three was the same: 11.7 seconds."[72]

Given that this was the 1936 Olympics, a great deal of media attention focused on the political, nationalistic, and racial undertones of the Games. The United States had a particularly deep and talented track and field team, headlined by Jesse Owens, whose dominant performance undercut Hitler's goal of the Games showcasing German, particularly Aryan, supremacy. Western media accounts tended to cover these aspects of the Games and little to no media attention was given to the use of the photographic or timing apparatus to determine placing.[73] Accounts of the women's 80m hurdles in the *New York Times* and *Toronto Daily Star* are indicative of the coverage, simply listing the finishers and their times with no explanation as to how the top finishers received the same time but were awarded different places.[74]

Electric eyes, eyes in the sky, and two eyes were variously employed to record and sometimes determine sporting contests during the opening decades of the twentieth century. Crucially, and in line with work in the history of photography and on objectivity, these mechanically produced images were not simply accepted as inherently truthful or as more accurate than human eyes. Instead, what we see over this period is a complex socio-technological system within which the status of human and machine vision is actively debated. Inventors, photographers, and sports officials and federations, as well as journalists and sports reporters, participated in this process. It is an example of what Nelly Oudshoorn and Trevor Pinch refer to as a "culturally contested zone" through which a given technology is variously adopted, adapted, used, and refuted. This is precisely the case with race-finish photography. There was no single system or practice that rose to prominence and became a standardized or universally accepted form. Instead, the period is marked by experimentation through which the status of the camera, its operators, and its product were being continuously redefined.

Lorenzo del Riccio and the Photo-finish

The second significant development for imaging and timing in the 1930s brings us in line with the earlier discussion on horse racing. On March 20, 1939, Lorenzo del Riccio, an optical engineer with Paramount Studios, filed two US patents, one titled "Camera" and the other "Method of Photographically Recording the Order of Passage of Moving Objects" (Figure 3.10).[75] The device was the product of an interesting collaboration between del Riccio and the entertainers Bing Crosby, Bogart Rogers, and William Lebron. Crosby and other Hollywood celebrities purchased a racetrack in Del Mar, California, and, prior to opening in 1937, enlisted del Riccio to develop a finish-line imaging and timing system. A 1939 article in *The Blood-Horse* shares an interesting origin story, as offered by del Riccio. While recuperating from a car accident, del Riccio followed the then-feverish debate over finish-line imaging in horse racing. And then, while "whiling away his time with the newspapers, Mr. del Riccio realized that he had already developed a camera for the job."[76] Del Riccio's existing camera was used for measuring time intervals in machinery but, according to the origin story,

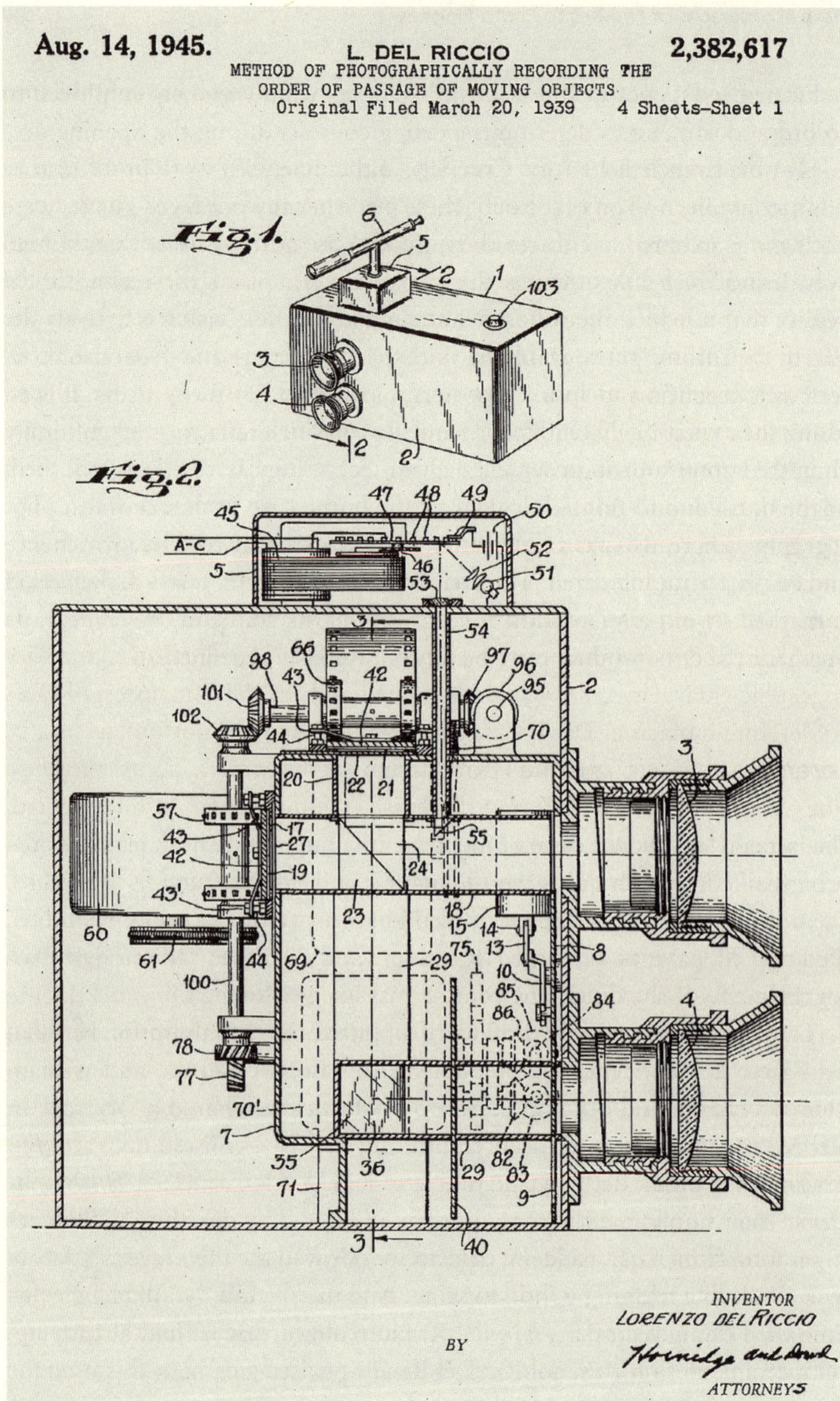

3.10 Lorenzo del Riccio's patent application for his "slit camera," 1939.

he recognized its potential for finish-line imaging and then brought the idea to Bing Crosby.

However much del Riccio's version of the invention is accurate, and as has already been shown, the debate over finish-line systems in 1930s horse racing was extensive. Though the potential problem of parallax had been solved and finish-line imaging systems were widely used, there was still the reality that movie-camera-based systems could never be perfectly accurate due to their frame-rates. Del Riccio's camera offered a solution to this problem. His invention included two lenses arranged vertically to be aligned along the axis of the finish line. The device was to be placed slightly higher than the contestants in order to effectively capture distances between them at the finish and to not be blocked by the body of an athlete or horse. The top lens used transparent film while the bottom one was loaded with sensitized photographic paper. The former would allow for prints and enlargements but could also be used for projections to be made (in del Riccio's view, for the entertainment of spectators), while the latter allowed for photographic enlargements to be made immediately at the conclusion of races to determine placing. Del Riccio also required that the bottom camera be trained on a "target" that was placed opposite the camera, across the finish line. As the competitors neared the finish, the device would be triggered, the bottom lens would capture images of the target, and both lenses would record all competitors crossing the line. Once all competitors had finished, the bottom lens would capture a second sequence of images of the target. This would serve as a "check" for accuracy so that the camera's position on the plane of the finish line could always be verified.

There are two especially noteworthy features of del Riccio's device that addressed key concerns in horse racing and athletics. First, his device included a type of "time-stamp" directly on the finish-line image. Whereas the Kirby "two eyes" camera recorded the athletes in one lens and a chronograph in the other, del Riccio's invention included a timing unit within the device that imprinted the time directly on both films. As shown in Figure 3.11, a rotating disc inside the camera was demarcated by units of parts of a second (ex. fifths). The individual units would be illuminated by a small lamp, fed by an electric pulse, with the illumination imprinting the time unit on the film. In this way, del Riccio's device merged timing and imaging in ways that previous systems such as Kirby's had not. The recording of timing and imaging data were internal to the apparatus, not accomplished through external means such as photographing a clock. Time became part of the finish-line image in a new and very literal way.

The second and more significant improvement by del Riccio came from a deficiency he found in Kirby's system and others that promoted the use of movie cameras. On these systems, del Riccio writes, "there is a space of time between successive individual pictures during which there is no record made of the position of the horses, which may be the precise moment in which the foremost horses crossed the line."[77] In other words, even at rates of 128, 200, or 360 images per second, each image created through the movie camera is nonetheless a still image with the minute physical distance between frames of film representative of distinct sections of race time and space that are not recorded. This was precisely the problem identified by those within the horse-racing community who were attuned to the finer details of race-finish imaging.

To correct this, del Riccio proposed to continuously record the finish. He described it thus: "instead of photographing the finish of the different contestants intermittently on a series of successive individual frames, the camera used in the present invention continuously photographs on a travelling film only the passage of the contestants across the finish line."[78] To do this, del Riccio created a slit aperture that was focused on the finish line. What was captured by the camera was only what passed through the narrow slit and was imprinted on film that ran at a parallel speed to the race participants. A 1938 article on the invention summarizes its key features: "it has no shutters, registers by means of photographs of a clock the exact time it takes each horse in a race to reach the finish, produces a picture in about 40 seconds, occupies half the space of other cameras, [and] eliminates background so that the images of the horses are set against a white background."[79] The "slit camera" invented by del Riccio is the basis of photo-finish imaging and its development marks a fundamental turning point in the use of the camera to determine placing.

Where a traditional photographic camera captures a distinct space in a moment in time, a slit camera captures the passing of time through a small, fixed space. I have referred to this distinction earlier as the difference between photographs *of* finishes and photo-finishes. Hemment's work, the use of chronophotograpy at the Paris Olympics, the judge's stand from the 1912 Games, and Kirby's "two eyes" all captured photographs *of* finishes, though

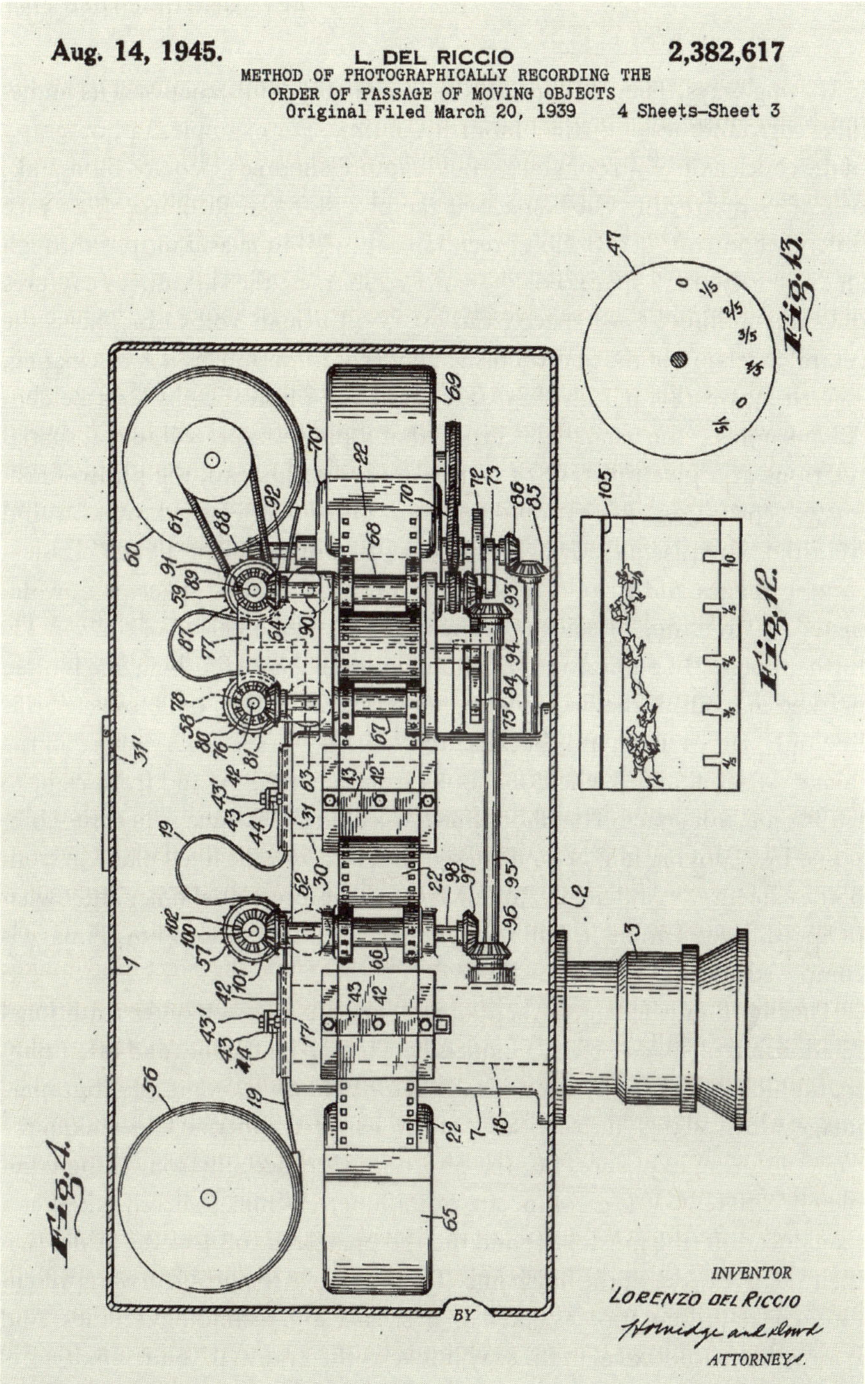

3.11 Lorenzo del Riccio, diagram from patent application showing the process for imprinting time intervals onto the film, 1939.

in varying ways. They all captured the space of the finish line and its immediate surroundings at distinct moments in time. For example, a photograph of the conclusion of a 100m race would capture hundreds, perhaps thousands, of square metres of visible space at the precise moment of 10:01.45 race time. By contrast, del Riccio's invention captured time as it moved through an extremely small space. For the same 100m race, the slit camera captures the same millimetres of space from 9:59.00 through 10:05.00. This is the central inversion of the photo-finish and it is as important as it is fascinating.

Writing on this paradoxical feature of the photo-finish, Kris Belden-Adams notes, "the usual expectation that a photograph will reveal spatial relations at a given instant of time is reversed. Instead, the photo-finish image depicts a fixed location – the finish line – over elapsed time."[80] And Maarten Vanvolsem describes it as such: "the difference between classical shutter images and strip images is that time, rather than space, is now depicted by stretching one line (a plane in space) over a period of time."[81] He further notes: "In publications of photo finish images, a finishing line is often marked in front of the first athlete, horse, cyclist and so on. However, this line only serves as an aid, because the finishing line is everywhere in the image. What changes when one looks from left to right and from right to left is time, not space. The photo finish is a continuous image in time, composed by a moving film behind a fixed slot, of a specific fixed plane in front of the camera."[82] And finally, John Marsden, a professional timer and owner of Speed River Timing in Ontario, explained that the photo-finish image is composed entirely of the finish line.[83]

The photo-finish image is therefore not just an inversion of the traditional relationship of space-time so eloquently taken up by Barthes and other photographic scholars; it is paradoxical.[84] It *looks* like a standard photographic image, albeit with some obvious distortions, as if someone had shaken the camera during exposure. But the photo-finish is actually something completely different. It is a composite of millimetres-thick "slices" taken at a fixed location (the finish line) and then re-presented to show the athletes in their relative order at the finish line. This is exactly the problem of representation or re-presentation as taken up in science and technology studies. And it is further paradoxical in the way it inverts the "normal" blurring of moving subject matter. In a traditional photograph, a quickly moving subject or object can create a blur in the final image. By contrast, blurs in a photo-finish are the result of objects that are relatively still compared to the fast-moving film within the slit camera. The stable and "normal"-looking parts of a runner in a photo-finish image are because the runner and film are moving at the same pace. The appearance of that same runner's leg as blurred and distended is due to it moving at a different pace from that of the film.

Much of the current public discourse about photo-finishes, ties, and dead heats fundamentally misunderstands this aspect of the technology. And so it is all the more interesting to note that some sports writers and enthusiasts at the time of del Riccio identified this aspect of his work. Clem McCarthy noted in a 1938 piece that "the calibrated film moves at the speed of the horses and photographs each as it enters a light 'field.' Developed, the tape shows the margins – in fractions of seconds – between every horse."[85] A 1939 piece on del Riccio offers considerable more detail: "The camera, now officially named the Photochart, has no shutter. Instead it has a small vertical slit (1/18,000 of an inch wide …), which is focused on the finish line, and covers a crosswise section of the race track about two inches wide."[86] The article then picks up on the key difference with del Riccio's camera, noting, "as the horses come to the finish they are photographed, so that the resulting picture is not one in which the winner is on the line, the second horse a bit back, the third perhaps a length from it, and so on. Instead, every horse is photographed on the finish line, and *every part of every horse is photographed on the finish line*" (emphasis in original). And after explaining how the device also records time, it offers a final example: "the photograph consequently does not show that Challedon finished a length and a half in front of Gilded Knight; it shows that he finished between one-fifth and two-fifths of a second in front of him." Del Riccio's device married imaging and timing and offered to contain all the labour involved in the two practices into a single, portable, and relatively small apparatus.

That del Riccio's system – and it is worth noting that he developed many different apparatuses and held numerous patents – emerged from within the Hollywood movie studios is important. Like the other movie-camera systems described earlier in the chapter, a key component of del Riccio's device was the ability to project recordings of races to a large audience. At Paramount del Riccio was a key person in the development of "magnafilm," which was an early iteration of wide-screen, using film twice the width of a traditional reel that "throws on a screen pictures that fill the stage like squawkies fill the auditorium."[87] By the 1940s, horse racing was a well-established, lucrative business and Crosby's track at Del Mar and his involvement with the track at Hollywood Park presented potential for significant revenue. The blending of entertainment and evidence provided for by del Riccio's device fit this burgeoning market perfectly.

The economic benefits of del Riccio's system were recognized from its origins and, in order to distribute and promote his apparatus, del Riccio and Bogart Rogers formed Photochart, Incorporated in 1937, which was also the name used to describe the camera system and its product. The name is significant. A "chart" is the term used for the official record of horse races and includes all essential information such as "order of finish, the positions of horses at various stages of a race, track conditions, purses, odds, and payouts."[88] In this way, the name "photochart" is a play on the etymology of "photography." Just as *photography* merges *photos* and *graphe* to form "writing with light," *photochart* suggests a racing record that is the product of nature itself, written by light onto film.

Del Riccio's relationship with Rogers and with Photochart, Inc. was complicated and contentious in large part due to the financial gains to be made in the emerging photo-finish business. Del Riccio and Rogers created Photochart, Inc. as an equal partnership in 1937, but on 25 June 1941, and in response to continued disagreements, entered into a formal licensing agreement. Del Riccio gave up his half of the company to Rogers and his associates (which included Bing Crosby), and in turn Photochart was granted exclusive licence to use "photochart" or the "photochart camera" to photograph horse or other races for seventeen years, with royalties paid to del Riccio. Del Riccio also agreed to not compete with Photochart for a period of five years. Numerous lawsuits followed, including an 11 October 1945 filing by Photochart against del Riccio, claiming that he had violated the agreement by working with other companies and producing new cameras. The judge placed an injunction on del Riccio, but by the time the case returned to court the five-year no-compete clause had expired and the judge ruled that del Riccio could compete. Del Riccio later sued Photochart for not providing royalty payments, and in 1947 del Riccio and Photochart united as plaintiffs against Photo Patrol Incorporated for patent infringement.[89] The specifics of the patent disputes and other litigations between del Riccio, Photochart, Inc., and other groups are beyond the scope of this project. Instead, it is sufficient to note that, by the 1940s, finish-line timing and imaging systems operated within a growing, competitive, and often contentious industry.

Conclusion

In the history of the photo-finish, the roughly forty-year period at the start of the twentieth century is marked by a gradual transition across four areas. First, the problems of human reaction time were addressed through the increased automation of finish-line photography. The continued use of electromagnetic shutter releases and photocells gave rise to "electric eyes" and eventually movie-camera systems so that the timing and imaging of a race was no longer dependent on human reaction time but could be recorded continuously, across time.

Second, the period marked the development of a more complete and precise racing record. Barber's patent to photograph the time alongside race participants was a key first step and was advanced through faster frame rates in cameras, automated systems of shutter release, and photocell "light beams" at the finish line, ultimately culminating in the photochart – an image-based finish-line document that gave detailed information on each participant. And finishing times that were recorded to the fifth of a second at the beginning of the century were being recorded to the hundredth or thousandth by mid-century. The tenth of a second that Canales equates with the modern era had moved two decimal places.

The formal use of the image as a decision-making tool in sport is the third area of development over this period. By the beginning of the twentieth century, cameras were employed in various ways across horse racing, athletics, and other sports, but their use as evidence developed gradually over the ensuing decades. The 1912 Stockholm Games was the first case of a photograph used to determine placing at the Olympics, but by the 1930s the Games in Los Angeles and Berlin show significant use of the photograph as evidence. The horse-racing community took up this debate in a significant way throughout the 1930s so that by the close of the decade the "eye in the sky" was generally accepted as an accurate record of the race.

The fourth development over this period was the emergence of a distinct commercial market for finish-line imaging. The work of instantaneous photographers and sports enthusiasts in the 1880s and 1890s signalled the possibility for this market, but it took until the 1930s and the then-burgeoning and highly lucrative horse-racing industry for it to be a reality. This facet of the photo-finish also importantly wedded the entertainment and evidentiary functions of the image, adding another layer to the complex, "culturally contested zone" of sport decision-making. Movie-camera systems enabled post-race projections of racing events for the viewing public, but they also enabled the projection of slow-motion replays during the live event. This was essential not just for public entertainment and amusement but for the sports gambling industry, as concerned bettors could see with their own eyes who had won and lost a given race.

These developments culminated in the creation of the slit camera, which constitutes a key shift from photographing finishes to photo-finishes. Many of the issues that had challenged earlier efforts in race-finish photography, primarily those tied to human reaction time and the technical constraints of still images, were solved with the slit camera. But it would be a mistake to attribute this process as one of pure technological transformation. Instead, the development of the slit camera has as much to do with a desire to determine accurate placing as it does with solving a human/technological problem. The modernization of sport, the move from amateurism to professionalism, the rise of nationalism with the Olympic movement, and the increasingly competitive commercial marketplace for sport were essential preconditions for the creation of the photo-finish.

Whether in the form of the electric eye, the eye in the sky, the two eyes, or the photochart, the camera did not fully replace the human eye in sport officiating and in determining the placing of participants. Instead, they merged into a reasonably complex and large officiating apparatus. An interwoven network of race officials, timers, judges, and photographers collected various forms of race data and collectively produced race results. Importantly, though, it was increasingly the photograph that carried the burden of proof. Human officials were still central to sport, and in fact increased in numbers as sport became more complex and professionalized, but over the course of forty years an increasing number of technological devices were created to fix what were perceived to be the problems of human vision. In this way, the opening decades of twentieth-century sport were essential in establishing the photograph's reputation as an accurate, mechanically objective record.

In the practice of mounting and officiating sports events and in the professional and public discourse that surrounded them, the mechanically produced image was used to make claims to objectivity in ways that human officials could not. Crucially, and in line with Daston and Galison's work on the topic, such objectivity was not due to the absence of the human but because of their non-intervention.[90] The camera was used to assist judges in decision-making in the early 1900s (and prior to this as in chapter 2) and was formally adopted in this capacity for the 1912 Olympic Games. By the 1930s, the image was finding increasing acceptance as an accurate and important part of judging sporting contests and was even used to overturn judges' decisions. This careful balance between the human eye and "electric eye" was gradually built over the opening decades of the twentieth century.

To conclude I turn to another invention of del Riccio, represented in Figure 3.12. The device pairs a set of binoculars with a small movie camera to be used by a set of race officials to continuously record portions of a race. The peculiar invention perfectly encapsulates the nexus of human and machine in the increasingly lucrative market of modern sport. In the opening paragraph of the patent application, del Riccio is clear about its rationale: "it is important that the horses and their jockeys be kept under observation as much as possible during the running of a race to guard against infractions of the rules and improper practices on the part of one jockey against another and his horse or with respect to his own horse." The device was a response to a growing problem in horse racing at the time: cheating or match-fixing. Del Riccio's solution was a form of mass surveillance: to photographically record the entire race so that infractions could be made visible and disputes resolved through recourse to the camera. Del Riccio's system brought together moving cameras and slit cameras to capture an ever more comprehensive racing record.

Patrol judges stationed around the track, who were already in existence at the time of del Riccio's invention, were equipped with a binocular-camera, and each would record one-eighth of a mile of the race, one-sixteenth as the horses approached, and one-sixteenth as they receded. The top images in Figure 3.12 show del Riccio's schematic for how the binocular-cameras would cover the entire field of the racetrack. The benefit, as del Riccio outlined, was the objectivity of the image in resolving disputes. He writes, "Since the reports made by such patrol judges are naturally the result of

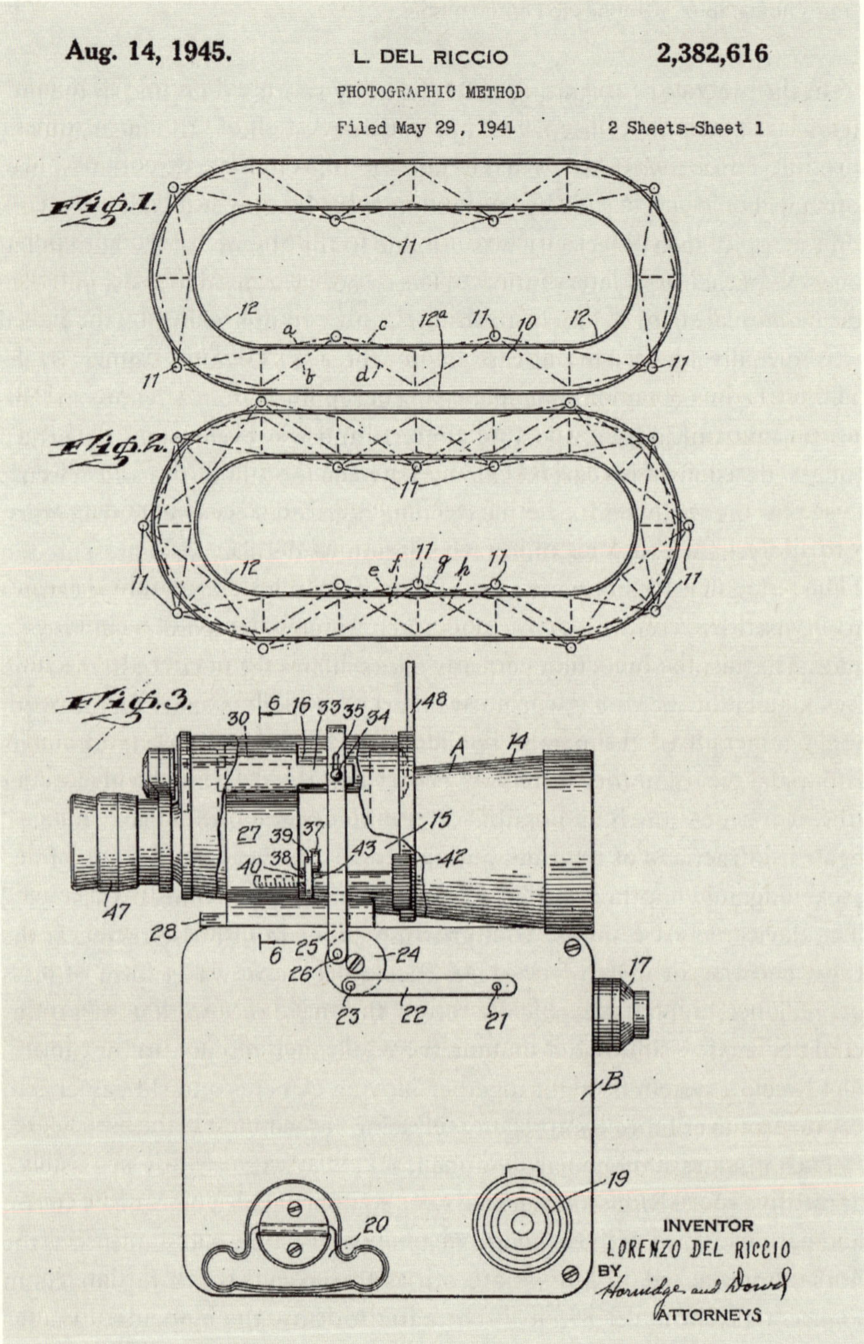

3.12 Lorenzo del Riccio, "Photographic Method." Patent, 1941.

personal observation and the judgment of the individual patrol judge in a particular division, the decision on a disputed question of fact may ofttimes be erroneous or unsatisfactory." He goes on to note that, by contrast, his system will produce "a length of motion picture film to which reference may be made on all questions as to what took place during each particular portion of the race." And later, he articulates a further benefit of his invention: "the individual strips of film comprising the photographs taken by the eight successive patrol judges are, after development, assembled into a single strip and there is thus obtained a complete photographic record of the race." Del Riccio's binocular-camera was officially adopted at Hollywood Park for their 1941 racing season. Del Riccio and track manager Jack Mackenzie were praised for the invention for both its technological advancement and its ability to address the problems of in-race infractions.[91]

The binocular-camera of 1945 is a material manifestation of the drive in early-twentieth-century sport to modernize through the use of technology. Central to this, the binocular-camera yielded an ever more detailed racing record, and it did so with the promise of mechanical objectivity. Paired with the slit camera used at the finish line, del Riccio's invention offered a complete visual record of the entirety of a horse race. Underlying the invention is the firm belief in a technological solution to not just one but two human problems. First, and as with previous practices, the vision and memory of patrol judges were prone to error compared to the mechanically objective binocular-camera. Second, humans were fallible in that they would cheat in order to affect the outcome of a race. Higher purses and stakes within horse racing led to charges of corruption and match-fixing, which in turn led to del Riccio's solution of making the whole race and not just the finish line visible.

A by-product of the modernization of sport – as manifest in the binocular-camera – was the development and regulation of an expanding, often highly competitive sports industry. Sut Jhally has written of the sports-media complex that developed with the marriage of sports (mainly NFL football) and television in the 1960s, but we can see its antecedents much earlier, from Hemment's work in the 1890s through to the development of a significant sport marketplace in the 1930s.[92] Mark Dyreson has addressed this in specific relation to image rights in the Olympic Games, showing that the Paris and Amsterdam Games in the 1920s were precedent-setting in that they established monopolies over the still and moving image rights of the Games.[93]

An essential but almost entirely ignored part of this industry is the growth and development of sports imaging and timing companies. Numerous race-finish photography systems developed over the opening decades of the twentieth century, and by the 1940s, several groups competed, sometimes in court, to have their systems installed at sport venues. In this way, increasing competitiveness on the field was matched by increasing competitiveness off the field.

CHAPTER FOUR

The Business of the Photo-Finish: OMEGA and the Olympic Games

As a young person watching sport on television, I often puzzled at the inclusion of "Swiss Timing" on scoreboards, display boards, or in other areas of the sports venue or the event's television broadcast. I wondered, "why did the Swiss have to do the timing for sports events?" "What was it about the Swiss that made them such good timers?" "Why wasn't there American Timing or Canadian Timing, particularly at American or Canadian events?" Now, many years later, the most immediate response to these questions is that Swiss Timing is a company and what I was seeing on TV was a company logo and not a statement about a nation and its characteristics. However, the reality is a little more complicated: the inclusion of "Swiss Timing" at sports venues and on television broadcasts was the promotion of both a corporation and a nation. And its particular dominance at sporting events during my childhood years in the 1970s and 1980s reflects the historically specific conditions of sports timing and the photo-finish.

Over nearly a century-long process, OMEGA has risen to a position of prominence in providing timing and photo-finish services for elite-level sport. Key to this are the corporate structure of OMEGA, its continued contract negotiations for the Olympic Games, and its competitive business practices. Drawing largely from contracts and correspondence in the Olympic archives in Lausanne, Switzerland, and from the Official Reports of the Olympic Games, this chapter traces the further development of the photo-finish, but with particular attention to its larger institutional context.[1] OMEGA and its affiliates have played an active role in defining and promoting the photo-finish as a largely infallible sport decision-making technology. Due to both its scale and its active history of timing, OMEGA has had an outsized role in shaping the discourse or narrative of performance measurement in elite-level sport.

Examining OMEGA's role in the history of the photo-finish shows direct parallels with the increasing professionalization and commercialization of sport. Importantly, over the mid-to-late twentieth century, the photo-finish itself came to be increasingly professionalized and part of a rapidly expanding and highly lucrative commercial market. Within such a context, OMEGA and related Swiss time-keeping companies both helped to build and benefited from a discourse that positioned timing and the photo-finish as increasingly unmediated indicators of athlete performance, and timing personnel as uniquely trained professionals. Nonetheless, and despite OMEGA's best efforts, increasingly precise timing and photo-finish systems did not replace human eyes as the ultimate source of decision-making. As with instantaneous photography at the turn of the twentieth century and the "electric eyes" and "eyes in the sky" of early-twentieth-century horse racing, the relationship between the camera eye and the human eye remained in dispute.

OMEGA: History and Structure

OMEGA was formally established as a company in 1903, though its roots extend to the mid-nineteenth century.[2] A year after its founding, OMEGA provided time-keeping for the 1904 Gordon Bennett Cup balloon race, which is one of the earliest formal relationships between a watchmaking company and a sports event. However, OMEGA's status as a world leader in sports timing developed alongside its formal relationship with the International Olympic Committee. That relationship began with OMEGA providing chronographs for the 1932 Olympic Games in Los Angeles, where Kirby's "two eyes" camera had debuted. Table 4.1 shows the timing providers for all Olympic Games. Of the forty Games listed, timing and photo-finish services for thirty-two were provided by OMEGA and related Swiss companies. As an example of the size and scope of the services provided by OMEGA, and in contrast to the chronographs for Los Angeles, for the London 2012 Olympics they provided 450 tonnes of equipment, more than 450 technicians, 70 display boards, and 175 kilometres of cable and optical fibre.

The development of OMEGA as a leader in sports timing and photo-finishes is a curious mix of business acumen, fortuitous timing, and national

Table 4.1
Official timing providers for the Olympic Games

Year	Summer/winter	Location	Provider
1932	S	Los Angeles	OMEGA
1936	S	Berlin	Zeis Ikon & Agfa
1936	W	Garmisch	n/a
1948	S	London	OMEGA
1948	W	St Moritz	OMEGA
1952	S	Helsinki	OMEGA
1952	W	Oslo	Longines
1956	S	Melbourne	OMEGA
1956	W	Cortina	OMEGA
1960	S	Rome	OMEGA
1960	W	Squaw Valley	Longines
1964	S	Tokyo	Seiko
1964	W	Innsbruck	OMEGA
1968	S	Mexico	OMEGA
1968	W	Grenoble	OMEGA & Longines
1972	S	Munich	Junghans & Longines
1972	W	Sapporo	Seiko
1976	S	Montreal	Swiss Timing
1976	W	Innsbruck	Swiss Timing
1980	S	Moscow	Swiss Timing
1980	W	Lake Placid	Swiss Timing
1984	S	Los Angeles	Swiss Timing
1984	W	Sarajevo	Swiss Timing
1988	S	Seoul	Swiss Timing
1988	W	Calgary	Swiss Timing
1992	S	Barcelona	Seiko
1992	W	Albertville	Swiss Timing
1994	W	Lillehammer	Seiko
1996	S	Atlanta	Swatch
1998	W	Nagano	Seiko
2000	S	Sydney	Swiss Timing
2002	W	Salt Lake	Seiko
2004	S	Athens	Swatch
2006	W	Torino	OMEGA
2008	S	Beijing	OMEGA
2010	W	Vancouver	OMEGA
2012	S	London	OMEGA
2014	W	Sochi	OMEGA
2016	S	Rio	OMEGA
2018	W	PyeongChang	OMEGA

pride. In 1930 OMEGA merged with another Swiss watchmaking company, Tissot, forming the Société Suisse pour l'Industrie Horlogère (SSIH). Another Swiss watchmaking group, the Allgemeine Gesellschaft der Schweizerischen Uhrenindustrie (ASUAG), was founded a year later in 1931. By the 1970s both SSIH and ASUAG were struggling as companies and faced liquidation, in large part because of the growth of the Japanese market with its use of quartz for time-keeping, which was both highly accurate and inexpensive. In response, Nicolas G. Hayek, then CEO of Hayek Engineering, was tasked to find ways to avoid this liquidation and to keep the two corporations and their brands in Swiss hands. A central result of Hayek's work was the merger of the two struggling units into the Swiss Corporation for Microelectronics and Watchmaking Industries Ltd (SMH) in 1983, renamed the Swatch Group in 1998. The Group's name stems from another of Hayek's recommendations, which was the production of a mass-market, high-quality, and "fun" Swiss Watch – which launched as Swatch in 1983 to tremendous success.

The Swatch Group is the single biggest watchmaking company in the world. In 2017 the Group posted net sales of CHF 7,989,000,000 and a net income of CHF 755,000,000.[3] The Group controls eighteen different watch brands: Balmain, Blancpain, Breguet, Certina, CK Calvin Klein, Endura, Flik Flak, Glashütte Original, Hamilton, Harry Winston, Jaquet Droz, Léon Hatot, Longines, Mido, OMEGA, Rado, Swatch, Tissot, and Union Glashütte. The Group also owns numerous production companies that are responsible for various watch movements, and it owns companies that research and provide electronic systems. One of these groups, Swiss Timing, is especially important in sports timing and imaging services. Swiss Timing was formed in July of 1972 by merging the sports timing sections of OMEGA and Longines. Prior to that, OMEGA and Longines competed against one another for sports timing contracts, including for the Olympic Games. Swiss Timing operates in the form of a quasi-independent third-party partner to the other Swatch Group brands, meaning that they share research and development in providing timing systems for sports but also serve as a direct provider to sports events.

The merger of SSIH and ASUAG into the Swatch Group with all of its subsidiary brands did much to centralize sports timing under a national umbrella, capitalizing on and contributing to Switzerland's reputation as a world leader in precision time-keeping. Prior to the 1970s and 1980s numerous Swiss watch brands competed against one another and against non-Swiss companies within the sports timing industry. In terms of the Olympic Games, as is illustrated in Table 4.1, OMEGA and Longines competed, with each winning contracts for several Games. From 1976 through 1988, and following the merger of the sports timing divisions of OMEGA and Longines, timing was provided by the resultant company, Swiss Timing. This centralization yielded advantages associated with economies of scale and a diversification of markets and products. Interestingly, this centralization is not immediately visible in the sporting world. The names Longines, Tissot, Rado, OMEGA, and Swiss Timing are highly visible at sporting events, often appearing as lead sponsors or providers. However, since the 1980s, it is important to remember that all of these brands operate as subsidiaries of the Swatch Group.

A former head of one of Swiss Timing's factories, J.P. Bovay, has written a significant number of pieces on Swiss Timing, OMEGA, and time-keeping more generally.[4] These documents, copies of which are held in the archives of the Olympic Studies Centre, are a curious mix of history and promotion. They were typically translated into a few languages, from the original French into English and German, with only a few hundred copies of each language produced, and many are richly illustrated, aesthetically beautiful objects. Their high production value, attention to historical detail, and overtly promotional tone are indicative of OMEGA's corporate and philosophical approach to time-keeping. The central theme throughout Bovay's work is that timing is both an art and a science and that Swiss Timers are both artists and scientists.

Just as the International Olympic Committee and the founder of the modern Olympic Games, Pierre de Coubertin, promote the Games as part of an historical trajectory from antiquity, so too does Bovay position timing in athletics within more universal quests for beauty and precision. For example, in *Coliseum '32–'84*, which is a glossy coffee-table-type book issued for the fiftieth anniversary of OMEGA's involvement in the Olympic Games, Bovay writes, "From Marcel Duchamp to Jean Tinguely, by way of Serge Eisenstein, Antonio Gaudi and Blaise Cendrars, the concept of purpose has always been considered as closely linked to artistic perception. The passage of time, the wisest of all judges, has proved that the anonymous craftsmen of yesteryear are truly the artists of today."[5] To this end, Bovay celebrates G.T. Kirby (creator of the "two eyes" camera discussed in chapter 3) as one such craftsman turned artist. He writes:

> patents files are the manuscripts of a new breed of poets of modern times: researchers and inventors. G.T. Kirby may be considered as the best example of the many researchers who, whether known or unknown, working alone or for an organisation, have never known wealth or celebrity but through their research, they have brought that impartiality and calmness so necessary in protecting the athlete faced with emotional and financial pressures.[6]

The positioning of timing as both an art and a science and as part of a larger universal quest for truth and knowledge is found throughout the timing contracts and promotional materials in the archives. And it is exemplified in the most recent annual report of the Swatch Group. Astronomical images such as galaxies, planets, and star-filled skies dominate the report, including its cover, and the headshots of Swatch Group executives are paired with icons showing their astrological signs. The report opens with the following text, set beneath an image of a Swatch watch face and under the headline "The Earth, the Sun, a Year":

> The Earth needs about 365.25 days to complete its gravity-assisted elliptical orbit of the sun. Of course, we generally round this number down and take care of that extra quarter day every four years. Typically, a day consists of 24 hours but we often record its two 12-hour halves. The 8760 hours in Swatch Group's 2017 were significant. This is their story.[7]

The text is telling as it speaks to the connection between the literal turn of the natural world and humans' attempts to record it and provide it a rationalizing structure (via time). The passage also personifies time, giving it agency and a voice, noting that the report is the story of 8,760 hours, not of the humans who populate the Swatch Group.

Bovay's writing and the Swatch Group report are component parts of a larger discourse surrounding the photo-finish, contributing to what Lisa

Cartwright terms a "cultural narrative."[8] In her essay on the Visible Human Project, Cartwright develops the notion of "cultural narratives" to describe the dominant stories that emerged in the academic, professional, and popular press following the release of the Visible Man and Visible Woman data sets. It is similarly possible to identify dominant cultural narratives that developed surrounding timing and the photo-finish. OMEGA's promotional writing as well as materials found in the contracts and correspondence of the Olympic archives reveal a distinct narrative related to timing which sees the practice as metaphysical and philosophical as much as it is technological. This cultural narrative also positions the Swiss as uniquely talented artist-scientists of time-keeping. In this way, the time-keepers who are identified and promoted through corporate communication reflect back to Daston and Galison's "truth to nature" episteme, whereby the metaphysically gifted scientist was able to extract truth from the natural world.

OMEGA at the Olympics: Developments in Photo-Finish Technology

The International Olympic Committee (IOC) awards the Olympics to various host nations through a competitive bidding process. Once awarded, the host nation's Local Olympic Organizing Committee (LOOC) is then responsible for planning, launching, and overseeing the Games. It is the responsibility of the LOOC to negotiate contracts and terms with various Olympic partners. In terms of timing and the photo-finish, this means that the contract for such services is negotiated for each Games between the LOOC and timing companies. And it is worth noting that, given the significant streams of revenue available through an Olympic Games, LOOCs often seek to employ local and national businesses. Adding to the complexity, the regulations governing individual sports are managed by international sports federations, including the International Association of Athletics Federations (IAAF) for track and field, the Fédération Internationale de Natation (FINA) for swimming, and the Fédération Internationale de Ski (FIS) for skiing. Providing timing and photo-finish services for an Olympic Games therefore involves collaboration and consultation between the IOC, the LOOC (with its preference to award contracts to host-nation companies), the international sports federations, and the timing companies. And given the increasingly complex and commercial nature of the Olympic Games, timing and photo-finish services (including the contracts that govern them) show a parallel trajectory of increasing complexity over the twentieth and early twenty-first centuries.

Though OMEGA's formal relationship with the IOC began with the 1932 Games, its first comprehensive participation was at the 1948 Games in London. Timing and photo-finish services for the 1936 Games in Berlin and Garmisch were provided by German companies under the direction of the Reich Institution for Physical and Technical Research. With the Games of 1940 and 1944 being cancelled due to war, the next Olympics were the 1948 Winter Games in St Moritz and Summer Games in London. In their promotional material OMEGA refers to this as the "birth of modern timing" and states that "it was at this Olympiad that machines began to out-perform human beings for accuracy."[9]

Finish-line systems for the 1948 Games in London – the "machines" said to outperform humans – were provided through a collaboration between OMEGA and the Race Finish Recording Company of London, UK. The latter was formed in 1946 in response to a request from the Jockey Club about using photography to determine placing in horse racing. For the 1948 Games, OMEGA provided the timing services, with the Race Finish Recording Company providing the photo-finish images. The Official Olympic Report for the 1948 Games includes four photo-finish images, the first time an actual photo-finish (i.e. one made with a slit camera) appears in an Official Olympic Report (Figure 4.1). The finishes of three track events are depicted (100m men's sprint, 110m men's hurdles, 80m women's hurdles) and one cycling event (1,000m men's sprint).[10] The report also includes brief but important sections on time-keeping and photo-finishes. The former notes that in early 1947 OMEGA had offered to supply all necessary timekeeping devices for the Games for free, and that the offer was accepted by the London Olympic Organizing Committee. OMEGA and the Organizing Committee worked with the existing sports federations to determine the specific number and precision of the timepieces needed, and OMEGA technicians also attended the Games providing support where needed.

The photo-finish services provided by the Race Finish Recording Company were sparingly used. After substantial discussions between the Olympic Organizing Committee and sports federations it was agreed that the photo-finish camera would be used for cycling events "but only as an aid to the judges in athletic track events when necessary."[11] The camera was installed

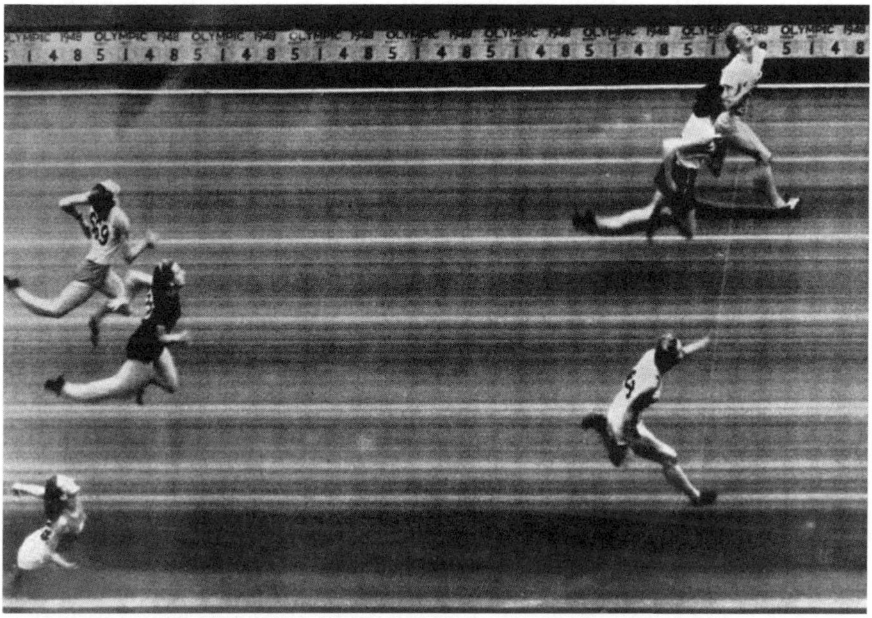

4.1 Photo-finish of women's 80m hurdles, 1948 Olympic Games in London.

60 feet above the track in the roof of Empire Stadium and prints could be created within 90 seconds. The images were sent along a hand-operated lift from the camera stand to the judges at the finish line. And, as later noted in the Official Report: "On the opposite side of the track to the camera, on the finishing line, was a revolving drum, synchronised to the camera speed. This ensured that every print showed a series of reproductions of the lettering on this drum, which carried the wording 'Wembley,' and the date and programme number of the event being photographed. This guaranteed identification of the photograph against the particular event."[12]

The revolving drum mentioned in the 1948 Report follows the practice discussed in chapter 3 in relation to Barber's and Petri's attempts to create a complete racing record. Whereas Barber and Petri created a board on which identifying information was written, the Race Finish Recording Company equipment used in London made its record by means of a spinning drum, timed with the speed of film in the slit camera. As shown in Figure 4.1, the drum for this particular race included "Olympic 48" and the numbers 4, 8, 5, and 1, with 4 and 8 corresponding to the date of the race,

4 August 1948. This effectively highlights a central role of the photo-finish: to provide a documentary record of the event. The use of the drum is also important as it foreshadows an issue that would become central to timing and imaging services in sports: sponsorship and advertising. In subsequent games, OMEGA was able to reproduce their company name in photo-finish images by including it on the rotating drum.

The Race Finish Recording Company continued to provide photo-finish services for Olympic Games in partnership with OMEGA. Their collaboration at the 1948 Games gave rise to the first complete photo-finish camera in 1949, the Racend OMEGA, which combined a quartz clock and slit camera. The Racend OMEGA was used again at the 1952 Games in Helsinki and was detailed in OMEGA's contract proposal for the Games (Figure 4.2). As with the 1948 Games, OMEGA provided all timing services. The Olympic Report includes a section, "Time-Keeping and Photo-Finish," which again stresses the uniqueness of the photo-finish:

> The camera with attached time-keeping device (Racend OMEGA Timer) used in the Olympic Stadium was similar to that used in London in 1948. This apparatus enables the order in which competitors finished to be established with absolute accuracy even though the human eye could detect no space between them. The picture taken by the camera resembles an ordinary photograph. Nevertheless, in it each competitor has been individually photographed at the instant he crossed the line. In reality, no such over-all situation ever existed as that shown in the photograph recorded by the camera.[13]

The Helsinki Report is illustrative of a larger trend in the treatment of the photo-finish during the middle decades of the twentieth century. There was a relatively nuanced discussion of the photo-finish as a unique visual form and as something that was not a traditional photograph but nonetheless had clear photographic properties. The uncertainty about what, exactly, the photo-finish was is evidenced by its slow and unequal adoption as a form of evidence in sport. As noted in the 1948 Olympic Report, "The I.A.A.F. [International Association of Athletics Federations] has so far not officially sanctioned the times recorded by the Racend OMEGA Timer, so that the times for the scoresheets are still taken with watches."[14] And so as with its adoption into horse racing during the opening decades of the twentieth

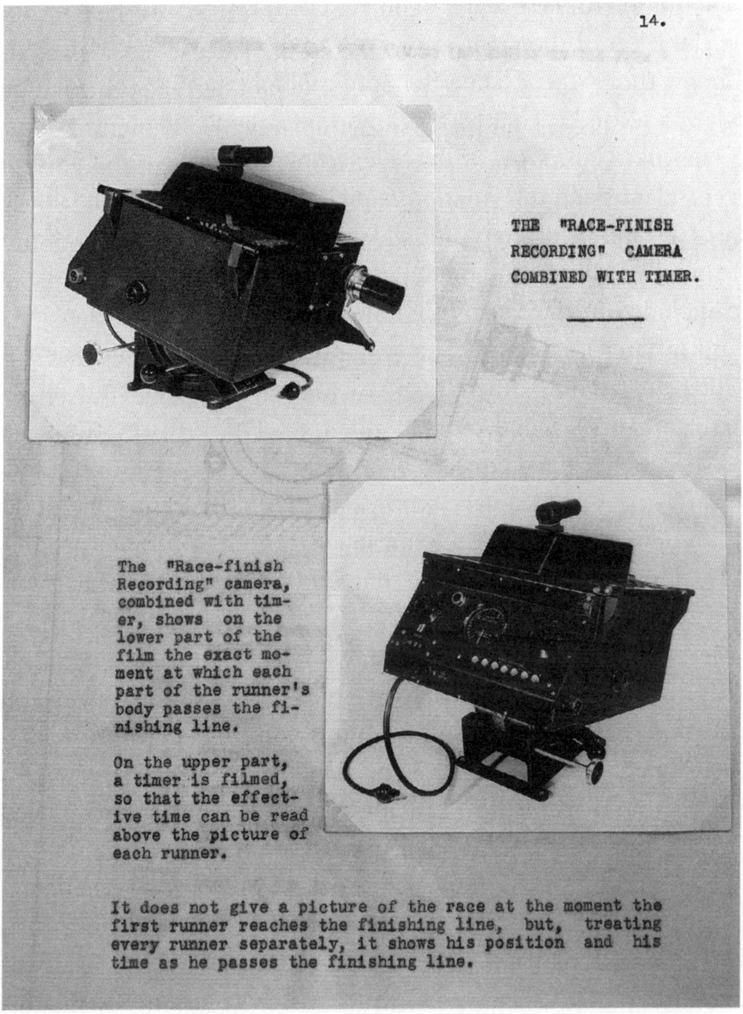

4.2 The "Race Finish Recording Camera," later renamed the Racend OMEGA.

century, the photo-finish was not quickly or easily accepted as a decision-making tool. Proponents employed the discourse of mechanical objectivity to argue for the infallibility of the camera, while opponents stressed the expertise of human officials.

For the Helsinki Games, OMEGA again provided their services free of charge.[15] This included over 2 tonnes of equipment, with 450 timepieces valued at US$200,000 and 3 Racend OMEGA Timers valued at US$7,000 each. In addition to these material objects, OMEGA provided ten technicians for the duration of the Games.[16] OMEGA also provided a new device for the Games, the OMEGA Time Recorder, which was capable of timing to 1/100th of a second.[17] Figure 4.3 is a photo-finish of a tandem cycling event at the Helsinki Games. As with the example of London discussed above, key event-identifying information is included in the photo-finish through the use of a spinning drum positioned opposite the camera at the finish line. Importantly, and unlike in London, the name of the Racend OMEGA Timer is also included in the finish-line record. OMEGA's inclusion of its name here and in later Olympic Games was the site of significant controversy, given the Games' commitment to amateurism and a non-commercial sporting environment. Official correspondence relating to the timing of the Games shows continued concern by the IOC, sports federations, and various corporations regarding OMEGA's tactics of inserting its name into Olympic competition. OMEGA's continued pattern of running afoul of IOC rules is less likely to be an accident than it is a strategic and largely effective business decision.

By the 1956 Games in Melbourne, the Racend OMEGA had been fully solidified as an instrumental part of the Games. The participation and specific identification of the Race Finish Recording Company waned from the 1948 to 1956 Games. The Race Finish Recording Company continues to provide photo-finish services for horse racing in the UK, though under the name RaceTech,[18] but their formal participation in the Olympics ended shortly after it began. OMEGA emerged as the de facto provider of both timing and photo-finish services. And it is worth noting that, following the 1956 Games, timing and photo-finishes were less likely to be separated in the professional and public discourse, with the latter generally being subsumed under the former. As such, and unless specified otherwise, the word "timing" used here refers to the comprehensive package of timing services which include timing, measurement, photo and video services, information and communication networks, and display boards.

OMEGA's position as the leader in sports timing was also actively being promoted through professional channels, seemingly outside the Olympic movement. A 1955 special issue of *La Suisse Horlogère* focused on "The Measurement of Time and the Olympic Games." The magazine was the official publication of the Swiss Watch Chamber of Commerce and, unsurprisingly, gave high praise to the importance and role of accurate timing in sport.

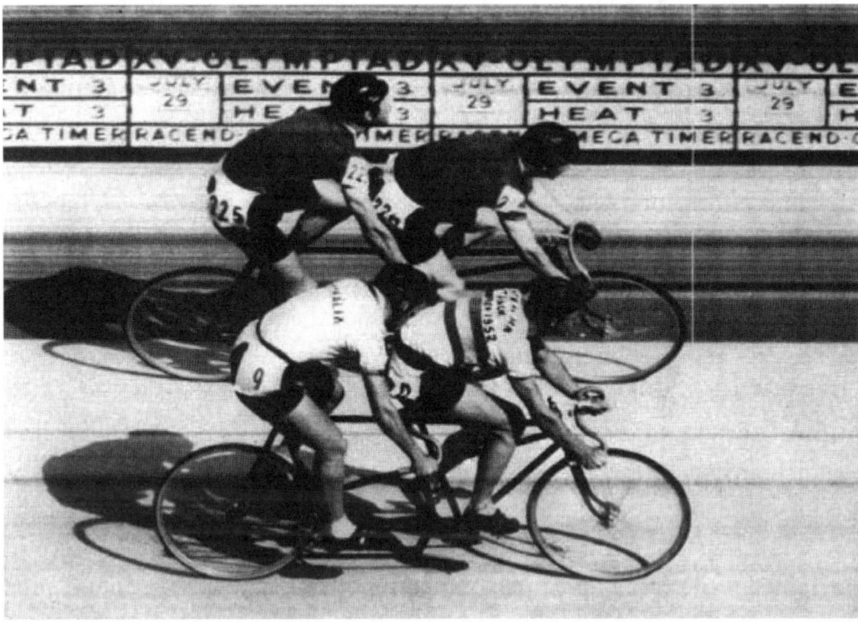

4.3 Photo-finish of a tandem cycling event, 1952 Olympic Games in Helsinki.

In his essay for the magazine, Avery Brundage, then president of the International Olympic Committee, wrote: "We of the world of sport today are greatly indebted to the watch industry. Indeed, it is difficult to envision some branches of sport today without a measure of time. It's true a race is a race and there is a winner and a loser whether there is a watch or not, but with a watch, the runners in any race have as competitors all other runners who have ever raced, any place or any time."[19] He goes on to stress that timing is one of the two key differentiators between the modern Games and its ancient precedent (the other being internationalization) and concludes with praise for the distinctly Swiss approach to timing: "The headquarters of the Olympic Movement are in Lausanne and all Swiss citizens have a great interest in Olympic affairs. The watch industry of Switzerland is famous. It is quite understandable that there has been close cooperation between some of the leading watchmakers of the world there and Olympic officials."[20]

What emerges from Brundage's article and the others in the special issue of *La Suisse Horlogère* is a common theme used in promoting the Olympic Games and its larger movement. The Games are positioned as distinctly modern but nonetheless a continuation of the Olympic "spirit" of antiquity. And with specific attention focused on timing, the modernization of the Games through technology is positioned as correcting human error. Brundage identifies the problems of human reaction time that plagued earlier timing efforts and twice claims that new timing systems eradicate human error and offer "complete accuracy."[21] Edmond Guyot offers a similar narrative in his essay on the evolution of timing in the Olympics, as does René P. Guye.[22] Guye even singles out the importance of formal training for time-keepers, referencing the professionalization of the role: "For certain sports such as car-racing, the timing operators have been specially trained and may be considered as professionals, for it has been amply proved that one cannot become a timing operator at a moment's notice but only after a period of complete instruction and experience."[23]

The article by Guye points to a key distinction in the discourse of the photo-finish as related to that of the preceding decades: the emergence of the trained professional. Hemment and other racetrack photographers of the early 1900s were identified as particularly skilled photographers, but Guye's passage identifies time-keepers as a new class of trained professionals. Daston and Galison's episteme of "trained judgment" with "pictorial presentation by (and for) the trained eye" is therefore visible in the discourse of timing and the photo-finish by the middle decades of the twentieth century.[24] This is a key aspect of OMEGA's rise to prominence in timing and photo-finish services – they provided not just highly precise and accurate equipment but the trained eyes of experts who could attest to the reliability and objectivity of the timing and photo-finish results.

The emergence of the trained expert and of a corporation with acknowledged expertise in timing and the photo-finish points to another concern in the history of the photo-finish and sport more broadly. As identified by Rayvon Fouché, the history of modern sport is intertwined with a history of technological and technoscientific development aimed at gaining competitive advantage.[25] Fouché's focus in tracing this development is on the body, specifically the athlete's body. He writes: "the history of sport in the twentieth century has been about gaining a competitive edge through the use of technoscientific artifacts attached to the body or integrated into the body or a change in body mechanics."[26] In a similar way, I argue that the history of modern sport is equally defined by the development of "technoscientific artifacts" designed to measure athlete performance. Timing and photo-finish systems are examples of such artifacts and OMEGA's rise to prominence in the industry must be seen within this larger context. As Adams and Hemment were key figures in promoting the use of the camera in sport, OMEGA and its partners were central in building sports timing into a professional, profit-driven practice.

Automation as Accuracy

A significant development in timing occurred with the 1960 Games in Rome. Combined with the steady advance in timing technology, collaboration and discussion between the International Olympic Committee and the various international sport federations led to a key change in timing practices. Prior to Rome, only the times of the top three competitors were recorded. By contrast, for the Rome Games the times of all competitors would be recorded. As noted in the Official Report: "In practice, for athletics on seven lanes, 21 timekeepers were necessary since it was even essential to take the times of the seventh runner to provide against the eventuality that the competitor might have equalled or beaten the record of his own country."[27] The ability to record each competitor and not just the winner extended sport's quest for records, enabling the accumulation of ever more information for sport and its audiences. By further relaxing the spatial and temporal boundaries of earlier sporting practices, racers were not racing just against each other, but against national or other records set at other meets in other places and times.

Although the 1960 change was in many ways driven by technological innovation, timing technology was still positioned as an aid to human officials. This meant a significant and seemingly paradoxical increase in the number of officials at the Games. The dramatic increase in human labour is exemplified in Figure 4.4. Captioned "Judges at the finish and timekeepers integrate electric timekeeping in the athletic events," the image is a strange amalgam of the old and the new. It follows the long-standing practice of officials in tiered seating at the finish line (see Figure 3.5 from the 1912 Stockholm Games) but shows the expanded labour pool resulting from the technological ability and desire within the sport community to record the times of all competitors. The image also speaks to the then-curious tension between new electronic timing systems and human officials, the former being positioned as an aid to the latter. The photo-finish was given similar status. As outlined in the Report, "all times taken and attributed to the various events were accompanied by photographic documentation at the finishes, this being effected by means of the Racend OMEGA Timer."[28] The phrasing here is important: the Racend OMEGA Timer provides a documentary record of the times taken and serves as an accompaniment to the timers rather than as its own evidentiary document. The tension between the human eye and the camera eye therefore remained, more than fifty years after the initial uses of the photograph to determine race results.

The 1972 Games in Munich saw the inclusion of in-field photo-finish cameras, which are now a mainstay in timing practices. That is, in addition to the typical positioning of a camera on the outside (stands-side) of the track, an in-field camera was used to give a second photo-finish perspective for races. Timing for the 1972 Games was awarded to Longines and the German company Junghans (discussed below) and so the Racend OMEGA was not employed at that Games. Junghans was in charge of timing athletic events and employed a modified Polaroid camera for the photo-finish, capable of recording to 3/1,000ths of a second. As with earlier Games, the uniqueness of the photo-finish image was described in the Official Report: "The film at the image plane of the camera moved past the lens at the same speed, in relation to the laws of optical images, as the objects it pictured. It ran so to speak across the finish line with the runners."[29] The Report goes on to explain: "thus the temporal events at the finish line were translated into a spatial order on the finish line film."[30] This last passage is particularly interesting as it highlights the continued attempt to understand the unique relationship of space and time in the photo-finish, contrasting it with the temporal fixity of a traditional photograph.

The modified Polaroid used for the Munich Games constituted the primary system of timing. The Organizing Committee also put in place secondary and tertiary systems that are of note. The secondary system required that two additional modified Polaroid cameras be installed on the infield side of the track. The rationale is described as such: "In the event of close decisions, the runners could overlap on the photo finish pictures. That impeded or completely hindered a clear decision."[31] And the tertiary system involved placing photoelectric cells at the 100m, 200m, 300m, and finish-line marks, capturing timing data for each runner as they tripped the beam. The importance of the secondary and possibly tertiary timing systems is

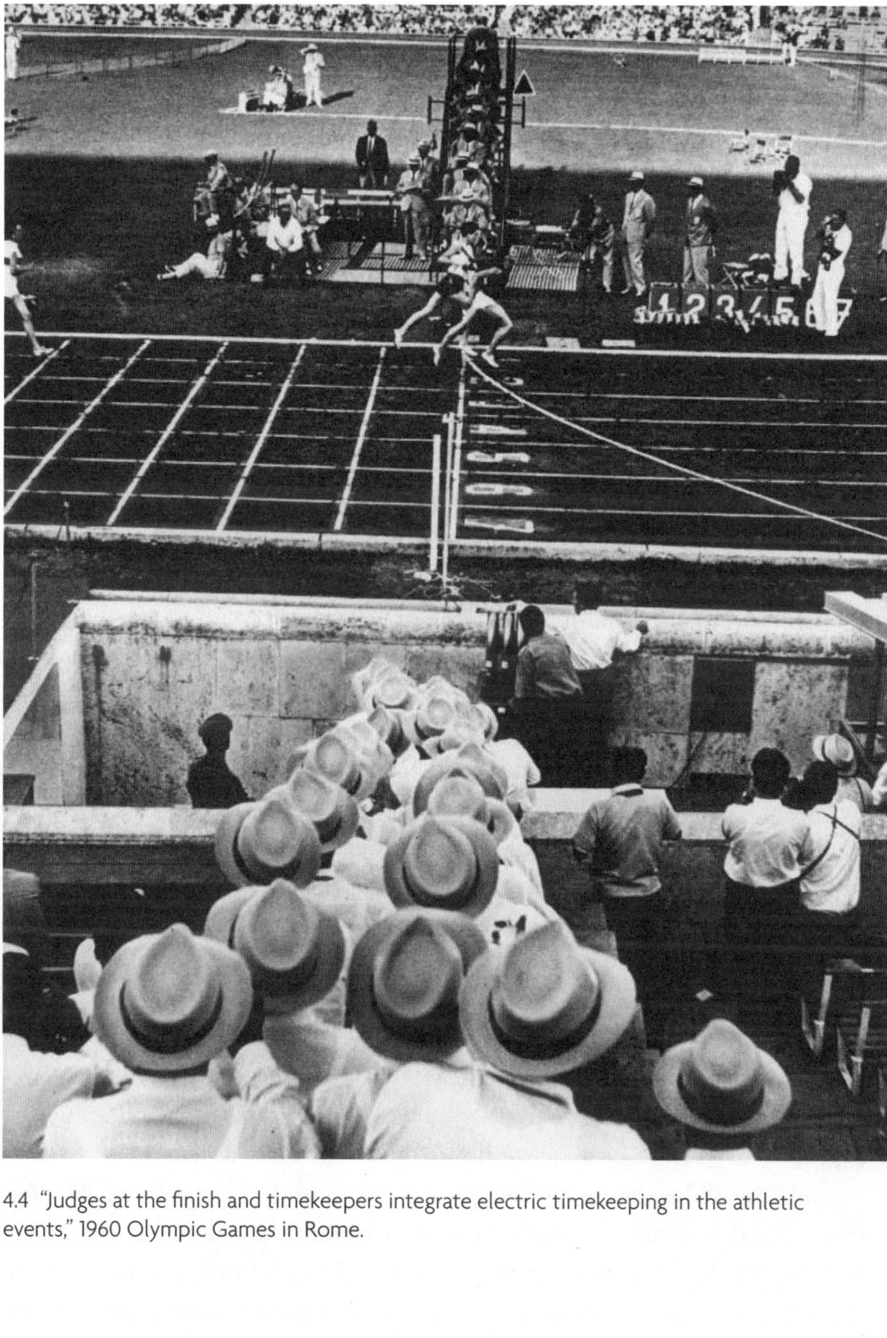

4.4 "Judges at the finish and timekeepers integrate electric timekeeping in the athletic events," 1960 Olympic Games in Rome.

evident in Figure 4.5, of the 100m race at the Munich Games. The method for determining placing and time is indicated by the inclusion of vertical lines leading to the two runners closest to the bottom of the image. The winner completes the run in 10.42 seconds with the sixth-place finisher arriving at 10.54. The first- and second-place runners can clearly be discerned in the image; however, the third- and fourth-place runners overlap each other. And despite continued advancements, the issue of obscured or obstructed body parts remains a key problem within the timing and photo-finish field.

The Olympic Games of the 1970s and early 1980s stand as a turning point for their emphasis on the "computerization" of the Olympics and, within that, on the automation of timing and photo-finish services. For the former, the once relatively disparate systems of the Games ranging from registration and athlete tracking to timing and media relations were increasingly brought together in large-scale digital networks. The Report for the 1972 Munich Games identifies the cautious desire to computerize the Games: "Besides the financial considerations, the [LO]OC had to take into account two requirements above all: on the one hand, they wanted to avoid 'overtechnologizing' the Games, but on the other hand, they wanted to fulfill the great expectations that had been spawned – especially in other countries – in technology as a means of organization and information."[32]

Timing and photo-finish services were similarly integrated into the new information networks, linking large electronic display boards, closed-circuit TV systems, media personnel, and broadcast networks. This is exemplified in Figure 4.6, which is a diagrammatic representation of the timing and information network for Alpine events at the 1984 Sarajevo Games. The diagram effectively shows timing and the photo-finish as part of Jhally's "sport/media complex."[33] Far removed from the set of chronographs provided for the 1932 Games, the Swiss Timing diagram shows timing and photo-finish systems as part of a highly complex information and communication network.

Automation became a key feature of sports timing and the photo-finish in this networked space. Use and acceptance of "fully automatic" timing (FAT) systems developed in the 1970s and 1980s, though "fully automatic" is a slight misnomer. FAT systems refer to a complete circuit uniting the start, finish, and timing and imaging equipment. As described in the Report for the

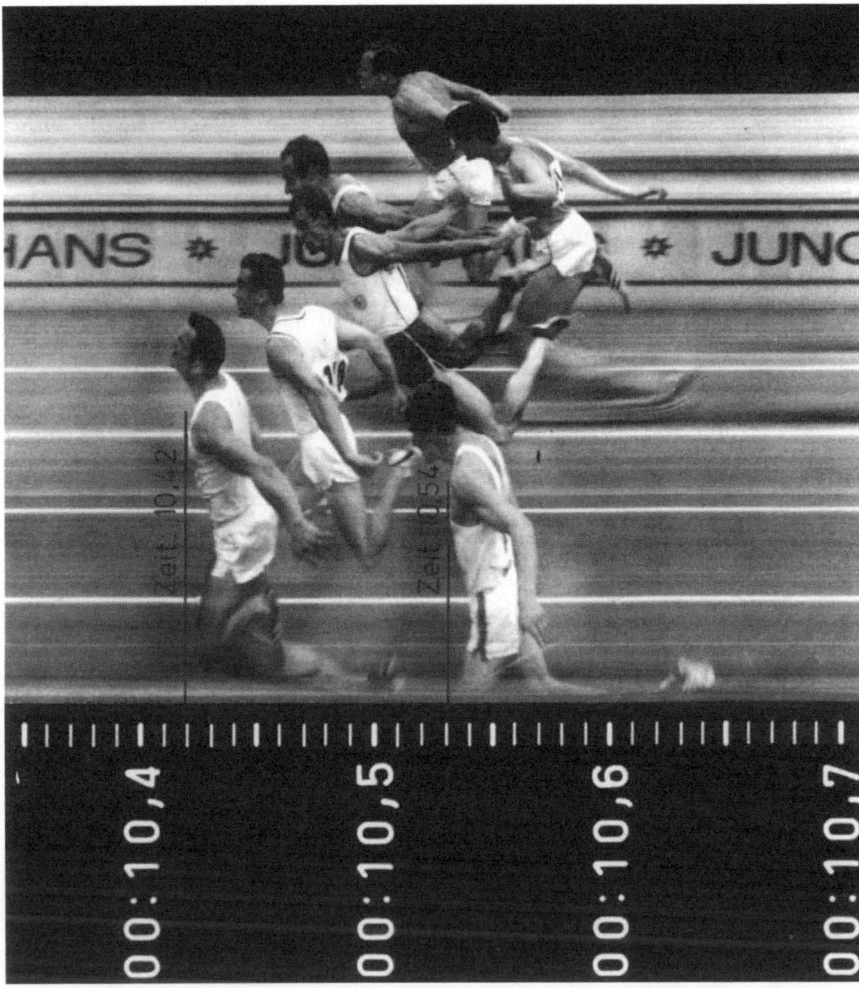

4.5 Photo-finish of the men's 100m at the 1972 Olympic Games in Munich.

1976 Games in Montreal, "the system approved for swimming included the full automatic timing system, with touch pads, false-start detection, transmission of the start signal to each starting block, and a video backup system for timing the race."[34] Importantly, all FAT systems still involve multiple human operators, officials, and interpreters. The particular configuration of event officiating, including human officials, FAT systems, and results interpreters, as well as the authority given to each, is governed by the individual sports federations. The differences between these configurations will be addressed in chapter 5; here it is sufficient to note the increasing reliance on and promotion of automation for timing and the photo-finish in sport.

The emphasis on automation was also continued in Moscow for the 1980 Games, with FAT systems used in thirteen sports, compared to seven in Montreal. And the Olympic Report is clear that automation is akin to accuracy: "As is well known, one of the criteria for judging the quality of information-measuring systems and the referee-information apparatus which forms part of them, is the degree of automation in determining and processing the results of events."[35] The Report goes on to stress the necessity of technological solutions: "The need to develop technical systems in order to make refereeing more objective has grown in urgency of late due to the increasing closeness of sportsmen's results. It has also been prompted by the need to increase accuracy and objectiveness in determining a sportsman's place in a run in cases when the gap between the athletes finishing is so tiny that it is beyond the capacity of the time-registering device."[36] One of the more interesting aspects of this section of the Report is the extent to which it parallels the discourse of instantaneous photography and early-twentieth-century horse racing with their emphases on visually recording what the eye could not see. Importantly, voices in the Official Olympic Reports were as confident (and incorrect) as Hemment in proposing a technological solution to a perceived human problem.

Olympic Reports following that of Moscow pay significantly less attention to questions of timing and measurement. Technical equipment and its providers are typically named, but the rationale driving the use of photo-finish or other timing equipment is no longer offered. The relatively nuanced debate about what a photo-finish was, which took place from the 1940s through the 1960s, dissipated over the 1970s and largely disappeared in the 1980s. And while it is overly simplistic to equate this with the full acceptance of the photo-finish as an evidentiary record in sport, it is nonetheless important to note that the practice was receiving less formal questioning within the sport community by the 1980s.

At least as it relates to the Olympic Games, OMEGA's advocacy and promotion of their product played a significant role in this stabilization. Key to this was an emerging discourse around automation which continued to champion the mechanical objectivity of the machine. However, equally im-

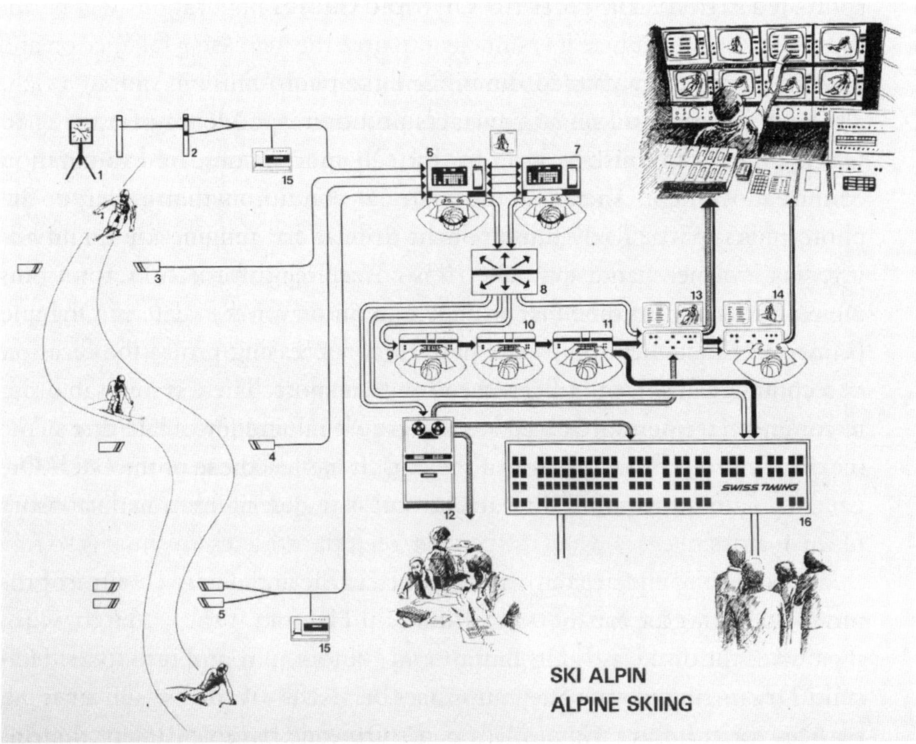

4.6 Timing and photo-finish as integrated in larger communications network. From Swiss Timing's proposal for the 1984 Olympic Winter Games.

portant was OMEGA's claim to professional expertise. The photo-finish became professionalized through the mid-to-late twentieth century and wedded the noninterventionist objectivity of timing technology to the trained expertise of the timing and photo-finish judge. Interestingly, unlike the trained professional of Daston and Galison's analysis, which emphasizes the individual, within the discourse of sports timing that attribute extended out to take on distinctly national characteristics. Precision timing was taken to be a birthright of the Swiss. In this way, all three of Daston and Galison's epistemic virtues are present at the Olympic Games in the mid-to-late twentieth century. Correspondingly, the objectivity of the photo-finish is produced through a mixture of mechanically objective technology and judges who were born, trained, and became professionals in Switzerland.

Exclusive Rights: Contracts for Olympic Games

The International Olympic Committee Historical Archives contain a rich, although incomplete, set of contracts and correspondence pertaining to timing and photo-finish services for the Olympic Games. An examination of these documents shows us the material conditions that underpin the photo-finish, particularly those related to financial remuneration and advertising and merchandising rights. It is unsurprising that contracts for timing services have become increasingly complex over the years of Olympic Games and that they follow the pattern of increasing professionalization and commercialization indicative of modern sport. There is a notable rise in commercial interests as well as extensive legal and financial agreements seeking to protect the interests of the IOC as well as those of the Local Organizing Committees and the various national and international sponsors of the Games.

The earliest complete contractual record in the archives is a contract proposal from OMEGA for the 1952 Games in Helsinki. On 25 March 1949, the owners of OMEGA, Louis Brandt and Frère, sent a proposal to the Helsinki Organizing Committee outlining their offer of timing and imaging services for the 1952 Games.[37] It is a thirty-one-page document that includes a proposal for a contract, suggestions of timepieces to use for the Games with accompanying photographs and descriptions, as well as discussion of the equipment used for the Olympic Games in London in 1948. There are twelve separate points in the contract proposal, which cover testing, delivery, and servicing of the equipment for the Games. In the proposal, OMEGA agrees to cover all costs related to their timing equipment, which include its testing, maintenance, and shipping to and from the Games. The Race Finish Recording Company of London agrees to do the same but with two caveats. First, the Organizing Committee of the Games must build, at their expense, the structures needed to house the cameras and develop the film, and must supply electricity and water. The second is that the Race Finish Recording Company would retain the rights to the photo-finish images created. Number 2, subsection e of the proposal reads: "The release rights to the press and sale to the public of all Race Finish photographs recorded at the Games are granted to the R.F.R.C., London, except in the event of a photograph being fairly and reasonably withdrawn on grounds of security."[38]

Item 9 of the proposal is particularly important as it foreshadows a central component of subsequent timing and imaging contracts. Titled "exclusive use," it reads: "The Organising Committee agrees to use OMEGA's time-pieces exclusively for the timing, by official time-keepers of the XVth Summer Olympic Games 1952. The same applies to the Race Finish Recording OMEGA Timer."[39] In addition to exclusive rights at the Games, the proposal requests that "both the R.F.R.C. and OMEGA should be given a credit line in the official programme."[40] OMEGA's contract proposal does indeed support the claim in the Olympic Report that timing services were provided free of charge. Beyond rights to exclusivity and being mentioned in the program, there is only one request for material remuneration, which is that the Organizing Committee cover the accommodation costs for the technicians of both the RFRC and OMEGA.

OMEGA's offer to provide timing services free of charge – as was the case in Helsinki – quickly proved to be untenable for the company. At the heart of this was a continued debate between OMEGA and the various Local Olympic Organizing Committees, as well as the International Olympic Committee, regarding OMEGA's desire to promote itself and its products as tied to the Olympic Games. The Olympic Committees were firm that no indication of sponsorship or advertising should be present in the Games. This debate is clearly illustrated in correspondence between A. Vallat, then Director of OMEGA, and Otto Mayer, Chancellor of the International Olympic Committee prior to the 1960 Winter Games in Squaw Valley, California.[41] On 23 April 1956, Mayer wrote a note to Vallat criticizing OMEGA's advertising in relation to the Olympic Games. Vallat's response on 7 May 1956 provides valuable insight into the costs associated with OMEGA's participation in the Games as well as the company's desire to mitigate these costs by marketing their affiliation with the Olympics. In his opening statement, Vallat stresses the difficulties of and expenses incurred by OMEGA in order to remain at the forefront of timing equipment and services. He writes, "First of all, I wonder if, in Olympic circles, one is really aware of the extraordinary expense incurred through being honoured with the timing of the Olympic Games."[42] Vallat then details the expenses: the total cost of their current timing equipment is 1,400,000 Swiss francs. Staff costs to keep updating and improving that equipment amounts to 600,000 to 700,000 Swiss francs per year. With the Olympics operating on a four-year cycle, Vallat notes the cost of timing the Games works out to 2,000,000 to 2,500,000

Swiss francs. He concludes noting that OMEGA's ability to advertise is needed if it wants to combat the high costs of timing for the Games and that, were he to eliminate the time-keeping department at OMEGA, he would no longer be able to offer free timing for the Games. And finally, Vallat expresses his anger that their time-keeping competitor (Longines) was allowed to promote itself as the official time-keeper for the Games.[43]

It is worth pausing to unpack the exchange between Vallat and Mayer, as it shows the rapidly changing landscape of timing and the photo-finish over the mid-twentieth century. A mere two decades prior to Vallat and Mayer's correspondence, OMEGA's presence at the Games amounted to a set of chronographs and accompanying technicians to ensure their effective operation. By the 1950s OMEGA claimed to be spending between CHF 2,000,000 and 2,500,000 to provide services for the Games, with a full-time staff dedicated to the research and development of timing technologies.

The financial difficulties signalled by Vallat were far from resolved following the 1960 Games. Correspondence between OMEGA and the Organizing Committee for the 1972 Munich Games shows that OMEGA decided not to submit a proposal for timing the Games.[44] A telegram from OMEGA to Agence France Press on 10 October 1969 announced, "OMEGA withdraws from Olympic time-keeping." The telegram offers a contextualizing statement: "From the 80 chronographs used for the Los Angeles Games in 1932 to the million dollars spent on the Mexico Games of 1968, the responsibilities accompanying the time-keeping have increased enormously. Moreover, like the President of the International Olympic Committee, Mr. Avery Brundage, the company believes that the spirit surrounding amateur sport is no longer the same." This is followed by the key complaint: "For the business in Bienne [the location of OMEGA's headquarters], this change belongs to the sphere of ever-increasing demands for more complex tasks in the field of time-keeping, which are in no way rewarded in respect of the recognition obtained." OMEGA then points to two recent examples where both the European Broadcasting Union and the International Association of Athletics Federations worked to have OMEGA's name and/or logo removed from broadcasts and media coverage of sports events. This meant blocking out the name/logo that would appear on timing equipment, scoreboards, and race results, including the photo-finish.

The awarding of contracts for the 1972 Games in Munich followed a curious process and is outlined in unusual detail in the Olympic Report for the Games.[45] Recognizing the need for highly precise and accurate measurement, the Organizing Committee sent a request for proposals to three timing firms: Longines, OMEGA, and the German company Junghans. Each firm expressed interest in timing the Games and each wanted exclusive rights in return. The Organizing Committee consulted with international sports federations to see if there was a consensus on a preferred company, but there was not. During this process, OMEGA withdrew its application, and the Organizing Committee, after some further information-gathering, awarded the contract to Junghans. This decision and the process through which it was achieved was objected to by sports federations, and the Organizing Committee struck a deal with Junghans and Longines that they would share timing duties. Each company was given charge over specific sports. The companies were forbidden from advertising at the Games but were allowed to promote their participation in the Games outside the Olympics and were able to use the Olympic symbol (the rings) in their marketing materials. Junghans received 290,000 DM remuneration for its services with Longines receiving 280,000 DM.

Following the 1972 merger of the timing units of OMEGA and Longines, the resultant company, Swiss Timing, provided the services for the 1976 Games in Innsbruck. Contracts between Swiss Timing and the Organizing Committee for Innsbruck continued to place strong limitations on Swiss Timing's ability to advertise its products and services. Specifically, the company was forbidden from advertising or otherwise showing the company name at competition sites other than on the time-keeping equipment.[46] But by the time of the 1980 Winter Games in Lake Placid and Summer Games in Moscow, Swiss Timing had negotiated considerably more favourable terms. For Lake Placid, the contract dated 19 June 1978 identifies that Swiss Timing would provide equipment, experts, printouts, and communication with display boards and TV, and that it would liaise with the various international sports federations to determine the specific needs for each event. For these services, the Organizing Committee agreed to pay Swiss Timing costs covering the transportation of equipment and personnel as well as the accommodations of the latter along with a US$50 per diem. Importantly, Swiss Timing was allowed to have its name appear on all devices and printouts/displays in competition. Crucially, the advertising, promotion, or sale of any watch or timing device other than those made by Swiss Timing and its affiliates was prohibited at all competition sites. And Swiss Timing was given exclusive rights to refer to itself as "Official Time-Keeper" and was able to use the Lake Placid Olympic Organizing Committee's Winter Games symbol in its own advertising. These last two provisions – exclusive rights to sell and advertise at the Games and rights to use Olympic symbols and logos in its products – remained central in future contracts and provided Swiss Timing and its affiliates with highly lucrative streams of revenue.

The contract for time-keeping at the Moscow Games, signed on 3 June 1977, followed the same basic parameters, but was more precise in its language. The contract noted that Swiss Timing would provide timing "in a number of sports on the programme of the Games of the XXII Olympiad in exchange for the right to be named 'Official Time-Keeper of the Games of the XXII Olympiad, Moscow, 1980.'"[47] The contract between Swiss Timing and the Moscow Organizing Committee specifies that fifty Swiss Timing technicians would attend the Games and that the Organizing Committee would cover flight and accommodation costs for the technicians as well as a 3 ruble per diem. The Organizing Committee also agreed to cover the transportation costs of the equipment. In relation to advertising and exclusivity, Swiss Timing was allowed to "identify the Swiss origins of its services" in competitions and in media outlets and PR materials for the Games, it was allowed to use the Olympic Rings in its own products and promotional material, and no other watch or clock maker was permitted to advertise at competition sites.[48] The provision to "identify the Swiss origins of its services" is interesting as it underscores the national-level interests in securing timing for the Games. And it is also interesting in that "Swiss Timing" is simultaneously a company name and a declaration of national origin.

Given that the 1984 Olympic Games in Los Angeles is understood as a turning point in the commercialization of the Olympic Games, it is no surprise that the contract between the Organizing Committee and Swiss Timing for the 1984 Games was considerably larger and more detailed than previous contracts.[49] Unlike previous contracts, which were between two parties (Swiss Timing and the local Olympic Organizing Committee), this contract, signed in 1981, includes Swiss Timing and Westinghouse Electric along with two of the latter's subsidiaries, Perrier mineral water and Office Furniture Worldwide. Swiss Timing was given exclusive rights to promote itself as Official Time-Keeper (including related phrases) and to use the

Olympic Rings in its promotional materials. There were two new items in the contract: first, that Swiss Timing would be given "priority treatment" with all other sponsors for hotel discounts and ticket purchases; second, that "Swiss Timing will supply timekeeping services and equipment for at least one pre-Games event in each of Athletics, Swimming, Cycling and Rowing/Canoeing."[50] This provision of pre-Games participation was mutually beneficial. It guaranteed highly reputable timing at major sporting events for the host nation, it allowed the equipment to be tested prior to the Games, and it provided Swiss Timing with another marketing and merchandising opportunity.

The contract for the 1988 Summer Games in Seoul offers yet another type of arrangement and provides specific financial numbers.[51] The provisional agreement was for Swiss Timing to be awarded contracts for the Asian Games of 1986 and the 1988 Seoul Olympics, with Swiss Timing responsible for all associated costs. The Agreement notes, "all the costs for the services set out above (including transportation, installation, dismantling and removal, insurance and rental of the equipment) shall be borne by Swiss Timing. The charge for such services shall amount to s.fr. 4,285,850 for the Asian Games and to s.fr. 5,890,000 for the Olympic Games."[52] Following this, the Agreement states that Swiss Timing would donate their services for the Asian Games (covering the s.fr. 4,285,850 cost) but that the Seoul Olympic Organizing Committee would cover the nearly s.fr. 6,000,000 cost of the Olympic Games. And as with previous timing contracts, Swiss Timing is given exclusive rights to promote their company and its products and services at both the Asian and Olympic Games. As such, Swiss Timing had secured the rights and provisions it had sought since the 1940s: to brand itself as an official Olympic affiliate, thereby gaining access to an increasingly lucrative commercial marketplace. Swiss Timing had also secured somewhat of a monopoly over Olympic timing and had developed a controlled and closed system for its services. As timing provider, Swiss Timing researched, built, and operated the equipment and provided extensive personnel and technicians for the Games. They negotiated with Organizing Committees, sports federations, and media corporations and provided, and controlled, the information and communication systems that united these groups. All of this took material form in comprehensive timing and photo-finish packages. The continued reach of OMEGA / Swiss Timing into the

Olympic Games solidified its status as the dominant provider of sports timing and it also gave them significant influence in shaping the discourse of timing and photo-finish in sport.

Competition

Table 4.1 shows the near-monopoly status that OMEGA and its affiliates hold over Olympic timing. For the 1936 Games, German companies were used, and Junghans (a German company) was awarded co-provider status with Longines in 1972. However, and within the Olympic Games specifically, the only true competitor to OMEGA has been Seiko. The Japanese company provided timing and photo-finish services for six Olympic Games: 1964 Tokyo, 1972 Sapporo, 1992 Barcelona, 1994 Lillehammer, 1998 Nagano, and 2002 Salt Lake. Though relatively slight, Swiss Timing did nonetheless face competition and sometimes pushed the boundaries of its affiliation with the Olympic movement.

As already noted, in correspondence surrounding timing for the 1960 Winter Olympics in Squaw Valley, OMEGA was criticized for advertising during the Games. These initial, early concerns centred on the notion that the Games were to be a celebration of amateurism and the Olympic ideal and were therefore to be free of commercial influence. With the continued expansion and commercialization of the Games and OMEGA / Swiss Timing's continued negotiation for advertising and other rights, the company was given increasing leeway to promote and advertise itself as the official Olympic time-keeper; however, even with these permissions in place, OMEGA / Swiss Timing faced criticisms for its marketing and advertising practices. Correspondence related to the timing of the 1988 Games in Seoul includes a letter of 17 October 1988 from Richard Pound of the IOC to Manfred H. Laumann, vice-president of Swiss Timing, noting that the timing company's marketing was in violation of IOC rules. The IOC rules were precise – for example, no more than one logo on any given side of a piece of equipment, and that logo could not be larger than 3–10cm – and as identified in Pound's letter, a representative from the IAAF noted many instances where OMEGA / Swiss Timing had violated these rules.

A more significant debate ensued around OMEGA / Swiss Timing's marketing during the 1992 Olympic Games in Barcelona and Albertville. A 30

March 1989 fax from Michael R. Payne of the International Olympic Committee to Ian T. Todd of the Albertville Organizing Committee and Antoni Rossich of the Barcelona Organizing Committee introduced that Seiko was interested in submitting a proposal for the timing of the Games.[53] The facsimile reads in full:

> Until recently, the appointed timing supplier has nearly always been a one horse race with Swiss timing!
>
> However, it would now appear that Hattori Seiko may well be interested in pursuing Olympic timing opportunities.
>
> Back in 1984, Seiko felt that the technical demands of Olympic games were beyond their ability. However, this would no longer appear to be true and the European Marketing Director has asked for a very general discussion with the IOC on the long term future. I would appreciate learning where you stand in your negotiations with Swiss timing and I can direct Seiko to you accordingly.

Seiko did submit a proposal to the Organizing Committee for the Barcelona Games and on 4 November 1990 a confidential memo from Michael Payne, IOC Marketing Director, to Juan Antonio Samaranch and other members of the IOC identified key differences between the bids.[54] Seiko offered free timing services for the Olympics, Paralympics, and pre-Olympic events in Spain, valued at $10 million (currency not specified but is presumed to be CHF) along with $1 million in cash and $3–4 million in support of National Olympic Committee (NOC) and IOC programming. By contrast, Swiss Timing offered $1.6 million "value-in-kind" and was to be paid $4 million by the local Olympic Organizing Committee for its services. It comes as no surprise that Seiko was awarded the timing contract for the 1992 Barcelona Games. In total, the contract is 74 pages in length with highly specific descriptions of the services Seiko was to provide, as well as the "hospitality package" that would be provided to Seiko by the Barcelona Olympic Committee. The latter includes "30 double rooms in 5-star or 4-star hotels" with an additional 180 rooms in 3-star hotels for the "service technicians." Sixty tickets to the opening and closing ceremonies would be reserved for Seiko, as well as sixty tickets for every athletic event, and Seiko was to have priority access to transportation and other hospitality- and tourism-related items.[55]

The contract between the Barcelona Olympic Committee and Seiko also specified that Seiko was given exclusive rights to promote itself as the official time-keeper of the Games and was permitted to use the Olympic Rings and related official symbols in its advertising and merchandise. In terms of the latter, the contract specified that Seiko could use Olympic symbols in consumer products including wristwatches, pocketwatches, pendant watches, stopwatches, wall clocks, table clocks, alarm clocks, "card" clocks, kitchen and other timers, as well as outdoor and indoor public area clocks, marionette clocks, and musical moving clocks. And Seiko was also able to use the Olympic Rings for its sports timing products including portable and fixed timing systems, printing timers, photo-finish systems, and touch-pad systems for swimming.[56] This long list of products highlights the tremendous merchandising opportunities of being an official Olympic partner. Such opportunities were necessary to offset the costs associated with providing timing services, including continued research and development between Olympic cycles.

With Seiko as the official time-keeper for Barcelona, concerns about Swiss Timing's (and its affiliates') advertising again surfaced.[57] A document internal to the IOC identified concern with an ad running in a German periodical where OMEGA promoted its sponsorship of the German Olympic team. The IOC's concern was that OMEGA was alluding to a formal tie to the 1992 Barcelona Games through its marketing of the German Olympic Team. A more substantive concern related to OMEGA's "Significant Moments" campaign that was running throughout Europe (including Spain) during 1992. As shown in Figure 4.7, the OMEGA ad includes the text: "OMEGA. The watch that records the world's significant moments. At the Olympic Games. In outer space. And exclusively for you." The Barcelona Olympic Organizing Committee protested to the IOC that OMEGA was violating IOC rules by suggesting a formal relationship with the Barcelona Games where none existed and where Seiko had been guaranteed exclusive rights.

Seiko was also awarded the contract for timing the 1994 Winter Games in Lillehammer, their bid again being accepted over that from Swiss Timing. Seiko reduced their bid, asking the local Organizing Committee for US$2.5 million from $3 million.[58] Seiko staff would also receive room and board up to US$200 per day. A 10 January letter from Michael Payne, IOC marketing director, to Juan Antonio Samaranch and others notes that the Organizing Committee was likely to select Seiko thanks to the IOC's efforts in lobbying

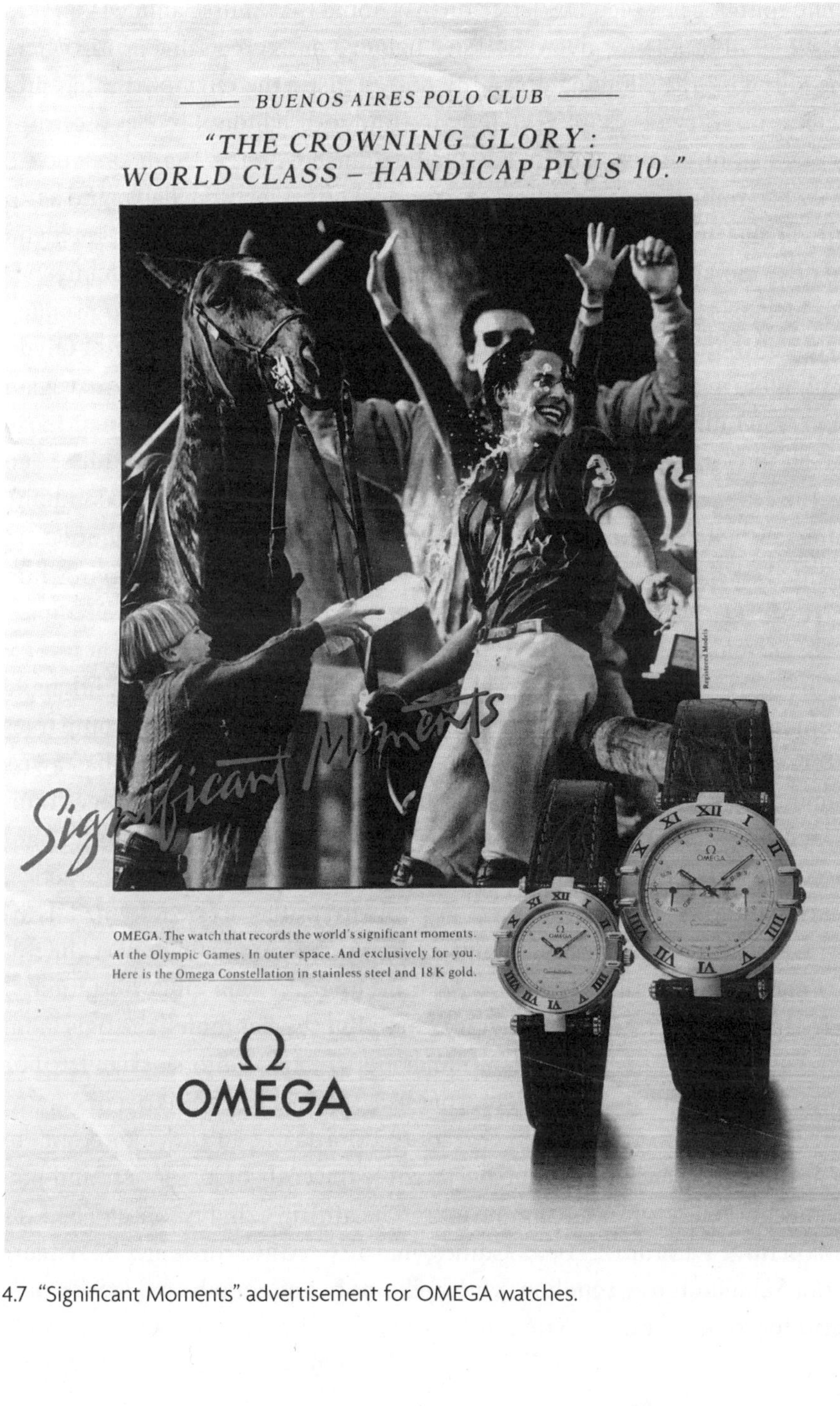

4.7 "Significant Moments" advertisement for OMEGA watches.

Seiko to reduce its bid. The letter further noted that Swiss Timing's bid was very high. But a letter two days later from Payne to the same group offers the following: "Following up on my note of last week re LOOC timing supplier appointment, Swiss Timing have now realised that Seiko is a serious contender, and consequently have halved the cost to be charged to LOOC from Sfr4million to Sfr2million. LOOC are now asking both Seiko and ST to submit their final offers, and a decision will then be taken. I will keep you posted!" Seiko did eventually win the contract, but not without an interesting hiccup. Correspondence between Seiko and the Olympic Organizing Committee notes that Seiko did not have permission to use the word "Olympic" in Norway in relation to its watches.[59] This was because a Norwegian man, Jon Lillebuen, had trademarked the use of the word "Olympic" in relation to watches in approximately 1980. The enterprising Mr Lillebuen was, in the early 1990s, in the process of selling his rights to a company called Brugaard that was making watches with the word "Olympic" in them. Seiko Europe reached an agreement with Lillebuen, paying him 64,750 NKr for the trademark, allowing Seiko to use the word "Olympic" in its merchandise.

In my research at the Historical Archives of the International Olympic Committee, I found no contracts or correspondence with timing companies from after the Lillehammer Games. However, Table 4.1 shows that Swiss Timing (now reverting to the name OMEGA) was able to regain its dominance in the Olympic timing market. Of importance here is the clear expansion of sports timing into a professionalized and commercialized practice. During the 1930s and 1940s OMEGA provided timing services to the Olympic Games for free. Significant contract negotiations took place over the following decades with differing concessions and financial and "hospitality" packages made in any given Olympic year. But the figures for the bids from the Barcelona and Lillehammer Games put the issue into stark relief. For 1992 OMEGA charged $4 million for their services, with Seiko agreeing to pay $4–5 million to be given the contract. That is, in order to compete against OMEGA, Seiko would have to cover the costs of its services and pay significant financial sums to the IOC and its affiliates. In response to Seiko's competitive win for the 1992 Games, in 1994 OMEGA dropped its request from $4 million to $2 million, with Seiko now asking to be paid ($2.5 million) for its services.

The competition between OMEGA and Seiko not only sheds light on the significant financial stakes of sports timing but adds further complexity to the photo-finish understood as a cultural artefact and collective practice. OMEGA, the IOC, LOOCs, Seiko, international sports federations, and their respective lawyers are added to the network of actors involved in the production of a photo-finish. And though the primary goal of this competition was financial, the winner was also able to gain influence in shaping the public and professional discourse of timing and the photo-finish.

Conclusion

While OMEGA and Seiko are relative giants in the timing industry, there are a plethora of small and mid-size businesses that offer race timing and photo-finish services. The Race Finish Recording Company that partnered with OMEGA in the 1930s and 1940s continues to provide timing and photo-finish services under the name RaceTech, but does so solely for horse racing in the UK.[60] FinishLynx Systems provides equipment and services to timing professionals across the world, and is a dominant presence at United States Association for Track and Field events.[61] And at the local level, Speed River Timing in Guelph, Ontario, provides timing services for the national champion Guelph Gryphons track and field team, including races hosted by the club.[62] Speed River uses equipment from Active Network I Ipico, a timing hardware provider used internationally including for the London and Tokyo Marathons.[63] These small-to-mid-size companies offer services similar to those of OMEGA, but with one very significant difference.

OMEGA retains full control over their products and services in what amounts to a closed system. This is an essential feature in OMEGA's gradual rise to prominence in the timing and photo-finish market. OMEGA's contracts with the IOC and LOOCs required the presence of OMEGA's trained professionals alongside their equipment. By contrast, providers such as FinishLynx and Ipico offer timing equipment for sale and use by anyone from hobbyists to international sports federations. FinishLynx offers everything from shoe-tags and timing mats to highly precise photo-finish cameras and scoreboards. Timers are encouraged to build their own packages from the hardware and software available in FinishLynx's product catalogue. In reality, in events where an exclusive contract does not exist, timers typically create their own timing and photo-finish services by employing a range of equipment and software. The Facebook Groups Racelresults Timers Group, FinishLynx Sports Timers, and Timers Talk host timing professionals who analyze the tools and practices of their profession, including the hardware and software of timing providers.[64] Timers Talk has a companion Group dedicated solely to the sale and exchange of timing equipment.[65] These differing organizational structures are important in understanding not just OMEGA's rise to prominence but also that, despite this prominence, timing and photo-finishes remain a highly varied practice.

There are two highly significant features of the development of timing and the photo-finish over the mid-to-late twentieth century. First is the slow and steady advance of precision and automation in timing and photo-finish services. The ability to time to the 10th, 100th, and 1,000th of a second developed over the middle decades of the twentieth century, though timing precision was not and is not universally applied across the various sports federations. The parallel move from hand-operated chronographs to the Racend OMEGA and FAT systems speaks to the attendant discourse of mechanical objectivity that remains a central feature in the contemporary timing and photo-finish scene. However much one agrees with OMEGA's claim that the 1948 London Games represented a turning point where machine accuracy surpassed that of human officials, the ascendancy of an automation-as-accuracy discourse in elite-level sport cannot be denied. OMEGA played a significant role in the simultaneous development of ever-more-precise timing equipment and in its promotion as the direct, unmediated measurement of athlete performance. Where Fouché has addressed the ascendancy of technoscientific artifacts used by athletes to gain competitive advantage, a similar drive took place in the measurement of athlete performance.

The second key development of this period is the growth of a competitive, professionalized marketplace, exemplified in the correspondence and contracts outlined above. After decades of negotiations and renegotiations, providing timing services in the form of timing and photo-finish equipment and personnel gave the timing companies exclusive rights to sell and advertise their products during the Olympic Games and at official Olympic venues. This provided the companies with a highly lucrative form of revenue, but it also prevented smaller companies from competing, as they would not have an extensive enough set of consumer products (such as watches) to offset the costs of timing for the Games. The 2017 Annual Report of the Swatch Group identifies that watch and jewelry sales netted the company CHF 7,702,000,000, whereas electronic systems (which is where timing and photo-finish equipment exist) netted CHF 267,000,000, or roughly 3.5 percent of the total of watches and jewelry.[66] These numbers represent all sales and not just those tied to sporting events, but they clearly indicate that the Group's revenues are tied to watch and jewelry sales. And it is not just during the Games that companies benefit from this relationship. During my research at the Olympic Studies Centre in July of 2017, the Olympic Museum gift shop sold a wide range of Swatch Group watches, all branded with the 2016 Rio Olympics colours and symbols. And the "PyeongChang 2018" Limited Edition series watches, still available for purchase on the OMEGA website, range from C$7,150 to $8,650.

Shortly after its initial participation at the Olympic Games, OMEGA began what would be a decades-long quest to have its name visibly affiliated with and promoted alongside the Olympic movement. During the mid-twentieth century, by including its name on equipment and, more cleverly, on the rotating drum of early photo-finish systems, OMEGA ran afoul of the IOC's commitment to an ethos of amateurism. In tandem with the growing commercialization and professionalization of the Games, OMEGA and its affiliates were able to secure exclusive rights contracts through which they were able to formally promote themselves as official Olympic partners. This gave the Swiss watchmaking companies access to highly lucrative merchandising opportunities. Yet even here, OMEGA and its affiliates pushed the boundaries of their Olympic affiliation through too-large signage at Games and through indirectly advertising their Olympic affiliation on the rare occasion when they weren't timing the Games.

The point here is not to denigrate OMEGA, Seiko, Swiss Timing, or any other sports timing company. Rather, the point is to stress the growth of a complex, competitive, professional marketplace for time-keeping services in elite-level sports. This of course is not limited to the Olympics but is the case with any timed sporting event, from Turkey Trots to the Tour de France. It follows that companies providing timing and photo-finish services have a vested interest in their product, in terms of both its promotion and its performance. This leads to one of the more fascinating questions regarding the photo-finish. Given the increasingly lucrative and competitive market of timing and photo-finishes and of sport more broadly, to what extent do developments in timing systems respond to a need in sport and to what extent do they create such a need? Phrased differently, this is a problem of representation versus co-construction. Photo-finishes are promoted as being representations of athlete performance. That is, they are understood to "re-present" infinitesimal differences between pieces of body or equipment as they cross over a specified finish line. But it could equally be argued that the infinitesimal differences are actually the product of the photo-finish. Differences of 1/1,000th of a second between athletes did not exist before timing and photo-finish systems could make them visible. In this way, the march of ever-finer gains in performance and in ever-more-precise measurement of that performance co-construct one another. As one changes, so must the other.

CHAPTER FIVE

Accuracy vs Precision: Interpretation, Nonintervention, and the Limits of Technology

Over a period of ten days from Saturday, 23 June to Monday, 2 July 2012, Hayward Field in "Tracktown USA" – Eugene, Oregon – hosted the United States Track and Field Trials, the purpose of which was to select the Olympic team for the coming London 2012 Olympic Games. The final for the women's 100m sprint took place on the first day of the Trials, Saturday, 23 June. Carmelita Jeter and Tianna Madison took first and second place in the women's 100m, their ranking and times posted to the on-field scoreboard almost instantaneously. After an approximately 20–25-second pause, Jeneba Tarmoh was listed in third with a time of 11.067 seconds and Allyson Felix in fourth place with a time of 11.068 seconds. The results were displayed on the stadium scoreboard for about a minute and then were taken down. Approximately forty-five minutes later, USA Track and Field (USATF) announced that, upon further review, third place in the women's 100m was declared a dead heat between Tarmoh and Felix, with both receiving a time of 11.068 seconds.

Athletes, fans, and media personnel were stunned by the turn of events, and the situation was made all the more complicated when it was revealed through a press release that the USATF did not have procedures in place for determining a winner in the event of a tie.[1] As has been noted throughout this book, ties or dead heats in elite-level sport are not uncommon, even for Olympic medals. In fact, at the same race (women's 100m) for the previous Games in Beijing (2008), Jamaican sprinters Kerron Stewart and Sherone Simpson both received silver medals as they tied in a time of 10.98 seconds.[2] However, the situation at Hayward Field was unique. Under USATF procedures, the US Olympic team is selected based on the top three finishers in each race or event. A tie for first or second would be easily resolved, as the top three finishers are easily identified (1st and 1st and 2nd or 1st and 2nd and 2nd). However, a tie for third is problematic as only the top two finishers are determined. This being the case, in order to send three US athletes to compete in the 100m, the placings of Tarmoh and Felix had to be resolved. Therefore, in announcing the dead heat the USATF noted that it would convene a group to meet that evening and draft procedures to solve the problem.

The following day, Sunday, 24 June, the USATF announced the newly minted procedures for resolving the tie in the Tarmoh/Felix case as well as any subsequent races at the Trials.[3] The procedures were roundly criticized within and outside the track and field community. There were three options identified in the procedures: one, an athlete could concede victory; two, the athletes could participate in a run-off; three, the athletes could participate in a coin-toss. The procedures further noted that if either athlete favoured a run-off, the other athlete had to concede or agree to the run-off. Adding to the confusion and complexity, Tarmoh and Felix had still to race in the 200m the following Saturday. Both athletes trained together and were coached by Bobby Keerse, and followed his recommendation that they not decide on the 100m until after completing the 200m. The day after the 200m finals, Sunday, 1 July, Tarmoh, Felix, and representatives for both athletes and from the USATF met to discuss the 100m dead heat. During that meeting Felix expressed an interest in a run-off, which, according to the newly drafted procedures, meant that Tarmoh either had to accept the run-off or concede. Tarmoh accepted and the run-off was scheduled for Monday, 12 July, and was quickly promoted as a prime-time televised battle. Twelve hours after the decision was made, Tarmoh withdrew from the run-off with little explanation and Felix was awarded the third and final spot on the Olympic team.

From the moment the 100m race concluded on 23 June, journalists, athletes, broadcasters, race officials, fans, and members of the general public took to mainstream, alternative, and social media outlets in an unusually large debate about the photo-finish. Camps formed in support of each athlete but the dominant discourse to emerge was that the USATF had handled the situation poorly. This was summed up by veteran sports reporter Tim Layden, who characterized the entire affair as "unseemly."[4] Rather than analyze the maelstrom of opinions, complaints, and rationalizations that quickly built up in the popular press surrounding the dead heat, this chapter focuses on the object at the centre of the controversy: the photo-finish image. The Tarmoh/Felix dead heat represents something of a "perfect storm" in the track and field and sporting community and, as such, is a particularly fruitful site of analysis for the photo-finish. One of the key, yet almost entirely unacknowledged, facets of the controversy was the way it revealed distinct technological limitations in using timing and photo-finish systems in the live environment.

A Rotated and Obscured Torso

The timing and photo-finish equipment at the 2012 US Olympic Trials was provided by Lynx System Developers and operated by Flash Results, a US-based company that has used Lynx equipment to provide photo-finish and timing services for the NCAA indoor and outdoor championships from 1994 to the present, as well as for the 2000, 2004, and 2008 US Olympic Trials.[5] The system operates similarly to the FAT (fully automatic timing) systems described in chapter 4. In the case of running events, the starter's pistol, timing system, and photo-finish cameras are all connected (wired and wirelessly) to computers running proprietary software under the control of the photo-finish judge. At Flash Results and in the case of the 2012 US Trials, that judge is/was Roger Jennings, a long-time and internationally known photo-finish expert, and one of seven such experts recognized by the International Association of Athletic Federations (IAAF). Flash Results was founded in 1992 by Jennings's father, Tom, who currently serves as the company president and is also a USATF official. As runners cross the finish line, images are sent to the judge's computer, where he/she clicks on the furthestmost point of each runner's torso and enters the corresponding lane number. From here the software produces a finishing time and rank which is instantaneously displayed on the scoreboards in the stadium. This all happens so quickly that it leaves the lay viewer – including me before researching the topic – with the impression that the entire process is fully automated and without human intervention other than the official operating the starting gun.

For the women's 100m at the US Trials, and following this specific procedure, Jennings identified (via a mouse click) the torsos of Jeter and Madison

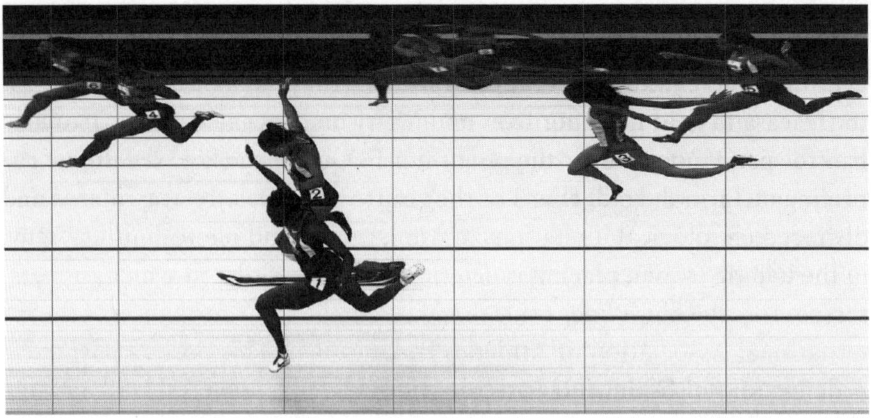

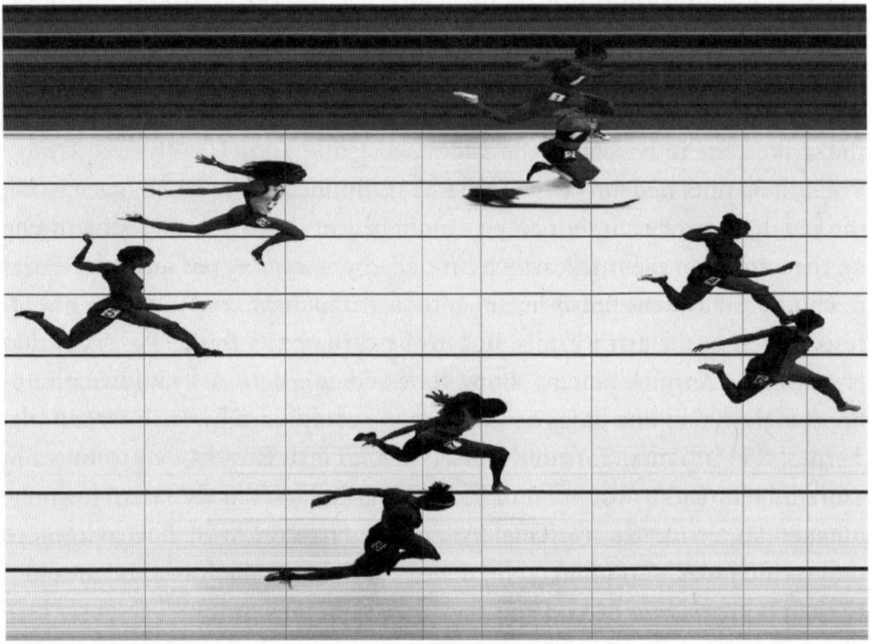

5.1 *Top* Inside camera photo-finish of women's 100m, 2012 US Olympic Trials. Photo courtesy and copyright of Lynx System Developers Inc.

5.2 *Bottom* Outside camera photo-finish of women's 100m, 2012 US Olympic Trials. Photo courtesy and copyright of Lynx System Developers Inc.

as crossing the line in first and second place, and this information was posted to the Hayward Field scoreboard. As noted previously, there was a significant delay in posting the times of the third- and fourth-place finishers. In contrast to the easy task of marking Jeter and Madison crossing the line, Jennings had to spend more time examining the finish-line images to determine the placing of Tarmoh and Felix. The root cause of the delay was a rotated and obscured torso.

In running events, placing is determined by the order in which runners' torsos cross the finish line, a rule that dates to the 1913 formation of the International Association of Athletics Federations.[6] This poses a particular problem for finish-line judges, as there is no precise, universal, and measurable standard for what constitutes a torso. As such, there is no algorithm available for finish-line imaging systems that can precisely and accurately identify the boundaries or edges of a torso. As a result, each photo-finish judge will have his or her particular way of defining and interpreting what constitutes an athlete's torso, making the determination similar to that of the strike zone in baseball.[7]

Flash Results had two Lynx cameras positioned at the finish line: one on the inside of the track, which produced 3,000 slices per second, and one on the outside of the track, which produced 5,000 slices per second. Figures 5.1 and 5.2 show the finish-line images from the inside and outside cameras respectively at the 2012 Trials. Images from the inside camera are typically enough to determine placing; however, in cases where more information is needed, the finish-line judge can access the outside camera. In the case of the Tarmoh/Felix finish, Tarmoh's raised arm and twisted body position obscured the furthestmost point of her torso and rendered the image from the outside camera ineffective. Thus Jennings had to work with the inside image only, which was also plagued by the problem of Tarmoh's raised arm and twisted body, shown here in Figure 5.3. To solve this problem, Jennings employed a process he terms "interpolation."

To interpolate the forwardmost point on Tarmoh's torso, Jennings identified two base points: one on the right of her race bib and another on her right bicep. From these two points, he interpolated – that is to say, he estimated based on prior knowledge – the forwardmost point of the torso. It is important to note that this process of interpolation is individual and is not a standard across athletics officiating. It is Jennings's particular method, and one that had been (and is) used successfully across numerous national and international competitions. In the finish-line image (Figure 5.3), the results of Jennings's interpolation yield a point that is obscured from view by Tarmoh's head. Using this manufactured point, Jennings marked the vertical line to indicate Tarmoh's torso and the computer assigned her a time of 11.067 seconds. Jennings next marked Felix's torso (which is clearly visible) and she was awarded a time of 11.068 seconds, one-thousandth of a second slower than Tarmoh. Tarmoh's name was listed on the scoreboard in third place, Felix in fourth. Tarmoh took a victory lap, donned a Team USA jacket, attended a post-race press conference for the top three finishers, and underwent mandatory drug-testing.

Unbeknownst to athletes and viewers, as soon as he made the determination of third and fourth position, Jennings protested his own read of the image and put in a call to the in-stadium officials asking for help in reviewing the race results. A group of officials responded, ultimately deciding that Bob Podkaminer, a senior USATF official and photo-finish expert, would represent the group.[8] Jennings and Podkaminer met for twenty minutes, looking over the finish-line image and ultimately deciding to declare a dead heat for third. The reasoning behind the decision – as explained by Podkaminer and Jennings in separate interviews – was that the process of interpolation, however accurate, still involved an element of subjectivity and would therefore leave the USATF open to protests or challenges around the decision. The two therefore decided to base the decision on what they could see in the image – unaided – with their eyes. In this way, the use of the image at the US Trials adhered to the long-standing practice of privileging machine-made images as arbiters of truth, objectivity, and accuracy. Unsurprisingly, a closer analysis of the deployment and interpretation of the finish-line image reveals a much more complicated picture.

Objectivity, Precision, and Accuracy

From Hemment's first experiments through those of Kirby to the creation of the Racend OMEGA Timer and the FinishLynx Pro camera, the photo-finish as an evidentiary object exemplifies the mutability of notions of objectivity and accuracy so clearly outlined by Daston and Galison. In terms of the Tarmoh/Felix dead heat, their work reveals the mutually constitutive forces of the image, its producers, and its users in the production of visual

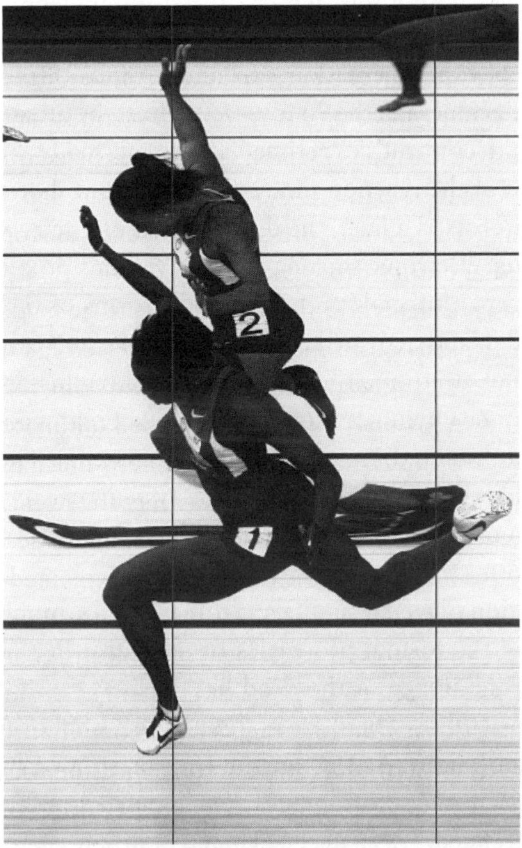

5.3 Close-up from Figure 5.1, showing Tarmoh (#1) and Felix (#2) dead heat.

evidence. The notion of nonintervention is particularly useful and important. Daston and Galison articulate the concept of nonintervention most clearly in their 1992 essay "The Image of Objectivity," where they write: "Nonintervention, not verisimilitude, lay at the heart of mechanical objectivity, and this is why mechanically produced images captured its message best."[9] Put simply, it was the scientist's lack of presence in the image (meaning that there were no signs of intervention in the form of annotations, clarifications, amplifications, etc.) that served to guarantee its objectivity.

It wasn't that scientists were physically absent from the production and interpretation of images, but that their involvement was increasingly less visible in the images in question.

Nonintervention is also central to the history of the photo-finish. The first several decades of experimentation – from the 1880s through to the development of the slit camera in the 1930s – are defined by attempts to automate the photo-finish. Hemment's experiments were marred by his physical presence in the form of the reaction time needed to trip a shutter at the precise moment a horse crossed a line. The development of electromagnetic shutter releases and, later, electronic starting gates solved this problem, but the tension between human officials and mechanical forms of timing and photo-finishes persisted. Hand-activated chronographs were increasingly challenged through the use of electronic timing systems, and the history of timing and photo-finishes at the Olympics shows a continued progression and emphasis towards more automated, noninterventionist systems. The use of the acronym FAT to describe contemporary timing systems encapsulates this drive towards more automated, "fully automatic," mechanical systems of recording athlete performance.

Nonintervention played a significant role in the Tarmoh/Felix dead heat both in terms of the formal properties of the finish-line image and in its interpretation. The image of the dead heat displays no visible trace of a human expert or author. There are no textual or visual overlays, no signature, and no annotations. As Daston and Galison show, Erwin Christeller's decision to not "clean up" his images, leaving pieces of tattered tissue untouched and unrefined, was a necessary step of nonintervention to guarantee the veracity of the object depicted. So too is the case with the 2012 dead-heat image. The distorted proportions of the athletes, including the long horizontal band that is Felix's shoe and the impossibly small left foot and lower left leg of Tarmoh, are not what we would see watching the live event or even in a photograph of the event; rather, these peculiar distortions, shapes, and forms are the product of a mechanical, noninterventionist vision and serve to testify to the evidentiary status of the image.

The interpretation of the finish-line image also strongly foregrounded a noninterventionist impulse. Immediately after using his interpolation method to identify Tarmoh in third and Felix in fourth, Jennings signalled to race officials that he was uncertain about the result. One of the chief officials, Bob

Podkaminer, then "read" the image with Jennings, the two ultimately deciding on a dead heat. In separate interviews with Tim Layden of *Sports Illustrated*, Jennings and Podkaminer explained the decision as being tied to the inherent subjectivity of Jennings's method. Podkaminer explained that "an interpolation is not a fact" and Jennings noted that "in the end, my read was subjective."[10] In my own conversation with Giles Norton, then of Lynx System Developers, Inc., he explained the situation by also highlighting the difference between interpretation and fact. He offered the example of a picture that depicts an elephant standing behind a building so that only the back end of the elephant is visible. Looking at this image, one could reasonably intuit that it is in fact a complete elephant and that the front is simply obscured by the building. But, he notes, you could not prove in a court of law that it was a complete elephant – it could be trunkless, missing a foot, or in some other way incomplete.[11] In the same way, Jennings can interpolate that Tarmoh's torso is indeed ahead of Felix's; however, that is an interpretation that is not verifiable in the image alone.

Jennings's method of interpolation has been used hundreds if not thousands of times and he is recognized as one of the foremost experts in his field; however, as this was a high-profile event with a great deal at stake, it was precisely his intervention that was cause for concern. A USATF press release by Communications Manager Katie Branham on the day of the race pointed to the differentiation between interpretation and evidence, while also foregrounding the specialized, mechanistic nature of the image: "The photo-finish image, shot at 3,000 frames-per-second, was then analyzed by timers and referees and unanimously ruled to be a dead-heat based on visual evidence."[12] Jennings's subjectivity in the form of his interpolation is not to be found in this statement. Instead, it speaks to visual evidence as tied to the image – in this case one produced by a camera with an incredibly high scan rate.

The final decision to declare third place a dead heat espoused the epistemic virtue of mechanical objectivity and ceded authority to the high scan rate of the machine-made image over the interpretation of the expert. However, what makes the example particularly interesting is the simultaneous foregrounding of Jennings's trained judgment. LetsRun.com, the source that carried the first post-race interview with Jennings, introduced him as being "considered by many to be the best timer in the world."[13] And in the most extensive interview with Jennings, Tim Layden of *Sports Illustrated* refers to him as "one of the most prominent photo-finish judges in the world."[14] Much of Layden's article provides a backstory of Jennings, documenting his long ties to the sport of track and field and his legitimacy as a photo-finish expert. Concluding his story, Layden writes of Jennings that "in the retelling [of the dead-heat controversy], Roger Jennings comes across as unfailingly professional."[15]

Jennings's intervention with the finish-line image was what initially constituted the evidence for Tarmoh being awarded third place. Jennings himself has said that if he were to review the image a hundred times, he would make the same determination every single time.[16] And only a few days after the dead heat was declared, Jennings's expertise and professionalism were lauded in the press. In this way, Jennings's work with the image – his trained judgment in the form of interpolation – was positioned as the necessary intervention of the expert to make the unreadable, readable. However, and true to the moral imperative of nonintervention, it was Jennings's own uneasiness with his interpolation and its subjectivity that led him to challenge his own decision. As a result, Podkaminer and Jennings both agreed that the decision should be made free of human intervention, choosing to allocate third and fourth place based on what the eye could see in the image, and not what the eye and mind could interpret. The paradoxical balance between letting the image speak for itself and Jennings's trained judgment is perhaps best exemplified in Jennings's post-race comments where he put this paradox in bold relief: "Looking at it the way that I read it, I still see lane one beating lane two from what I [was doing at first] using an educated guess on torso position, but on visual evidence, on what I can actually see in the picture, it's a dead-heat so I'm comfortable with that decision."[17]

This is not to suggest that the reading of the image was free of other influences. If it was a moral process of nonintervention, it was also political and economic. A central part of Podkaminer's own rationale to ignore Jennings's interpolation of the image was that its inherent subjectivity would open the USATF to formal challenges and protests. Jennings was also subject to external pressure from both the USATF and NBC, the network covering the Trials. He was connected via headset to on-field officials as well as to the NBC broadcast support crew, to whom he provided results and commentary. Although Jennings has said that he did not feel pressure to make a decision one way or another, his colleague Bob Podkaminer identified pressure from both the USATF and NBC, noting, "As soon as there was a delay, there were voices in that booth who wanted something. The meet announcer wanted something. NBC wanted something. Those voices were loud."[18]

My point here is to highlight the stress and also the gravity of the situation. Jennings analyzed and interpolated the finish-line image within twenty-five seconds, and, consciously or not, was under what must have been intense pressure by both the USATF and NBC. And as this was the Olympic Trials the decision was particularly important. The top three finishers go the Olympics, with all the material and cultural capital that that entails, and all other athletes must wait four years for the next opportunity. Add to the fact that Felix was a decorated, veteran track star and Tarmoh was a relative newcomer, and that the compensation and sponsorship packages of the two differed by hundreds of thousands of dollars, and it is clear that Jennings's decision had both immediate and far-reaching ramifications.[19] Finally, Jennings's own status as an internationally known photo-finish expert, and as one of the public faces of his father's company, would surely have added to the weight of the moment. In other words, it wasn't just the placing of Tarmoh and Felix that was at stake but also the reputation of Jennings, his company, Lynx Systems equipment, and the USATF, together with the contracts and sponsorship agreements these individuals and groups would have with sport and media corporations.

There was, therefore, a great deal involved and at stake in the deployment and interpretation of this particular photo-finish image. One way to explain Jennings's paradoxical position to trust his own judgment but to let the image speak for itself is that it satisfied the varied actors in play. On the one hand, following the epistemic virtue of mechanical objectivity and letting the image speak for itself freed the USATF, Flash Results, and Jennings from any further controversy or potential litigation. On the other, Jennings's reputation as one of seven internationally recognized finish-line experts required that his trained judgment remain intact. In this way, the defining features of two epistemic virtues – mechanical objectivity and trained judgment – come together in the interpretation of the finish-line image in ways that simultaneously reinforce the evidentiary authority of the machine-made image and the specialized, trained capacity of photo-finish judges to read such images.

The Limitations of Timing and the Photo-Finish

As evidenced in the Tarmoh/Felix dead heat, athlete placing at the Trials was determined by timing to the 1/1,000th of a second. To comply with international standards and to participate in an Olympic Games, the USATF (as well as all other national track and field associations) must comply with the rules and regulations of the governing international body, in this case the International Association of Athletics Federations (IAAF). The IAAF sets the rules for the sport, including the application and precision of timing and photo-finish systems. This brings us to another important aspect of the photo-finish as a cultural artefact – its differential application across sports. To examine this aspect of the topic, I will first introduce two other notable race finishes contemporary to the Tarmoh/Felix dead heat.

The first race finish is Michael Phelps's record-setting seventh gold medal at the 2008 Beijing Olympic Games. Phelps won the 100m butterfly over Milorad Cavic by 0.01 of a second, in 50.58 to 50.59.[20] Under the regulations of the Fédération Internationale de Natation (FINA), placing is determined when athletes hit a touch pad placed at the end of each lane and connected to a digital timing system. The specific system in Beijing was provided by OMEGA, though it is worth noting that touch pads in swimming had been in use since the 1968 Mexico Olympics and OMEGA had even offered them for use in the 1952 Helsinki Games.[21] In other words, the touch-pad system in Beijing, though refined, was not a new invention.

A key narrative that emerged from the Phelps/Cavic decision foregrounded the infallibility of the timing system, especially as it compared to the fallibility of the human eye. Accounts of the race in the media firmly separated what the eye saw and what the timing system proved. For example, writing for the *Montreal Gazette*, Cam Cole opens his story by noting, "A photo-finish. A 1/100th of a second margin. A race he appeared to lose in real time, on replay, even in super slow-motion. But the timer evidently doesn't lie."[22] Michelle Kaufman wrote that "[e]ven Michael Phelps couldn't believe his eyes" and that he had to consult the scoreboard to see who had won the race. She further pointed to the difference between what one could see and what the timing system proved: "To the naked eye, it was nearly impossible to tell who won. And from some camera angles, it appeared Cavic had the gold. But the electronic clock read Phelps 50.58, Cavic 50.59."[23]

Few commentators picked up in any significant way on the issue of the timing. Thomas Boswell addressed some of the issue in the *Washington Post*, noting that FINA examined replays run at 1/10,000th of a second, and he quotes Ben Ekumbo from FINA as noting, "There are no doubts: It was very clear that the Serbian swimmer touched second."[24] In a prelude to a rematch approximately one year later, Cavic came out as critical of the decision, noting that he touched first but did not touch hard enough to activate the sensor. Cavic claimed, "I did touch the wall first, but I didn't activate the wall first," concluding that "this is FINA and OMEGA's problem."[25] For its part, and in line with the discussion of chapter 4, OMEGA issued a press release in 2008 under the title "Great Moments," explaining the technology used at the Beijing Games and noting that their timing and imaging systems provide rankings "which are beyond doubt and dispute." As if channelling Daston and Galison, the press release put the issue of human and non-human capacities in stark relief, noting that a key feature of their timing and imaging system is that "there is no human intervention between the athlete and the measurement of his or her performance."[26] This suggests that human officials and human interpretation are entirely absent from the process, as if the times of Cavic and Phelps were automatically recorded from sensors planted in their bodies. This was clearly not the case in the men's butterfly, yet it is interesting to ponder if and when such a "noninterventionist" timing system will be proposed.

The second race finish to add is the tie for gold in the women's downhill at the 2014 Sochi Olympic Games between Dominique Gisin of Switzerland and Tina Maze from Slovenia. Under Fédération Internationale de Ski (FIS) rules, placing is determined according to the net time of racers taken from the moment they cross the starting gate to when they trigger a beam connected by sets of photocells at the finish line. Gisin and Maze covered the approximately 2.7km-long course in 1:41.57, the decision again based on timing to the hundredth of a second. The dominant narrative that emerged in the coverage of this event was that this was a feel-good moment in the Games. Maze's often-cited remarks that "two happy faces" were better than one became a shorthand for the event, as did photos of the two with hands joined and raised on the Olympic podium. The question of timing and how two skiers could tie to the hundredth of a second over such a distance was alluded to in many accounts but was only brought up for serious discussion in a few cases.

In cases where the tie was discussed commentators pointed to a distinction between what was technologically possible with the timing system and what was permissible under FIS regulations. Writing in the *New York Times*, Bill Pennington set it up most dramatically:

> In a glass-enclosed timing booth perched at the top of the grandstand next to the finish, the times for Maze and Gisin were measured and recorded to the 10,000th of a second: four digits to the right of the decimal point, not just two. As Daniel Baumat, vice president of Swiss Timing, the company that administers the timed results for the Olympic Games and many other sports, said late Wednesday: "There is a more precise number, to the 10,000th. But the rule is to report to the hundredths. We follow the rule."[27]

Peter Hurzeler from OMEGA also highlighted the difference, noting that the OMEGA timing system can calculate to the millionths of a second but that the FIS does not accept such precise measurement.[28] And an unauthored piece in the *Irish Times* picks up on the same issue but goes further, with another quote from Daniel Baumat, who noted that an actual winner was determined: "Still, in the timing control booth, three people – the head timer, a backup timer and a computer operator – saw who won the race according to the timing data." Baumat added, "No one, including FIS, was informed of the actual winner. That is forbidden."[29] Lastly, the former American ski racer, Picabo Street, who was working for Fox Sports at the event, had the most emphatic response. Directing her attention at the timers in the booth, she exclaimed, "I want to get that person and just like beat it out of 'em."[30] Her rationale was that, if the timing data was available, it should be used. "If it's gauge-able, let us have it," she is quoted as saying, adding, "give it to me. Give me that thousandth."[31]

The two events described above, along with the Tarmoh/Felix dead heat discussed previously, are three from a vast set of possible examples of the role of timing and photo-finishes to determine placing in elite-level sport. They are representative inasmuch as they highlight the often idiosyncratic nature of decision-making in sport (both within and between sports) and the many parameters at work in producing timing and image-based evidence. Here I want to call attention to a key disconnect in contemporary timing and photo-finish discourse between technological precision and accurate measurement.

Timing Regulations: Humans and Machines Make Decisions

The particular and often peculiar relationship between human officials and electronic timing and imaging equipment that was foregrounded in the events described above is also manifest in the regulations governing athletics, swimming, and alpine ski racing. USATF rules allow for manual, semi-automated (electronic systems controlled by human officials), and fully automated timing and imaging systems for competitions, though preference is given to fully automated systems. Importantly, and as has been shown in the Tarmoh/Felix dead heat as well as in the previous chapter, fully automated systems still require the participation of human officials. The ultimate result of automation – the photo-finish image – still requires the active participation and interpretation of a human judge. This is summarized in Rule 126 on Judges: "When an approved imaging device is properly functioning at the finish of an event, the image must be referred to the Photo-finish Judges for the primary determination of the order of finish. In the absence of such a device, the primary determination of the order of the finish shall be made by the Judges at the finish."[32] In this way, USATF rules effectively merge the electronic system with the human in determining placing, with authority ultimately vested in the latter.

Like in the USATF, under FINA regulations, races can be timed and officiated manually, semi-automatically, or automatically, again with a preference for fully automated timing. The rules governing timing outline the relationship between automated and human time-keepers, in which the former are privileged. Rule SW 11.1 reads:

> The operation of Automatic Officiating Equipment shall be under the supervision of appointed officials. Times recorded by Automatic Equipment shall be used to determine the winner, all placing and the time applicable to each lane. The placing and times so determined shall have precedence over the decisions of timekeepers. In the event that a break-down of the Automatic Equipment occurs or that it is clearly

> indicated that there has been a failure of the Equipment, or that a swimmer has failed to activate the Equipment, the recordings of time-keepers shall be official.[33]

As this rule makes clear, ultimate evidentiary authority rests with the timing system. The human official serves as a backup in the event that the electronic system fails. Similarly, photo and video services are not mandatory in FINA-sanctioned races but are often employed as a back-up to aid judges in making decisions. This was the case in the Cavic/Phelps race, where underwater video was reviewed at 10,000 frames per second.

The timing and imaging systems for alpine ski races, as set out in FIS guidelines, are considerably more nuanced and thorough than those of the USATF and FINA. This is because, unlike the USATF and FINA, the FIS has a specialized and designated "Timing Working Group" to oversee, assess, and ultimately create policies and regulations towards "the correct evaluation of human performance through fundamental timekeeping concepts."[34] FIS guidelines require that both fully automatic electronic timing and hand timing be used in all major competitions. Rule 611.2 notes that "[f]or all events in the FIS calendar, electronic timers, start gates and photocells homologated by the FIS must be used."[35] The FIS requires two separately wired systems be used, with System A as the default and System B as the backup. And Rule 611.2.2 specifies that hand timing must also be used: "Manual (hand) timing, completely separate and independent of the electronic timing, must be used for all competitions listed in the FIS calendar."[36] As with FINA, the mandatory inclusion of hand timing devices is primarily for backup purposes in case both of the electronic systems fail.

In all three events – athletics, swimming, and alpine skiing – evidence in the form of timing and imaging is the result of a combination of human and machine. Timing and photo-finish systems used by the USATF, FINA, and the FIS bring together the automated image and timing data with the trained judgment of race officials, time-keepers, and other personnel to produce evidence in the form of athlete placing. And just as the three sports federations have different rules governing the relationship of humans and machines in determining results, so too do they have different rules on the precision to which athletes are to be timed and results to be fixed.

Precision vs Accuracy: Hundredths of a Second and Beyond

In each of the events addressed here, athlete placing is determined by timing and imaging to the hundredth of a second. Timing to the hundredth of a second has been practised for decades, which may seem paradoxical given that timing companies now offer data to the ten thousandth, hundred thousandth, or even millionth of a second. And so it is important to take up the question of why each of these sports determines placing based on the hundredth of a second. The regulations of the USATF, FINA, and the FIS all clearly stipulate the requirements for timing and imaging systems and generally coalesce at the level of the hundredth of a second, but with curious and important differences.

The USATF determines placing based on the hundredth but stipulates that times are recorded to the thousandth. As identified in Rule 165 Subsection 11 a):

> Fully automatic timing for races on the track up to and including 10,000 meters shall be read to 0.001 of a second, when possible. When the last digit is zero, that digit shall be dropped and the official time recorded in hundredths of seconds. Otherwise, the time shall be rounded to the next longer hundredth of a second and so recorded. When the fully automatic timing device cannot be read to 0.001 of a second, it shall be read and recorded in hundredths of seconds, rounded up to the next longer hundredth when the time is between hundredths indicators.[37]

In this way, runners with times of 10.001 and 10.009 both receive a time of 10.01; the 8/1,000ths of seconds that separate them are erased. However, and as found in Rule 167, the thousandth of a second is used to determine placing in the event of ties: "In determining whether there has been a tie for a qualifying position for the next round based on time, the Photo-finish Judge shall consider the actual time recorded by the competitors without regard to the rule that the time should be read to the next longer 1/100th of a second."[38] This being the case, the runner with a time of 10.001 would win over the competitor with 10.009. This was the case in the initial read of the Tarmoh/Felix decision, with Tarmoh awarded third place in a time of 10.067 to Felix's 10.068.

In contrast to the USATF, FINA expressly forbids recording data beyond the hundredth of a second. Rule SW 11.2 sets out its policy, also noting the result in terms of ties:

> When Automatic Equipment is used, the results shall be recorded only to 1/100 of a second. When timing to 1/1000 of a second is available, the third digit shall not be recorded or used to determine time or placement. In the event of equal times, all swimmers who have recorded the same time at 1/100 of a second shall be accorded the same placing. Times displayed on the electronic scoreboard should show only to 1/100 of a second.[39]

This FINA rule is particularly clear in noting that in both recording and public display (via scoreboard), swimming races are to be timed to the hundredth of a second. And the language is equally clear that any timing beyond hundredths is not to be taken into consideration nor used in determining placing. And this was the case in the Cavic/Phelps race, as times were recorded and decisions made to the hundredth of a second with no recourse to more precise numbers to justify the decision.

And finally, FIS policy adds further nuance, stipulating that, while results are recorded to the hundredth, races are timed to *at least* the thousandth of a second, meaning that times can be recorded to the ten thousandth of a second or beyond. Rule 611.2.1 notes:

> All time of day times must be immediately and automatically sequentially recorded on printed strips to at least the 1/1000th (0.001) precision. Both systems must allow for the calculation of net times by the mathematical comparison of each competitor's start time to finish time. The final result for each skier's run is then expressed to 1/100th (0.01) precision by truncating the calculated net time on course.[40]

Whereas in USATF rules, truncating times involves rounding up to the next nearest hundredth, in FIS competitions, truncation is done by deleting any digits beyond the hundredths column, so that a skier with a time of 1:21.011 and a skier with a time of 1:21.019 will both receive times of 1:21.01.[41] In relation to the Gisin/Maze tie, the thousandths column was not communi-

Table 5.1
Timing regulations

	USATF	FINA	FIS
Timing to:	Thousandths (0.001)	Hundredths or thousandths (0.01 or 0.001)	At least thousandths (≥ 0.001)
Results to:	Hundredths (0.01)	Hundredths (0.01)	Hundredths (0.01)
Third digit (thousandth):	Rounded up to next hundredth	Dropped	Dropped
Tie determined by:	Thousandths	Hundredths	Hundredths

cated, so that both received a time of 1:41.57 even though, by FIS policy, the race was timed to at least three decimal places.

As discussed above, and as summarized in Table 5.1, regulations governing athletics, swimming, and downhill skiing all stipulate that placing is determined to the hundredth of a second. However, each regulating body has slightly differing policies regarding the precision of the equipment used and what, if anything, is done with data that is recorded to the thousandth of a second or beyond. FINA is the most straightforward, with timing and decision-making done at the level of 0.01 of a second, regardless of the capabilities of the timing and imaging equipment to deliver more precise numbers. The USATF records times to the 0.001 of a second but determines placing based on 0.01 of a second. The FIS records times to at least 0.001 of a second but also determines placing to 0.01. And when dealing with timing data beyond 0.01 of a second, FINA does not record it, the USATF rounds up to the next longest 0.01 of a second, and the FIS simply eliminates all digits beyond the hundredths column. The end result is a set of procedures that are often confusing and, in some cases, seem contradictory.

The confusion within the differing regulations was also manifest in the public and professional discourse surrounding the three events, most notably in the Gisin and Maze tie. Recall that a theme in the commentary surrounding the race distinguished between times recorded to 0.0001 (ten thousandths) of a second, OMEGA's ability to record to 0.000001 (millionths) of a second, and FIS regulations that results be recorded to 0.01

(hundredths) of a second. This led some commentators to argue that one of the two skiers had actually won the race (according to timing done to the 0.0001 of a second), but that this result was not allowed by FIS policy. Most importantly, two OMEGA executives – Daniel Baumat and Peter Hurzeler – gave public interviews in which they made such claims. This insinuates that the FIS policy is flawed and that the more precise timing data was accurate. By contrast, in what follows I argue that claims by OMEGA and others for timing beyond 0.01 of a second can and do lead to public and professional misunderstandings of the capabilities of timing and imaging systems. And I further argue that they obfuscate the limitations of timing and photo-finish systems as they are applied in the live environment.

Measurement Error and Dimensional Tolerances

Given the speeds at which athletes travel, the closeness of race results, and the tremendous amounts of money, national pride, and cultural capital involved in sports competition, timing and imaging systems have to be able to capture highly precise data across different, and sometimes difficult, environmental conditions. In concert with the increased emphasis on "marginal gains" in athlete training and the goal of shaving thousandths and hundredths of seconds off of a performance, OMEGA offers the Quantum Timer and Lynx System Developers the EtherLynx Pro Photo-Finish Camera, which split the second into millionths and ten-thousandths respectively. However, what I stress here is that there are limits to the accuracy of such timing and imaging systems as they are employed in the natural world. Advanced timing and imaging systems capture information beyond what can be guaranteed in the live environment.

The required physical dimensions and properties of sport venues – in this case a track, a pool, and a ski course – are precisely defined within the regulations governing each sport. Importantly, as these venues are composed of, exist in, and function in the natural world, each sport federation allows for slight variation or "dimensional tolerances" in the configuration of the venue/course. This means that, though runners, swimmers, and ski racers cover the same course, there are very slight differences between each athlete's particular lane or route and these differences are permissible under USATF, FINA, and FIS regulations. And these differences, which at first blush appear inconsequential, can have very significant impacts. Giles Norton, formerly at Lynx Systems, explained with the example of swimming, noting that the difference between first and second place could come down to the difference in the thickness of paint on the pool walls.[42] The end result of this is that the differences revealed by timing and imaging systems operating in the hundredths, thousandths, or millionths of a second are not necessarily evidence of differences in athletic performance, but might instead indicate differences in the physical configuration of the event venue. More precise numbers do not mean more accurate measurement of athlete performance.

To understand the issue more completely, it is important to outline the speed and distance that athletes travel as well as the "dimensional tolerances" of individual sporting venues. Table 5.2 presents the time and distance travelled for each of the events described above. Times are shown in whole seconds for ease of explanation. For the physical configuration of running tracks, the USATF follows the guidelines prescribed by the International Association of Athletics Federations (IAAF). The IAAF requires that track measurements be accurate to within +/-0.01m, or 10mm. As shown in Table 5.2, in 0.01 of a second, Tarmoh and Felix covered 100mm, which is ten times the allowable difference in the track's configuration. At that level of precision, placing can accurately be attributed to athlete performance. However, in 0.001 of a second the runners covered 10mm, which matches exactly the allowable differences in the physical measurement of the track. Therefore, at 0.001 of a second or beyond, differences between runners cannot confidently be attributed to differences in performance, but could instead be due to allowable differences in the physical configuration of the track (i.e. Tarmoh's lane vs Felix's lane).

In relation to the Cavic/Phelps race, in 0.01 of a second the swimmers travel a distance of 1.667cm (16.67mm) and in 0.001 of a second they travel 0.1667cm (1.667mm). FINA regulations governing the physical configuration of event venues (in this case the pool) provides for a dimensional tolerance of 30mm between the end walls of a given lane. As identified in FR 2.2.1: "Against the nominal length of 50.0 meters, a tolerance of plus 0.03 metre in each lane minus 0.00 metre on both end walls at all points from 0.3 metre above to 0.8 metre below the surface of the water is allowed." Therefore, any two lanes in a swimming pool and any two straight lines within a single lane can range in length from 50.00m to 50.03m, meaning that any two measurements can differ in length by 30mm.

Regarding the Cavic/Phelps decision, timing to 0.01 of a second captures 16mm of the athletes' movement and timing to 0.001 of a second captures 1.6mm. Adding to the complexity is that the Cavic/Phelps race was 100m (double the length of the pool), meaning that the allowable differences in lane length would double so that one racer might swim 100.00m and the other 100.06m. At the level of 0.001 of a second or beyond, the differences captured by the timing system exceeds what can be guaranteed in the physical configuration of the pool. Differences in athlete placing at that level of precision can be due to allowable differences in the length of each lane rather than the distance travelled by the swimmers. Timing to 0.01 second captures 16.6mm, which far exceeds the dimensional tolerances of the pool. At that level of precision, differences in placing can confidently be attributed to the differences between swimmers covering the race distance. As such, FINA's policy accurately accounts for the limitations to technological precision, though this is not made clear in the rules and regulations.

The issue of dimensional tolerances is different in alpine ski racing for at least two reasons. First, with the exception of parallel events, athletes do not race beside one another as in swimming and athletics, but race individually down the mountain. Times are recorded at the start when the athlete trips a wand at the starting gate and again at the finish when they break a beam of light between photocell receptors. The start and finish-line systems are connected directly by cable, and there are two, independently wired systems attached to the start and finish gates. A second difference is that the distance travelled by skiers will vary considerably more than that in a 100m swimming or running race. A skier's finishing time is directly dependent on the "line" that they take down the course in a way that is fundamentally different from that of swimmers and sprinters. This means that the issue in alpine skiing is less one of dimensional tolerances than it is a question of an agreed-upon threshold used to determine placing. This threshold is pointed to in a comment by the communications manager of the FIS, Jenny Wiedeke, following the Gisin/Maze tie.[43] Speaking specifically to the FIS regulation to time to the hundredth and not the thousandth, Wiedeke noted: "when you start getting into such small numbers you cannot guarantee the integrity of that number. It's an outdoor sport in a winter climate; a piece of flesh could be the difference."[44] Wiedeke's reference to a "piece of flesh" separating competitors is a slight exaggeration. As shown in Table 5.2, at 0.01 of a sec-

Table 5.2
Timing and distance travelled

	Tarmoh/Felix	Cavic/Phelps	Maze/Gisin
Time	10.00	60.00	1:42.00
Distance	100m	100m	2,719m
Distance per second	10m	1.667m	26.67m
Distance per 1/10th (0.1)	100cm (1,000mm)	16.67cm (166.7mm)	266.7cm (2.667mm)
Distance per 1/100th (0.01)	10cm (100mm)	1.667cm (16.67mm)	26.67cm (266.7mm)
Distance per 1/1,000th (0.001)	1cm (10mm)	0.1667cm (1.667mm)	2.667cm (26.67mm)

ond Maze and Gisin cover 26.67cm and at 0.001 they cover 2.667cm. While 2.667cm is clearly thicker than a "piece of flesh," the difference between Gisin and Maze at that level is extremely slight given the distance and variable conditions of the racecourse. What is missing, however, from both FIS regulations and their comments following the Gisin/Maze tie is a clearer, more full explanation for why placing is awarded based on the hundredth of a second, especially when racers are timed to at least the thousandth.

The issue of dimensional tolerance as outlined above and the differential application of timing and imaging systems in athletics, swimming, and alpine ski racing brings to light another central aspect of the photo-finish: that there are distinct limits to the use of timing and imaging systems as evidence in sport. These limitations speak to a fundamental disconnect in timing and the photo-finish between precision and accuracy. Whether in athletics, swimming, or alpine ski racing, there is a threshold of precision beyond which the timing and imaging data cannot accurately be said to represent differences in athlete performance. The ability to divide the second into millionths is indeed an impressive technological accomplishment; however, greater levels of precision do not necessarily correspond to more accurate measurement of athlete performance.

The disconnect between technological precision and its application in the live environment is captured in Lev Manovich's writing on the paradoxes of digital photography.[45] The author critiques accounts of digital imaging that compare it to traditional, film-based photography, arguing that each is a unique form of image-making. Of Manovich's claims, the one most pertinent in understanding the photo-finish is his positioning of the digital image and the photographic image as constituting different realities. He writes: "A synthetic computer-generated image is not an inferior representation of our reality, but a realistic representation of a different reality."[46] This is indicative of the disconnect in timing and photo-finish systems that time to the thousandth, ten thousandth, and millionth of a second: though they can accurately subdivide the second into increasingly infinitesimal amounts as part of a digital reality, these micro-measurements do not correspond to the lived reality of sporting competition. It is not just that the human eye cannot perceive differences in placing beyond a single decimal place; it is that bodies competing in the live environment cannot be separated by such infinitesimal margins. Neither is more or less accurate: instead, they are different realities.

Conclusion

Daston and Galison refer to the process through which scientists and nonhuman actors build the images and knowledge of their disciplines as "collective empiricism."[47] Despite all pronouncements of "fully automated" timing systems and measurements produced directly from the athletes themselves, the phrase equally describes the process of determining placing in sport, with an important caveat. In contrast to the more specialized and closed practice of scientific atlas–making, the photo-finish includes a considerably more diverse set of actors. As is evident in the Tarmoh/Felix dead heat, the photo-finish is a collective process that involves advanced imaging and timing hardware and software, a photo-finish judge, competition officials, federation rules, and the architectural configuration of the venue. It also often indirectly (and sometimes directly) involves sponsors, broadcasters, athletes, fans, and industry professionals.

Given the diversity of actors at work in the production and use of the photo-finish, it might better be described as existing in a "mediation junction" as identified by Johan Schot and Adri Albert de la Bruheze. They define the mediation junction as "the place at which consumers, mediators, and producers meet to negotiate, articulate, and align specific technical choices and user needs."[48] Returning to the Tarmoh/Felix dead heat we can see Jennings, Flash Results, Lynx Systems, the USATF, the IAAF, NBC, Nike (the athlete sponsors), sports journalists, and fans at work in a mediation junction to articulate the specific meaning and impact of the photo-finish.

The steady march of timing technology has meant that timers can now divide the second into millionths, which is a far cry from the fifths used to determine placing in the first several Olympic Games of the modern era. However, timing to the hundredth or thousandth of a second and beyond does not necessarily provide a more accurate result, a fact that is readily acknowledged in the timing community. Why then would Daniel Baumat and Peter Hurzeler of Swiss Timing / OMEGA claim otherwise? And why would Picabo Street demand to know who "really" won the race? The most immediate and at least partially correct answer is that such claims and demands are good for business, in this case the businesses of sports timing and sports entertainment. Baumat and Hurzeler were advocating for their specific product and Street was adding drama to Fox's sports broadcast.

Claims about a "real" winner or about the pure measurement of athlete performance reinforce a discourse as old as race finish photography: namely, that technology will solve perceived human problems. More specifically, in the history of the photo-finish this discourse has manifested itself as equating accuracy with technological advancement and precision, such that greater precision must necessarily mean more accurate race results. This teleological view is categorically false. Despite the increased technological precision of timing and photo-finish systems, there is a limit to such precision when used to measure sporting contests. This is because sport is still a human pursuit and sporting events take place within the natural world. This means that imperfect actors such as bodies, precipitation, and the construction of sports venues with materials such as dirt, sand, concrete, wood, rubber, and paint negate technological attempts at perfect measurement of athlete performance. They are two different realities, a fact that is readily acknowledged by sports federations in the form of dimensional tolerances in the regulations governing the construction of sport venues, but remains largely unacknowledged in the broader sporting community. This often leads to confusion regarding how race results are determined, and demands – such as those by Picabo Street – that a winner be identified.

At the London Olympic Games, on Saturday, 11 August 2012, Mo Farah became one of the most celebrated English athletes in Olympic history. He won the 5,000m race that day, after winning the 10,000m earlier in the Games.[49] Farah's "double" put him in the company of a select few running legends including Emil Zatopek, Lasse Viren, and Kenenisa Bekele. The mostly hometown English crowd of 80,000 was so loud that the cheering reached levels of 140 decibels, the equivalent of a jet engine at take-off. The noise was so strong that it literally shook the stadium and, with it, OMEGA's timing and photo-finish equipment, fastened as it was to the Olympic venue. The result was a unique but not anomalous photo-finish.[50] In contrast to the clean, precise horizontal lines characteristic of the photo-finish as manifest in the Tarmoh/Felix image, the lines in Farah's photo-finish are wavy, the result of a literally shaking sport venue.

The Farah photo-finish provides another example of the disconnect between precision and accuracy in timing and the photo-finish. The dimensional tolerances of track measurement as governed by the IAAF can account for the minuscule differences inherent to the human creation of a running track, but there are no such guidelines to accommodate crowd noise. Fortunately, Farah won the race clearly and the photo-finish was not needed to determine placing. What would have happened had the race come down to a result as close as that of Tarmoh and Felix? What if the decision, in front of 80,000 fans, cheering at levels ten times the threshold for human pain, had come down to the interpolation of an obscured and rotated torso? What if, under those conditions, Farah had lost by a thousandth of a second? Perhaps more importantly, would his accomplishments and the remuneration that followed have been any less had he tied for first? As part of Guttman's "quest for records," the measurement of athlete performance is an essential component of modern and contemporary sport. Indeed it is inimical to think of sporting contests without clear winners and losers. The photo-finish was designed with the promise of enabling if not guaranteeing such clear decision-making. But, as has been shown throughout this book, the use of the photo-finish in sport has fallen far short of this promise. And as the concluding chapter takes up, the continued promise and promotion – over nearly 150 years – of technology to solve the dead heat is underlain by mythical notions of pure performance and its equally pure measurement.

CHAPTER SIX

Beyond the Finish Line: Decision Aids and the Myth of Pure Measurement

The Tarmoh/Felix dead heat, as well as the Cavic/Phelps and Gisin/Maze finishes addressed previously, contain within them many of the key debates and issues from the history of the photo-finish in sport. They speak to a historical trajectory of using imaging technologies to make the unseen seen in the hopes of uncovering an irrefutable truth. They speak to the situatedness of human vision and the resultant mutability of seemingly stable concepts such as objectivity, truth, and visual evidence. And they speak to the broad material and cultural influences and impacts of images used as evidence in sporting contests.

Discussion of the capabilities of using the photograph to determine placing in sport began as early as the 1870s and developed significantly through the instantaneous photography movement over the decades bridging the turn of the twentieth century. The discussion took on considerably more nuance following the invention of the slit camera in 1937, particularly as the new invention differed from its traditional photographic counterpart. The status and evidentiary weight of the photo-finish was the subject of relatively nuanced discussion over the middle decades of the twentieth century, and by the 1980s the practice had gained general acceptance within the sporting world. Save for truly anomalous cases such as the Tarmoh/Felix dead heat, the photo-finish has become an accepted, even mundane, part of elite-level sport.

The examples of photographs of finishes and photo-finishes throughout this book – from the Salvator vs Tenny Match Race of 1890 to the 2012 Tarmoh/Felix dead heat – are a tiny fraction of the mass of close and/or controversial calls within the history of sport. Indeed, one of the paradoxes in the history of the photo-finish is that, despite ever more advanced technological capabilities, and the ever more precise measurement of space and time, we are no closer to eradicating the dead heat than were the instantaneous photographers of the late nineteenth century. But to focus solely on this aspect of the dead heat is to miss the photo-finish's function within a larger sports/media/culture landscape.[1] The history of the photo-finish intersects with the histories of numerous other pursuits and professions including journalism, film and television, watchmaking, gambling, and sports entertainment. And the history of the photo-finish is bound to changing conceptions of objectivity, accuracy, and human performance. Finally, the history of the photo-finish is tied to a modernist "quest for records" in sport with its emphases on regulation and standardization and a teleological view of sport performance and its measurement.

The limitations and fallibility of human vision has been a key presumption throughout the history of the photo-finish. Hemment's race finish photography, Kirby's "two eyes" camera, the Racend OMEGA, and the Finish-Lynx Pro camera were/are all promoted as fixing the inherent limitations of humans. Importantly, the history of the photo-finish is not a steady march from subjective human vision to objective machine vision; rather, it shows the continued interaction of Daston and Galison's epistemic virtues. The metaphysical-based expertise of the "truth to nature" episteme is present in the discourse surrounding Hemment and other instantaneous photographers of the late 1800s and early 1900s, and throughout the history of OMEGA and its affiliates. "Mechanical" or "noninterventionist objectivity" has played a significant role throughout the history of the photo-finish. As was the case in other social institutions, the use of the camera to determine placing in sport both contributed to and benefited from the photograph's cultural legacy of objectivity. Lastly, the epistemic virtue of "trained judgment" emerged over the middle decades of the twentieth century with the professionalization of photo-finish and is exemplified in the figure of Roger Jennings, the photo-finish judge who presided over the Tarmoh/Felix dead heat.

Daston and Galison are clear that these epistemic virtues are not mutually exclusive and that they do not exist sequentially. They write, "epistemic virtues do not replace one another like a succession of kings. Rather, they accumulate into a repertoire of possible forms of knowing."[2] The history of the photo-finish, then, is also a history of "possible forms of knowing."

Camera lenses, photosensitive paper, photographers, sports federations, fans, materials engineers, athletes, journalists, and sport/media corporations are among the many players at work in the production of the photo-finish, helping to determine what can be known from a given image.

My aim in this book has been to position the photo-finish not just as an apparatus – a set of gears, circuits, lenses, and other materials – but as a cultural artefact and as a collective practice that brings together many, often disparate human and non-human actors. The photo-finish (the literal image produced by a slit camera) is not nearly the closed system that it often appears. Instead, it is the product of more than a century of experimentation, invention, debate, and discussion, and its meaning – its evidentiary capacity – is not fixed but is built in the moments surrounding its use. In what follows I conclude the book by addressing two key issues "beyond the finish line." The first is more pragmatic in that it responds to the concrete limitations of the photo-finish, calling for their clear and transparent articulation. The second is more philosophical and positions the photo-finish within a larger mythical quest of pure performance and pure measurement.

Photo-Finishes and/as Sports Decision Aids

The debates that animated the early use of the photo-finish, such as the relationship between the camera eye and human eye and the evidentiary value of photomechanical images, still play a strong role in the sporting world as it explores newer technologies such as instant replay, goal-line cameras, and decision review systems. The continued adoption of these technologies in the twenty-first century has resulted in a sporting landscape that is increasingly fraught with tension between fans, referees, and others in the sport community. Two particularly notable cases from 2010 exemplify the issue. The first was a World Cup match between England and Germany, where referees missed a goal by England's Frank Lampard that was clearly visible to television viewers through instant replay.[3] The second was the denial of a "perfect game" by Detroit Tigers pitcher Armando Galarraga after a bad call by umpire Jim Joyce, again visible to television viewers and stadium fans through recourse to instant replay.[4] Lampard's missed goal and Galarraga's near-perfect game led to widespread debate in football and baseball communities about the need or not to include goal-line technology and instant replay as part of officiating.[5] The discussion ranged from the highly offensive (calling for the death of the referees/umpire), through issues of money, prestige, and nationalism, to quite nuanced discussions about the role of human error in sport. In total, the discussion shows fascinating parallels to those surrounding the photo-finish in the 1950s, '60s, and '70s.

Another example adds further complexity to the sports decision-making problem. In the sport of professional golf, Tiger Woods was the seat of controversy when television viewers called in to report an infraction he made during the 2013 Masters tournament that was missed by tournament officials.[6] Woods's case at the Masters speaks to an entirely new phenomenon where television viewers use the visual technologies afforded through sports broadcasting, High Definition and instant replay, to play a part in the officiating of sports events (a rule that was only recently removed by the PGA). That is, in contrast to the Lampard and Galarraga examples where the official call stood but was shown to be inaccurate, in Woods's case the official call came after the fact and directly due to infractions spotted only by television viewers. This complicated practice is made all the more problematic by the differential treatment of golfers in sports broadcasting. Because televised broadcasts of golf focus most of the coverage on top-ranked players such as Woods, some critics argue that that places an unfair burden on these golfers, as television viewers are less likely to see and report infractions from lower-ranked players, not because they aren't making mistakes but because those mistakes are not caught on camera. This is another, admittedly simple, example of the burden of representation identified by John Tagg.[7]

Most recently, video-assist-referee technology (VAR) was unveiled at the 2018 FIFA World Cup, where it was hailed by some and criticized by others.[8] VAR did successfully show infractions that were missed by the referees, but in other cases its use simply slowed the game, muddied otherwise clear decisions, or gave rise to controversial calls. As exempla of the controversies surrounding the use or suggested use of (visual) technologies for decision-making in sport, the cases cited here, as well as those addressed throughout this book, illustrate a continued drive to develop technological systems to supplement and sometimes replace the human in sports officiating. Such practices receive healthy debate in the popular press, but minimal scholarly attention. Fortunately, and because of the scale on which decision-aid technologies have developed as well as their import in the sporting world, new decision-aid systems are receiving at least some scholarly attention, whereas the photo-finish has received almost none.[9]

The most thorough, significant, and sustained critical examination of the evidentiary use of decision-aid technology in sport is found in the independent and collaborative work of Harry Collins, Robert Evans, and Christopher Higgins.[10] Using Hawk-Eye as their primary object of analysis, the authors have called for greater critical analysis of what they term "sports decision aids" (SDAs). Their work analyzes the predictive algorithms of Hawk-Eye as applied in both tennis and cricket to make transparent that SDAs are not infallible. Rather, such technologies include "measurement error" (much like that identified in chapter 5) and so cannot provide fully determinate answers in sporting events. For the authors this leads to public misunderstandings of SDAs. Hence, a primary recommendation of theirs is that the measurement errors inherent in any technological system should be made clear and transparent in its use. In a 2011 essay on the topic, Collins and Evans applaud the use of Hawk-Eye in cricket for meeting this goal, but are critical of its use in tennis because it is presented as making fully determinate decisions (the ball is in *or* out).[11] For the authors, this results in something akin to a "CSI effect" in professional sport, where the technology is presented as being infallible and ridding the game of (human) error.

In a similar way, I argue that the uses and limitations of timing and the photo-finish in sport should be made clear and transparent. The regulations governing timing and photo-finish systems in each sport discipline should make clear the reasons for timing to tenths, hundredths, thousandths, or beyond with specific reference to the issue of dimensional tolerance and the limits of technological precision in a live environment. Clarifying the capabilities of timing and photo-finish systems in the regulations of the USATF, FINA, the FIS, and other sports federations should be a relatively simple task. The FIS Timing Working Group is an example in this regard. Their 2014 Timing Booklet for Alpine Skiing far surpasses the guidelines of other sports in its thoroughness and nuance; yet it could do more to explain – in layman's terms – the rationale for timing to .01 of a second. There is no explicit statement in any of the regulations governing swimming, track and field, or alpine skiing that provides a rationale for the level of precision used. A simple, concise statement noting the threshold beyond which timing is no longer accurate in determining placing would go a long way to prevent confusion in the professional and public communities that interact with SDAs. Without such a statement and with counter-statements put forward by timing and imaging companies, broadcasters, journalists, athletes, and fans, professional sports fall prey to the "CSI effect," where a technological solution is always around the corner.

Collins, Evans, and Higgins also recommend that the limits of SDAs should be communicated to the public, including as part of the live sports broadcast. On this recommendation I am considerably more skeptical. As Jhally and later Rowe, Wenner, Whannel, and others have so clearly outlined, by the 1970s sports, commerce, and television broadcasting had developed a fully symbiotic relationship, with each depending on the others for survival in the highly competitive, for-profit sports entertainment industry.[12] The resulting sports/media or sports/media/culture complex is a tangled web of human and non-human actors within which the technological limitations of sports decision aids may not find a welcome home. OMEGA, Lynx Systems Developers, Seiko, and other timing and photo-finish equipment providers vie for lucrative contracts and merchandising opportunities and so must advertise their technology as being more accurate and more precise than that of their competitors. And broadcasters must produce the best sports entertainment package they can in order to increase market share and sell advertising space to corporate sponsors. Hence the OMEGA press release following the 2008 Beijing Games and the Phelps/Cavic controversy that their equipment provides results "which are beyond doubt and dispute."[13] And hence Picabo Street's remarks following the Gisin/Maze tie demanding to know who *really* won.[14] Understood within the framework of the sports/media complex, OMEGA's remark is good for business and Street's is good for television. Communicating the results of races on TV broadcasts and at the live event as being accurate +/-5% would betray the win-at-all-costs attitude central to contemporary sports entertainment.

The Myth of Pure Measurement

Apart from the more pragmatic concerns identified above, critical analysis of the photo-finish points to larger, more philosophical questions related to sport and its underlying narratives and myths. Michael Real first brought attention to the mythical structures of sport in his 1975 essay on the Super-

Bowl.[15] He argued that the SuperBowl was a spectacle that revealed the dominant myths and values in American culture, including the quest for property (possession on the field) and control (of time) in the pursuit of economic gain (team revenues). Numerous scholars have extended Real's work to address the myths underlying other sports and in other nations. Two particularly strong accounts in this regard are those by Tara Magdalinski and Rayvon Fouché.

In her 2009 book, *Sport, Technology and the Body: The Nature of Performance*, Magdalinski highlights the false binaries, primarily that of nature/artifice, that have animated modern and contemporary sport.[16] She traces the complicated and often contradictory quest to rid performance of artificial enhancement through forms such as equipment, doping, prosthetics, and even genetics. As she shows, the continued battle against such enhancement is predicated on the belief that such a thing as "pure performance" exists. In such a space, bodies completely free of technological or other enhancement compete in a perfectly fair environment, under perfectly standardized conditions. As Magdalinski shows, such a "pure" sporting space is a myth for several reasons, chiefly because notions of what constitutes the body, technology, nature, and performance are mutable. Erythropoietin (EPO) use, cooling vests, altitude simulation tents, Fastskin swimsuits, asthma inhalers, and prosthetic legs all enhance or in some way add to the sporting body, but only some of these are considered artificial and/or illegal. As Magdalinski shows, whether a technology is considered natural or artificial is bound up with historically specific notions of the body, health, and performance that are both ideological and moral.

Rayvon Fouché takes up a similar argument in his book, *Game Changer: The Technoscientific Revolution in Sports*.[17] Fouché identifies the notions of pure performance and fair competition as constitutive, but false, narratives in sport. A central theme of his book is the ways in which "sporting communities," composed of publics, governing bodies, competitors, and technoscientific actors, respond to technological innovation through recourse to these narratives. He notes that any technoscientific enhancement of the athlete's body or performance – from Speedo LZR swimsuits and leather vs synthetic basketballs to gender testing and the current use of athlete biological passports – is often vetted and made legal or illegal in ways that allow sport to maintain its mythological narratives of pure performance, natural bodies, and fair competition. Fouché's book offers in-depth analyses of numerous technoscientific developments in sport and the ways in which they were accepted or refuted in order to maintain these myths. It is interesting to note that in comparison to the extensive amount of time spent on regulating sport's bodies (i.e. the athletes), there is relatively little attention paid to how those bodies' performances are measured. In other words, given the limitations and problems associated with timing and finish-line systems, should we not see a significant level of attention in regulating how sport performance is measured, defined, and awarded?

Less academic but no less rigorous examinations of the drive towards enhanced sport performance have emerged in best-selling popular texts and films, including David Epstein's *The Sports Gene*, Mark McLusky's *Faster, Higher, Stronger*, Bryan Fogel's *Icarus*, and Alex Hutchinson's *Endure*.[18] All of these accounts chronicle a continued drive across sports to find ways – sometimes illegal and deadly – to maximize an athlete's performance. The most recent of these analyses – Hutchinson's – is particularly interesting as it focuses on "brain doping," or attempts to circumvent the brain's regulatory system such that the athlete can "push through" or overcome their brain's early warning systems. This is a fascinating development in sports science as it seeks to separate the body and mind, removing the latter so that the former can perform at its absolute physical limit: pure physical output devoid of mental constraint. It is unsurprising that Hutchinson's book includes examples of athletes sustaining serious injury and even death when "practising" such extreme forms of performance enhancement.

The point in highlighting these texts is to illustrate the drive towards "pure" performance that animates much of modern and contemporary sport. I am not suggesting that the contemporary sporting landscape is a technophilic dystopia, but that there is a clear trajectory in sports science and technoscience that aims to find the absolute limits of human performance through research and experimentation with nutrition, training, attire, and even genetics. Nike's Breaking2 is a perfect example: millions of dollars were spent in an attempt to control every "natural" variable of the event from the athletes' bodies (inside and outside) to the running surface, pace, wind, and humidity. Importantly, it is not just placing or the all-important record that is at stake but, at larger institutional and national levels, extraordinarily large sums of money, cultural capital, and the resultant power that flows from each.

My focus complements those of Magdalinski, Fouché, Epstein, McLusky, Fogel, and Hutchinson but resides on the other side of the finish line. That is, where these authors focus on the drive for perfect or pure performance, I argue that the history of the photo-finish has in part been animated by a drive towards the perfect or pure measurement of athlete performance. As I hope to have made clear, the perfect or pure measurement of athlete performance is not a practical reality in a sporting environment that is by definition imperfect. Even if we were to ensure that sporting bodies were somehow "pure" and that all such bodies and the venues in which they compete were perfectly similar and equal, awarding placing based on timing and imaging data at hundredths of a second and beyond betrays the reality of the limits of technological precision as applied in the natural environment. This is because bodies and the natural world are not pure, fixed, and immutable but are highly variable and imperfect.

And so where Magdalinski, Fouché, and others identify the myth of "pure performance," I argue that the use of increasingly precise timing and photo-finish systems contribute to a myth of "pure" or "perfect measurement." Such a myth promotes timing and photo-finish systems as producing ever more precise, definitive results that are unmediated and infallible measurements of athlete performance. Returning to Guttmann, "pure measurement" is the apotheosis of the quest for records – it is a pure, noiseless record of athlete performance – a Peircean indexical sign that is the direct, unmediated consequence of the athlete's body.

The drives for pure performance and pure measurement result in a chicken-and-egg problem. Do timing and photo-finish companies and practitioners develop ever more precise technology as a response to the increasingly minuscule differences in athlete performance? Or do athletes and their coaches and sponsors adopt such extreme training regimens and technoscientific R&D programs because differences in placing are measured in the thousandth of a second? Regardless, these parallel drives reinforce one another such that sports federations are now routinely embroiled in scandal as one team, group, or nation after another is found to be violating regulations in the pursuit of extracting every last ounce of athlete performance. While this practice is as old as sport, it has scaled up exponentially into a technoscience arms-race, as clearly articulated by Fouché. Read optimistically, our techno-sport landscape produces an array of astounding athletic performances as new records are set and seemingly impossible barriers are surpassed. Read pessimistically, athletes, teams, and nations adopt increasingly dangerous training practices in the pursuit of "marginal gains" and a win-at-all-costs attitude. Whatever the stance taken, it is hard not to see these co-drives as increasingly abstracting the human and the "liveness" from sport.

But isn't a defining feature of sport the imperfect, fallible, and limited human body? Would a sporting contest between two perfectly identical bodies in identical physiological and mental condition racing in exactly similar environments and timed to the millionth of a second be of any interest? Should we pursue further noninterventionist approaches to measuring athlete performance by embedding chips or sensors under the skin as has been done in soccer balls and hockey pucks? Would this finally rid us of human error in sport or would it bring about new forms of error, perhaps related to the sensitivity or reliability of the sensor? Is any of this worth doing?

In his critique of internet-centrism and technological solutionism Evgeny Morozov cautions: "We must not fixate on what this new arsenal of digital technologies allows us to do without first inquiring what is worth doing."[19] He uses the term "technological solutionism" to describe society's fascination with finding technological fixes for its problems. But, key for Morozov, this technological impulse sometimes sees or assumes problems where they don't exist. Later in the book he identifies what is at stake:

> To succumb to the solutionist temptation to recast the new digital platforms as just more objective and efficient versions of the older, inefficient, human-drive alternatives is to opt for an adversarial and counterproductive approach that refuses to acknowledge the immensely important roles that subjectivity, inefficiency, and ignorance have been playing in our culture and public life as a whole.[20]

He goes on to say that technological solutions to these "deficiencies" miss the mark because they are not deficiencies but are fundamental parts of the human condition.

Morozov's words are instructive in helping us think through what is at stake in the winner-take-all approach that guides contemporary sport and the photo-finish's role within that space. In many ways the history of the photo-finish is a history of technological solutionism, one in which the next technological development is presented as more objective, more accurate, more able to "fix" human error than its predecessor. Within the specific context of timing and the photo-finish, such a discourse promotes a direct correlation between accuracy and the number of digits to the right of the decimal. But greater precision does not mean greater accuracy.

The myths of pure performance and pure measurement are bound in an interesting paradox. The drive to eradicate perceived human deficiencies in sport, to achieve pure performance and pure measurement, finds its logical conclusion in the dead heat. Within such a space, and freed of all the messiness of bodies and the natural world, these utopian athletes and their performances would be equal in every way. And so what is lost when we strive to eradicate the limitations inherent to the performance and measurement of sport? What do we achieve by measuring athletic performance to the hundredth, thousandth, or millionth of a second? And what do we lose? Morozov compels: "It's time to give up this talk of 'Technology' with a big *T* and instead figure out how different technologies can boost or compromise the human condition."[21] This book offers one such attempt – to think of the photo-finish not as Technology but as, among other things, a technological solution to a problem that may or may not exist.

Notes

Chapter One

1 "Canada's Kripps, Kopacz Tie Germany for 2-Man Bobsleigh Gold," CBC *Olympics*, 19 February 2018, https://olympics.cbc.ca/news/article/kripps-kopacz-secure-man-bobsleigh-gold-for-canada.html.
2 Cathal Kelly, "All Olympic Golds Are Special, but a Tie Is Sweeter," *The Globe and Mail*, 19 February 2018, https://www.theglobeandmail.com/sports/olympics/canadian-german-bobsleigh-pairs-rejoice-in-shared-olympic-gold/article38020829/.
3 Adams, "Photography and Athletics: First Paper," *Outing* 19 (1892): 406.
4 Morozov, *To Save Everything, Click Here*, 5.
5 King, *The Inconvenient Indian*.
6 Jordanova, *The Look of the Past*.
7 Belden-Adams, *Modern Time*.
8 Ivins, *Prints and Visual Communication*.
9 Peirce, "What Is a Sign?"
10 Barthes, *Image, Music, Text*.
11 Ivins, *Prints and Visual Communication*.
12 Batchen, *Burning with Desire*, 213.
13 Snyder, "Picturing Vision."
14 Tagg, *The Burden of Representation*; Sekula, "The Body and the Archive"; Rafter, "Criminal Anthropology in the United States"; Gilman, *Difference and Pathology*; Gilman, *Seeing the Insane*; Bassnett and Goss, *Picturing Toronto*.
15 Finn, *Capturing the Criminal Image*.
16 Mitchell, *Picture Theory*.
17 Huggins and O'Mahony, "Special Issue on Sport and The Visual"; Huggins and O'Mahony, *The Visual in Sport*.
18 Latour and Woolgar, *Laboratory Life*.

19 Lynch and Woolgar, *Representation in Scientific Practice.*

20 Dumit, *Picturing Personhood*; Joyce, *Magnetic Appeal.*

21 Coopmans, *Representation in Scientific Practice Revisited.*

22 Oudshoorn, *How Users Matter*, 7.

23 Ibid., 1.

24 Fouché, *Game Changer.*

25 Ibid., 4.

26 Real, "Super Bowl," and see Real's 2013 essay for an update on his earlier work and its relationship to the field of communication and sport: Real, "Reflections on Communication and Sport." See also Parente, "The Interdependence of Sports and Television"; Williams, "The Structure of Televised Football"; Bryant, Comisky, and Zillmann, "Drama in Sports Commentary"; Comisky, Bryant, and Zillmann, "Commentary as a Substitute for Action"; Goldstein and Bredemeier, "Socialization"; Horowitz, "Sports Telecasts"; Siegfried and Hinshaw, "Professional Football and the Anti-Blackout Law."

27 McChesney, "Media Made Sport," 61.

28 Jhally, "The Spectacle of Accumulation."

29 Barnett, *Games and Sets*; Gruneau, *Class, Sports, and Social Development*; Rowe, *Sport, Culture and the Media*; Wenner, ed., *Media, Sports, and Society*; Wenner, ed., *MediaSport*; Whannel, *Fields in Vision.*

30 Creedon, *Women, Media, and Sport*; Daddario, *Women's Sport and Spectacle*; Davis, *The Swimsuit Issue and Sport*; Fuller, *Sport, Rhetoric, and Gender*; Jhally, *Playing Unfair*; Messner, *Out of Play*; Miller, *Sportsex*; Watson and Scraton, eds., *Sport, Leisure Identities and Gendered Spaces.*

31 Back, Crabbe, and Solomos, *The Changing Face of Football*; Bloom and Willard, eds., *Sports Matters*; Hylton, *Critical Race Theory in Sport*; King, *Sport and Race.*

32 Blain, Boyle, and O'Donnell, *Sport and National Identity in the European Media*; Chandler, *Television and National Sport*; Hundley and Billings, eds., *Examining Identity in Sports Media*; Whitson and Gruneau, eds., *Artificial Ice.*

33 Huggins and O'Mahony, *The Visual in Sport*; Huggins and O'Mahony, "Special Issue on Sport and The Visual."

34 Brown, "The Modern Romance of Mountaineering."

35 Brown, "Modern Sport, Modernism and the Cultural Manifesto."

36 Veder, "Seeing Your Way to Health."

37 Barnett, "Girls Gone Web"; Dumont, "The Beautiful and the Damned." For a similar discussion but in relation to digital media, see Thorpe, "Foucault, Technologies of Self, and the Media."

38 Mnookin, "The Image of Truth."

39 Becker, "Photojournalism and the Tabloid Press."
40 Daston and Galison, *Objectivity*, 372.
41 Ibid., 204.
42 Ibid., 125.
43 Daston and Galison, "The Image of Objectivity."
44 Daston and Galison, *Objectivity*, 355.
45 Davies, *Sports in American Life*; Gruneau, *Class, Sports, and Social Development*; Gruneau, "Aesthetics and the Politics of Representation"; Gruneau, *Sport and Modernity*; Guttmann, *From Ritual to Record*; Guttmann, *Sports*; Howell and Howell, eds., *History of Sport in Canada*; Morrow, ed., *A Concise History of Sport in Canada*.
46 Gruneau, *Sport and Modernity*; Gruneau, "Aesthetics and the Politics of Representation."
47 Gruneau, *Sport and Modernity*, 62.
48 Ibid.
49 Guttmann, *From Ritual to Record*, 55.
50 Mumford, *Technics and Civilization*, 306.
51 Guttmann, *From Ritual to Record*, 61.
52 Howell and Howell, eds., *History of Sport in Canada*; Morrow, ed., *A Concise History of Sport in Canada*, 2000.
53 For a discussion of Debord's notion of spectacle as it aligns with sport and specifically the Olympics see Kellner, *Media Spectacle*.
54 Nike, "Just Do It. Breaking2"; Nike, "Nike Introduces Breaking2"; Caesar, "The Epic Untold Story of Nike's (Almost) Perfect Marathon."
55 Mumford, *Technics and Civilization*, 306.
56 Magdalinski, *Sport, Technology and the Body*; Fouché, *Game Changer*.
57 Epstein, *The Sports Gene*; McClusky, *Faster, Higher, Stronger*; Fogel, dir., *Icarus*; Hutchinson, *Endure*.
58 Fouché, *Game Changer*, 208.
59 Ibid.

Chapter Two

1 "Progressive Photography," *The Spirit of the Times*, 11 October 1879.
2 Muybridge, "A Dead Heat."
3 Toby, "History of Racing Photography: The Days of the Daguerreotypes," *The Blood-Horse* (25 April 1981): 2397.
4 "The Camera on the Racecourse."
5 Underwood, *Thoroughbred Racing & Breeding*; Hervey, *Racing in America 1922–1936*.
6 Adams, "Instantaneous Photography," *Outing* 15 (1889–90): 221.

7 O'Neill, "The History of Race Photo Finish Photography," 6.
8 Bovay, *Photosprint*, 5.
9 Blackwell, "The Rowing Clubs of Canada," *Outing* 18 (1891): 123.
10 Adams, "Photography and Athletics: First Paper," *Outing* 19 (1892): 405.
11 Von Borries, *RaceLens*, 35.
12 Bovay, *Photosprint*, 2.
13 Canales, *A Tenth of a Second*, 107–8.
14 Rosenblum, *A World History of Photography*, 249.
15 Wade, "Capturing Motion and Depth Before Cinematography"; Aubert, "From Photography to Cinematography"; Prodger et al., eds., *Time Stands Still*; Braun, "The Expanded Present."
16 Galton, "Conventional Representation of the Horse in Motion"; Galton, "A Rapid-View Instrument for Momentary Attitudes."
17 Braun, "The Expanded Present," 150.
18 Daston and Galison, "The Image of Objectivity"; Daston and Galison, *Objectivity*.
19 "Instantaneous Photography," 366.
20 Prodger et al., eds., *Time Stands Still*, 25.
21 "Lantern Slide and Camera," *New York Times*, 10 May 1891.
22 Abney, *Instantaneous Photography*.
23 Adams, *Amateur Photography*, 55.
24 Muybridge, "A Dead Heat," 81.
25 "The Camera on the Racecourse," 401.
26 "Instantaneous Photography"; Adams, "Some Modern Achievements of the Camera," *Outing* 18 (1891): 481–2.
27 Adams, "Instantaneous Photography," *Outing* 15 (1889–90): 221.
28 Ibid.
29 "Quick as Lightning: Instantaneous Picture of the Finish of the Fastest Race of 1888," *The Seattle Post-Intelligencer*, 9 January 1889.
30 "Skating Records Broken," *The New York Times*, 25 January 1895; "Skating," *The Sporting Life* 20, no. 22 (25 February 1893): 15.
31 Adams, "Photography and Athletics: First Paper," *Outing* 19 (1892): 404–8; "Decided by the Camera," *Brooklyn Eagle*, 2 August 1891.
32 Hemment, *Cannon and Cameras*, x.
33 Ibid., 264.
34 "Pershing's Men Well Fed," *The New York Times*, 29 October 1917.
35 "About Shooters," *The Sporting Life* 60, no. 23 (8 February 1913): 18; "In Re Shooters," *The Sporting Life* 58, no. 3 (23 September 1911): 28.
36 "Only the Photographer," *Technical World Magazine* 19, no. 6 (1913): 812–13; "Brooklynite Starts on Troglodyte Hunt," *Brooklyn Eagle*, 2 November 1913; "Jack Hemment Back with Tse-Tse Films," *Brooklyn Eagle*, 4 Septem-

ber 1914; "Great Animal Picture Show in Aid of the Red Cross," *Brooklyn Eagle*, 29 October 1914; "J.C. Hemment Bitten By Tse-Tse Fly, Fears 'Sleeping Sickness,'" *Brooklyn Eagle*, 21 January 1916.

37 Hemment, "My Search for the Missing Link," 77.

38 "A Unique Picture Run," *Brooklyn Eagle*, 28 April 1897.

39 Vera, "J.C. (John Charles) Hemment."

40 Adams, "Some Modern Achievements of the Camera," *Outing* 18 (1891): 482.

41 Adams, "Photography and Athletics: First Paper," *Outing* 19 (1892): 404.

42 Ibid., 405.

43 Ibid.

44 Ibid., 406.

45 Adams, "Photography and Athletics: Second Paper," *Outing* 19 (1892): 449.

46 Ibid.

47 Ibid.

48 Hemment, "Photography Applied to Sports," 198.

49 Ibid., 201.

50 Ibid.

51 Hemment, "Rapid Photography," 216.

52 "Decided by the Camera," *Brooklyn Eagle*, 2 August 1891.

53 "Marginalia: Close Finishes and Other Matters," *The Thoroughbred Record* 129 (10 June 1939): 346.

54 Von Borries, *RaceLens*; Vanvolsem, *The Art of Strip Photography*.

55 "Decided by the Camera," *Brooklyn Eagle*, 2 August 1891.

56 Sekula, "The Body and the Archive," 16.

57 Hemment, "Photography Applied to Sports," 202.

58 "The Camera on the Racecourse," 401.

59 "Decided by the Camera," *Brooklyn Eagle*, 2 August 1891.

60 "World Beaters!"

61 Adams, "Instantaneous Photography," *Outing* 15 (1889–90): 221.

62 "Instantaneous Photography," 366.

63 "Decided by the Camera," *Brooklyn Eagle*, 2 August 1891, 13.

64 "W.C. Downs' Record. The Camera to Be Used Still Further to Settle the Dispute," *The Sporting Life* 16, no. 9 (29 November 1890): 12; "Athletic," *The Sporting Life* 16, no. 10 (6 December 1890): 12.

65 "W.C. Downs' Record," *The Sporting Life* 16, no. 9 (29 November 1890): 12.

66 "Athletic," *The Sporting Life* 16, no. 10 (6 December 1890): 12.

67 "Gossip about the Turf: Review of the Past Week at the Monmouth Track," *New York Press*, 15 July 1888.

68 "Photographing Close Finishes," *The Thoroughbred Record* 42 (24 August 1895): 104.

Chapter Three

1 Both Bovay and O'Neill identify Petri's and Barber's patents as key in the development of the photo-finish. See Bovay, *Photosprint: History*; Bovay, *Time and Sport Story*; and O'Neill, "The History of Race Photo Finish Photography."
2 Barber did not invent the use of an armband in racing. The 1893 American Racing Rules of the American Turf Congress required riders to wear armbands, predating Barber's patent. Thank you to Roda Ferraro of the Keeneland Library for this clarification.
3 Sekula, "The Body and the Archive," 16.
4 Mumford, *Technics and Civilization*.
5 Canales, *A Tenth of a Second*.
6 Baylis, "Electric Timing," *Outing* 10 (1887): 59.
7 Ibid., 61.
8 O'Neill, "The History of Race Photo Finish Photography," 1.
9 Simon, *Racing through the Century*.
10 Ibid., 105.
11 "Marvels of the Magic Electric Eye," *The Salt Lake Tribune*, 30 July 1933, 72; Goldberg, "Mr. Televox Acquires an Eye: New Photo-Electric Device May Be Called on For Many Uses," *The Baltimore Sun*, 7 April 1929, 109; "How the 'Electric Eye' Now Protects Human Eyes," *Daily Press*, 24 May 1934. There are hundreds of newspaper articles from the late 1920s throughout the 1930s which marvel at the various uses of the new 'electric eye.'
12 Simon, *Racing through the Century*, 105.
13 Hervey, *Racing in America 1922–1936*.
14 Ibid, 208.
15 Ibid.
16 Ibid.
17 Ibid., 207–8.
18 Ibid., 208.
19 Rosebud, "Odds and Ends: Another Customer," *The Blood-Horse* (25 July 1936): 87.
20 "Florida," *The Blood-Horse* (18 December 1937): 910.
21 "New Jones Camera," *The Blood-Horse* (25 December 1937): 967.
22 "Cameras for Maryland," *The Blood-Horse* (29 January 1938): 224.
23 Palmer, "Sidelights: Hialeah's Camera," *The Blood-Horse* (22 January 1938): 174.
24 "Race-Finish Photography," *The Blood-Horse* (25 January 1936): 144.
25 Ibid.

26 "Finish Photography," *The Blood-Horse* (20 June 1936): 743.
27 Ibid.
28 Becker, "The Camera and the Eye," *Thoroughbred Record* (8 August 1936): 97.
29 "Florida," *The Blood-Horse* (18 December 1937): 910.
30 "Camera Wins," *The Blood-Horse* (21 November 1936): 558.
31 "Camera's Accuracy," *The Blood-Horse* (31 May 1941): 835.
32 "Florida: Camera Speed," *The Blood-Horse* (21 January 1939): 127.
33 "Cover Picture," *Thoroughbred Record* (23 August 1941): 124.
34 Mérillon, "Concours Internationaux D'Exercices Physiques et de Sports: Rapports."
35 Ibid., 390–1. Translated by Nicole Boulet.
36 Ibid., 403. Translated by Nicole Boulet.
37 Lucas, "The Olympic Games 1904," 42.
38 Cook, "Official Report Olympic Games of 1908."
39 Guttmann, *From Ritual to Record*, 61.
40 Bergvall, ed., *The Official Report of the Olympic Games of Stockholm 1912*, 110.
41 Ibid.
42 Ibid., 111.
43 The use of a device by a Swedish inventor is indicative of a practice found throughout the Olympic Reports which is to employ inventors and staff from the host nation in the production of materials for the Games.
44 Bergvall, ed., *The Official Report of the Olympic Games of Stockholm 1912*, 349.
45 Ibid.
46 Ibid., 366.
47 "New Record Set," *Topeka Daily State Journal*, 10 July 1912.
48 "England Wins Thrilling Victory in 1,500 Metre Race," *Lake County Times*, 11 July 1912.
49 "England Wins Big Race at Stockholm," *New York Tribune*, 11 July 1912.
50 "U.S. Bested in 2 Olympic Events," *San Francisco Call*, 11 July 1912.
51 Bovay, *Photosprint*, 6.
52 "Olympic Games Antwerp 1920: Official Report."
53 "Les Jeux de La VIII Olympiade, Paris 1924: Rapport Officiel," 712.
54 Fleming, trans., "Official Report of the Olympic Games of 1928 Celebrated at Amsterdam."
55 "Gustavus Kirby, Leader in Sports," *New York Times*, 29 February 1956; Fetter, "A New Way of Splitting Seconds."
56 Fetter, "A New Way of Splitting Seconds," 295.
57 Ibid.

58 Ibid., 298.
59 Ibid.
60 "Olympic Games Official Report Los Angeles 1932," 803.
61 Fleming, trans., "Official Report of the Olympic Games of 1928 Celebrated at Amsterdam."
62 "Change in Hurdles Made at Olympics," *New York Times*, 5 August 1932.
63 Marsh, "With Pick and Shovel: Knocks and Boosts, Slams and Salve," *The Toronto Star*, 5 August 1932.
64 Ibid.
65 "Olympic Games Official Report Los Angeles 1932," 379.
66 Ibid., 384.
67 Fetter, "A New Way of Splitting Seconds," 299.
68 "The XIth Olympic Games Berlin, 1936 Official Report," 633.
69 Ibid., 634.
70 Ibid., 650.
71 Ibid., 922.
72 Ibid., 609.
73 This was also the Games that was extensively recorded by still and moving cameras under the direction of Leni Riefenstahl. The allowances made for Riefenstahl, including physical changes to the venues to accommodate her equipment and crew, are fascinating and detailed in the Official Olympic Report, but are outside the scope of this project.
74 "Summaries in Olympics," *New York Times*, 7 August 1936; Gibb, "No Man's Land of Sport," *Toronto Daily Star*, 10 August 1936.
75 Del Riccio, "Camera"; Del Riccio, "Method of Photographically Recording the Order of Passage of Moving Objects."
76 Palmer, "Maryland, My Challedon," *The Blood-Horse* (20 May 1939): 715.
77 Del Riccio, "Method of Photographically Recording the Order of Passage of Moving Objects," col. 1.
78 Ibid., col. 2.
79 "California: Inglewood's Camera," *The Blood-Horse* (26 March 1938): 541.
80 Belden-Adams, "A Wrinkle in Time"; see also Belden-Adams, *Modern Time: Photography and Temporality*.
81 Vanvolsem, *The Art of Strip Photography*, 35.
82 Ibid.
83 Personal communication, 20 February, 2018.
84 Barthes, *Image, Music, Text*; Barthes, *Camera Lucida: Reflections on Photography*.
85 McCarthy, "At the Races," *The Globe and Mail*, 23 November 1938.
86 Palmer, "Maryland, My Challedon," *The Blood-Horse* (20 May 1939): 715.
87 "Bigger Movies," *Oakland Tribune*, 31 July 1929.

88 Personal communication, 8 March 2018.
89 "Photo-Finish Camera Inventor Facing Suit," *Los Angeles Times*, 4 September 1948; "Photo-Finish Contest to Be Viewed in Court," *Los Angeles Times*, 29 December 1948; "Photo-Finish Inventor Wins Camera Suit," *Los Angeles Times*, 9 April 1949; Photochart et al. v. Del Riccio; Photochart v. Del Riccio; Del Riccio et al. v. Superior Court of California.
90 Daston and Galison, "The Image of Objectivity"; Daston and Galison, *Objectivity*.
91 "Hollypark Judges to Introduce Binocular-Camera," *Wilmington Daily Press Journal*, 10 May 1941; "Hollywood Park Opens 1941 Horse Racing Season Today," *San Bernardino County Sun*, 23 May 1941; "Jerry Giesler Praises Jack Mackenzie's Work," *Los Angeles Times*, 2 June 1941.
92 Jhally, "The Spectacle of Accumulation."
93 Dyreson, "Aggressive America."

Chapter Four

1 As noted on the LA84 website: "Olympic Games official reports are the most comprehensive historical documents of each Olympic Games. Prepared by the host organizing committee, the report typically provides detailed information on Games, planning, construction, operations, budget, Olympic-related cultural activities, and competition results." The Olympic Studies Centre in Lausanne also has a complete collection of Official Reports available through their website. Though every Official Olympic Report was examined for this book, for brevity's sake only those which are borrowed from directly will be cited. See http://digital.la84.org/digital/collection/p17103coll8 and https://library.olympic.org/.
2 The history of OMEGA presented here is drawn from many sources including several in-house publications, a self-published book by an OMEGA engineer, and the websites of OMEGA and the Swatch Group, as well as the various contracts and related documents in the International Olympic Committee Historical Archives that are cited throughout this chapter. See: Bovay, *Photo-sprint*; Bovay, *Coliseum '32–'84*; Bovay, *Time and Sport Story*; Cheng, *Splitting the Second: My Wacky Business in Olympic and Sports Timing*; OMEGA Sports Timing, *The Art of Timing Sports Events*; "History – Swiss Timing"; "Olympic Games"; "Swatch Watch History – Past – The Swatch Group – Swatch Group"; Gomelsky, "How Switzerland Came to Dominate Watchmaking," *The New York Times*, 20 November 2014, https://www.nytimes.com/2014/11/21/style/international/what-enabled-switzerland-to-dominate-watchmaking.html.
3 Swatch Group, "Swatch Group Annual Report 2017," 169.

4 Of Bovay's publications, the most significant are *Photosprint: History*; *Coliseum '32–'84*; and *Time and Sport Story*.
5 Bovay, *Coliseum '32–'84*, 8.
6 Ibid., 12.
7 Swatch Group, "Swatch Group Annual Report 2017," 2.
8 Cartwright, "A Cultural Anatomy of the Visible Human Project."
9 "Olympic Games."
10 "The Official Report of the Organising Committee for the XIV Olympiad."
11 Ibid., 58.
12 Ibid.
13 Kolkka, "The Official Report of the Organising Committee for the Games of the XV Olympiad, Helsinki, 1952," 72.
14 Ibid.
15 Ibid., 71.
16 Collett, "Journal of Sports," *The Journal Herald* (Dayton, OH), 17 July 1952; "Morning After," *The Tampa Tribune*, 13 July 1952.
17 Kolkka, "The Official Report of the Organising Committee for the Games of the XV Olympiad, Helsinki, 1952," 72.
18 RaceTech, "History of RaceTech."
19 Brundage, "Time and the Olympic Games," 4.
20 Ibid., 6.
21 Ibid.
22 Guyot, "Evolution in the Timing Methods of the Olympic Games"; Guye, "Modern Timing Instruments for the Olympic Games and Other Important International Sporting Events."
23 Guye, "Modern Timing Instruments for the Olympic Games and Other Important International Sporting Events," 22.
24 Daston and Galison, *Objectivity*, 355.
25 Fouché, "Aren't Athletes Cyborgs?"; Fouché, *Game Changer*.
26 Fouché, "Aren't Athletes Cyborgs?" 282.
27 "The Games of the XVII Olympiad Rome 1960: The Official Report of the Organizing Committee. Volume 1," 172.
28 Ibid., 174.
29 "Die Spiele," 158.
30 Ibid.
31 Ibid.
32 Ibid., 156.
33 Jhally, "The Spectacle of Accumulation."
34 "Games of the XXI Olympiad Montréal 1976: Official Report. Volume 1," 413.

35 "Games of the XXII Olympiad Moscow 1980: Official Report. Volume 2," 206.
36 Ibid.
37 Brandt, "Timing at the 1952 Olympic Summer Games in Helsinki."
38 Ibid., 4.
39 Ibid.
40 Ibid., 5.
41 "Correspondence about Timing at the 1960 Olympic Winter Games in Squaw Valley, OMEGA."
42 Ibid., 1.
43 Longines was not specifically named by Vallat in the correspondence, but we know from the Olympic Report that Longines provided timing for the Games.
44 "Timekeeping at the 1972 Olympic Summer Games in Munich."
45 "Die Spiele," 156–75.
46 "Correspondence between the OCOG and Swiss Timing on Timing during the 1976 Olympic Winter Games in Innsbruck."
47 "Contracts Signed between the Organizing Committee of the 1980 Olympic Summer Games in Moscow and Various Firms," 1; "Correspondence between the OCOG and Swiss Timing on Timing during the 1976 Olympic Winter Games in Innsbruck."
48 "Contracts Signed between the Organizing Committee of the 1980 Olympic Summer Games in Moscow and Various Firms," 9.
49 "Contracts Signed between the Organizing Committee of the 1984 Olympic Summer Games in Los Angeles and Various Firms."
50 Ibid., D-5.
51 "Marketing (Official Time Keeper) of the 1988 Olympic Summer Games in Seoul."
52 Ibid., 3.
53 "Marketing (Official Time Keeper) of the 1992 Olympic Summer Games in Barcelona: Correspondence and IOC Approval Form Concerning Seiko."
54 Ibid.
55 "Marketing (Official Time Keeper) of the 1992 Olympic Summer Games in Barcelona: Contract Concerning Seiko."
56 Ibid., 35–6.
57 "Timing (Swiss Timing) at the 1992 Winter Olympic Games in Albertville."
58 "Marketing (Official Suppliers – Timing) of the 1994 Olympic Winter Games in Lillehammer."
59 Ibid.
60 RaceTech, "About RaceTech."

61 "FinishLynx Sports Timers."
62 Speed River Timing, "Speed River Timing."
63 "ACTIVE Network | IPICO Race Timing Systems & Chip Timing."
64 "Race|result Timers Group"; "FinishLynx Sports Timers"; "Timers Talk."
65 "Timers Talk Sales."
66 Swatch Group, "Swatch Group Annual Report 2017," 170.

Chapter Five

1 Branham, "USA Track & Field – Women's 100m Update – Dead-heat for Third Place."
2 "100 Metres Result | The XXIX Olympic Games | IAAF.org."
3 USATF, "USA Track & Field – Dead-Heat Procedures Announced."
4 Layden, "Tim Layden."
5 Flash Results, "Flash Results, Inc."
6 Zemper, "The Evolution of Track and Field Rules During the Last Century," 6.
7 Giles Norton, personal communication, 12 November 2013.
8 There are competing accounts of who was called to assist Jennings. I follow Layden's account, as he had the closest contact with Jennings and Podkaminer. See Layden, "Tim Layden."
9 Daston and Galison, "The Image of Objectivity," 120.
10 Layden, "Tim Layden."
11 Personal communication, 12 November 2013.
12 Branham, "USA Track & Field – Women's 100m Update – Dead-heat for Third Place."
13 "An Exclusive Interview with the Man Responsible for Reading the Allyson Felix 100m Finish Picture."
14 Layden, "Tim Layden."
15 Ibid.
16 Ibid.
17 "An Exclusive Interview with the Man Responsible for Reading the Allyson Felix 100m Finish Picture."
18 Layden, "Tim Layden."
19 Layden notes the differences between the financial packages of the two athletes.
20 Bell, "Lucky No. 7 for Phelps; U.S. Swimmer Comes from Back of Pack to Win by One-100th of a Second," *Ottawa Citizen*, 16 August 2008; Boswell, "By the Smallest of Margins, a Magnificent Seventh for Phelps," *Washington Post*, 17 August 2008; Coffey, "Phelps Wins a Magnificent 7. Ties Spitz Mark – by a Fingertip," *New York Daily News*, 16 August 2008; Cole,

"Last-Second Surge Gives Phelps Seventh Gold to Tie Record; Only Medley Relay Stands between Him and History," *Montreal Gazette*, 16 August 2008; Kaufman, "Phelps Stretches for His Seventh Gold, Tying Spitz's Record," *St. Paul Pioneer Press*, 15 August 2008; Maki, "Phelps Keeps Streak Alive, Barely; U.S. Wonder Swimmer Captures Seventh Gold Medal, but Serbs' Protest that Cavic Touched First Is Denied," *The Globe and Mail*, 16 August 2008; Reid, "With .01 to Spare, Phelps Beats O.C. Native Cavic to Tie Spitz at Seven Golds," *The Orange County Register*, 16 August 2008.

21 Brandt, "Timing at the 1952 Olympic Summer Games in Helsinki: Correspondence and Offer from OMEGA."

22 Cole, "Last-Second Surge Gives Phelps Seventh Gold to Tie Record; Only Medley Relay Stands between Him and History," *Montreal Gazette*, 16 August 2008.

23 Kaufman, "Phelps Stretches for His Seventh Gold, Tying Spitz's Record," *St. Paul Pioneer Press*, 15 August 2008.

24 Boswell, "By the Smallest of Margins, a Magnificent Seventh for Phelps," *Washington Post*, 17 August 2008.

25 Crouse, "Phelps Rival Speedy with His Lips; Bashful He's Not, Cavic Is a Verbal Typhoon ahead of Rematch with American," *The International Herald Tribune*, 1 August 2009.

26 Omega Watches, "Great Moments!"

27 Pennington, "First Tie for Alpine Gold, though Not Precisely," *New York Times*, 13 February 2014.

28 Fendrich, "Maze and Gisin Tie for Downhill Gold," *The Scotsman*, 13 February 2014.

29 "It's a Double Gold as Clock Stops Short of Splitting Maze and Gisin after Historic Run; Tie for Gold Medal in an Alpine Olympic Event Had Never Occurred before Yesterday," *The Irish Times*, 13 February 2014.

30 Svrluga, "Too Close to Call," *Washington Post*, 13 February 2014.

31 Chadband, "Gold Shared in Downhill Drama," *The Daily Telegraph*, 13 February 2014.

32 United States of America Track and Field, *2012 Competition Rules*, 49.

33 Fédération Internationale de Natation, *Constitution and Rules 2009–2013*, 169.

34 Fédération Internationale de Ski, *Timing-Booklet: Alpine Skiing. Version 2.52*, 35.

35 Fédération Internationale de Ski, *The International Ski Competition Rules (ICR): Book IV Joint Regulations for Alpine Skiing*, 51.

36 Ibid., 52.

37 United States of America Track and Field, "2012 Competition Rules," 80.

38 Ibid., 89.

39 Fédération Internationale de Natation, "Constitution and Rules 2009–2013," 169.
40 Fédération Internationale de Ski, *The International Ski Competition Rules (ICR): Book IV Joint Regulations for Alpine Skiing*, 51.
41 Ibid.
42 Personal communication, 12 November 2013.
43 Pennington, "First Tie for Alpine Gold, Though Not Precisely," *New York Times*, 13 February 2014.
44 Ibid.
45 Manovich, "The Paradoxes of Digital Photography."
46 Ibid., 248.
47 Daston and Galison, *Objectivity*, 48.
48 Schot and Albert de la Bruheze, "The Mediated Design of Products," 234.
49 Longman, "Mo Farah Wins 5,000 Meters at London Olympics," *New York Times*, 11 August 2012, https://www.nytimes.com/2012/08/12/sports/olympics/mo-farah-wins-5000-meters-at-london-olympics.html.
50 OMEGA / Swiss Timing would not allow me to reproduce the image in this book. It can be readily found in media accounts of the race. See Hart, "Olympics Hero Mo Farah Aiming to Break Steve Ovett's 34 Year-Old British Record at Aviva Birmingham Grand Prix," *The Telegraph*, 25 August 2012, https://www.telegraph.co.uk/sport/othersports/athletics/9499185/Olympics-hero-Mo-Farah-aiming-to-break-Steve-Ovetts-34-year-old-British-record-at-Aviva-Birmingham-Grand-Prix.html.

Chapter Six

1 Jhally, "The Spectacle of Accumulation"; Wenner, ed., *Media, Sports, and Society*; Wenner, ed., *MediaSport*; Whannel, *Fields in Vision*.
2 Daston and Galison, *Objectivity*, 113.
3 Armstrong, "Time for Football to Embrace Technology?"; Marcus, "Referees Talk Openly, but Not about that One Call," *New York Times*, 21 June 2010, https://www.nytimes.com/2010/06/22/sports/soccer/22referees.html; Vecsey, "An Obvious Case for Instant Replay," *New York Times*, 27 June 2010, https://www.nytimes.com/2010/06/28/sports/soccer/28replay.html.
4 Blair, "Blown Call Becomes a Lesson in Sportsmanship," *Globe and Mail*, 3 June 2010, https://www.theglobeandmail.com/sports/baseball/blown-call-becomes-a-lesson-in-sportsmanship/article1372323/; Lage, "Blown Call Costs Galarraga Perfect Game," *Globe and Mail*, 3 June 2010; Vecsey, "Worst Call Ever?" *New York Times*, 3 June 2010, https://www.nytimes.com/2010/06/04/sports/baseball/04vecsey.html; Weber, "Armando Galarraga

and the Perfect Asterisk," *New York Times*, 5 June 2010, https://www.nytimes.com/2010/06/06/weekinreview/06weber.html.

5 Bell, "Soccer to Adopt Goal-Line Technology," *New York Times*, 5 July 2012, https://www.nytimes.com/2012/07/06/sports/soccer/soccer-to-adopt-goal-line-technology.html; C.S.W., "Ins and Outs: Goal-Line Technology in Football," *The Economist*, 12 April 2013, https://www.economist.com/game-theory/2013/04/12/ins-and-outs; Hoffman, "Primer on How Expanded Instant Replay Will Work," *New York Times*, 17 August 2013, https://www.nytimes.com/2013/08/18/sports/baseball/primer-on-how-expanded-instant-replay-will-work.html.

6 Pennington and Crouse, "By Phone or by Text, Golf Entertains Second-Guessers," *New York Times*, 13 April 2013, https://www.nytimes.com/2013/04/14/sports/golf/television-viewers-flag-rule-violations-as-golf-officials-take-note.html; Tierney, "PGA to Discuss Reducing Viewers' Impact on Penalties," *New York Times*, 17 September 2013, https://www.nytimes.com/2013/09/18/sports/golf/pga-to-discuss-reducing-viewers-impact-on-penalties.html.

7 Tagg, *The Burden of Representation.*

8 Belam, "VAR at the World Cup," *The Guardian*, 22 June 2018, https://www.theguardian.com/football/2018/jun/22/var-at-the-world-cup-the-big-decisions-game-by-game; Clarey, "Video Review Will Make the World Cup Better, but Not Quieter," *New York Times*, 27 June 2018, https://www.nytimes.com/2018/06/17/sports/world-cup/world-cup-referee-var.html; Kelly, "Video Review Works, and It's Going to Ruin the World Cup," *The Globe and Mail*, 17 June 2018, https://www.theglobeandmail.com/sports/article-video-review-works-and-its-going-to-ruin-the-world-cup/.

9 Dyer, "The Controversy of Sports Technology"; Nafziger, "Avoiding and Resolving Disputes during Sports Competition"; Nlandu, "The Fallacies and Assumptions behind the Arguments for Goal-Line Technology in Soccer"; Steen, "Going Upstairs."

10 Collins and Evans, "You Cannot Be Serious!"; Collins and Evans, "Sport-Decision Aids and the 'CSI-Effect'"; Collins, "The Philosophy of Umpiring and the Introduction of Decision-Aid Technology"; Collins, Evans, and Higgins, *Bad Call.*

11 Collins and Evans, "Sport-Decision Aids and the 'CSI-Effect.'"

12 Jhally, "The Spectacle of Accumulation"; Rowe, *Sport, Culture and the Media*; Wenner, ed., *Media, Sports, and Society*; Wenner, ed., *MediaSport*; Whannel, *Fields in Vision.*

13 Omega Watches, "Great Moments!"

14 Svrluga, "Too Close to Call," *Washington Post*, 13 February 2014.

15 Real, "Super Bowl."
16 Magdalinski, *Sport, Technology and the Body*.
17 Fouché, *Game Changer*.
18 Epstein, *The Sports Gene*; McClusky, *Faster, Higher, Stronger*; Fogel, dir., *Icarus*; Hutchinson, *Endure*.
19 Morozov, *To Save Everything, Click Here*, 124. A special thank you to my colleague Ian Roderick for pointing me to Morozov's work.
20 Ibid., 179–80.
21 Ibid., 323.

Bibliography

"100 Metres Result | The XXIX Olympic Games | IAAF.org." https://www.iaaf.org/results/olympic-games/2008/the-xxix-olympic-games-3659/women/100-metres/final/result (accessed 24 July 2018).

"The XIth Olympic Games Berlin, 1936 Official Report." Berlin: Organisationskomitee für die XI. Olympiade Berlin 1936 e. V., 1937. http://library.la84.org/60ic/OfficialReports/1936/1936spart1.pdf.

Abney, Captain. *Instantaneous Photography*. New York: E. & H.T. Anthony & Co., 1896.

"ACTIVE Network | IPICO Race Timing Systems & Chip Timing." http://www.activeendurance.com/products/ipico (accessed 1 August 2018).

Adams, W.I. Lincoln. *Amateur Photography: A Practical Guide for the Beginner*. New York: Baker & Taylor Co., 1893.

"An Exclusive Interview with the Man Responsible for Reading the Allyson Felix 100m Finish Picture." http://www.letsrun.com/2012/felix-0623.php (accessed 18 July 2018).

Armstrong, Paul. "Time for Football to Embrace Technology?" http://www.cnn.com/2010/SPORT/football/06/28/football.goal.line.technology/index.html (accessed 28 August 2018).

Aubert, Genevieve. "From Photography to Cinematography: Recording Movement and Gait in a Neurological Context." *Journal of the History of the Neurosciences* 11, no. 3 (2002): 255–64.

Back, Les, Tim Crabbe, and John Solomos. *The Changing Face of Football: Racism, Identity and Multiculture in the English Game*. Basingstoke, UK: Berg, 2001.

Barnett, Barbara. "Girls Gone Web: Self-Depictions of Female Athletes on Personal Websites." *Journal of Communication Inquiry* 41, no. 2 (2017): 97–123.

Barnett, Steven. *Games and Sets: The Changing Face of Sport on Television*. London: British Film Institute, 1990.

Barthes, Roland. *Camera Lucida: Reflections on Photography*. Translated by Richard Howard. New York: Hill and Wang, 1981.

– *Image, Music, Text*. Translated by Stephen Heath. New York: Hill and Wang, 1977.

Bassnett, Sarah, and Arthur S. Goss. *Picturing Toronto: Photography and the Making of a Modern City*. McGill-Queen's University Press / Beaverbrook Canadian Foundation Studies in Art History. Montreal, Kingston, London, and Chicago: McGill-Queen's University Press, 2016.

Batchen, Geoffrey. *Burning with Desire: The Conception of Photography*. Cambridge, MA: MIT Press, 1997.

Becker, Karin E. "Photojournalism and the Tabloid Press." In *The Photography Reader*, edited by Liz Wells, 291–308. New York: Routledge, 2003.

Belden-Adams, Kris. "A Wrinkle in Time." *Cabinet*, 2007. http://www.cabinetmagazine.org/issues/25/belden-adams.php.

– *Modern Time: Photography and Temporality*. New York: City University of New York, 2010.

Bergvall, Erik, ed. *The Official Report of the Olympic Games of Stockholm 1912*. Translated by Edward Adams-Ray. Stockholm: Wahlstrom and Widstrand, 1912. http://library.la84.org/6oic/OfficialReports/1912/1912.pdf.

Blain, Neil, Raymond Boyle, and Hugh O'Donnell. *Sport and National Identity in the European Media*. Leicester, UK: Leicester University, 1993.

Bloom, John, and Michael Willard, eds. *Sports Matters: Race, Recreation, and Culture*. New York: New York University, 2002.

Bovay, J.P. *Coliseum '32–'84: Ars et Scientia Temporis Mensurae*. Bienne, Switzerland: Omega Electronics, 1985.

– *Photosprint: History*. Bienne, Switzerland: Omega Sports Timing, 1980.

– *Time and Sport Story*. Bienne, Switzerland: Omega Sports Timing, 1991.

Brandt, Louis and Frère. "Timing at the 1952 Olympic Summer Games in Helsinki: Correspondence and Offer from Omega." 25 March 1949. CIO JO-1952S-OMEGA. International Olympic Committee Historical Archives.

Branham, Katie. "USA Track & Field – Women's 100m Update – Dead Heat for Third Place." http://www.usatf.org/news/women%E2%80%99s-100m-update-%E2%80%93-dead-heat-for-third-place.aspx (accessed 18 July 2018).

Braun, Marta. "The Expanded Present: Photographing Movement." In *Beauty of Another Order: Photography in Science*, edited by Ann Thomas, 150–85. Ottawa and New Haven, CT: National Gallery of Canada and Yale University Press, 1997.

Brown, Douglas. "Modern Sport, Modernism and the Cultural Manifesto: De Coubertin's Revue Olympique." *The International Journal of the History of Sport* 18, no. 2 (June 2001): 78–109.

– "The Modern Romance of Mountaineering: Photography, Aesthetics and Embodiment." *The International Journal of the History of Sport* 24, no. 1 (2007): 1–34.

Brundage, Avery. "Time and the Olympic Games." *La Suisse Horlogère*, special issue, "The Measurement of Time and the Olympic Games," no. 4 (December 1955): 4–6.

Bryant, Jennings, Paul Comisky, and Dolf Zillmann. "Drama in Sports Commentary." *Journal of Communication* 27, no. 3 (1977): 140–9.

Caesar, Ed. "The Epic Untold Story of Nike's (Almost) Perfect Marathon." *Wired*. https://www.wired.com/story/nike-breaking2-marathon-eliud-kipchoge/ (accessed 25 June 2019).

"The Camera on the Racecourse." *British Journal of Photography* 35, no. 1469 (29 June 1888): 401.

Canales, Jimena. *A Tenth of a Second: A History*. Chicago: University of Chicago Press, 2009.

Cartwright, Lisa. "A Cultural Anatomy of the Visible Human Project." In *The Visible Woman: Imaging Technologies, Gender, and Science*, edited by Paula Treichler and Lisa Cartwright, 21–43. New York: New York University, 1998.

Chandler, Joan M. *Television and National Sport: The United States and Britain*. Urbana-Champagne: University of Illinois, 1988.

Cheng, Alex. *Splitting the Second: My Wacky Business in Olympic and Sports Timing*. Bloomington, IN: Authorhouse, 2008.

Cole, Simon. "Witnessing Identification: Latent Fingerprinting Evidence and Expert Knowledge." *Social Studies of Science* 28, no. 5–6 (1998): 687–712.

Collins, Harry. "The Philosophy of Umpiring and the Introduction of Decision-Aid Technology." *Journal of the Philosophy of Sport*, no. 37 (2010): 135–46.

Collins, Harry, Robert Evans, and Christopher Higgins. *Bad Call: Technology's Attack on Referees and Umpires and How to Fix It*. Cambridge, MA: MIT Press, 2016.

Collins, H.M., and R. Evans. "Sport-Decision Aids and the 'CSI-Effect': Why Cricket Uses Hawk-Eye Well and Tennis Uses It Badly." *Public Understanding of Science* 21 (2011): 904–21.

– "You Cannot Be Serious! Public Understanding of Technology with Special Reference to 'Hawk-Eye.'" *Public Understanding of Science* 17 (2008): 283–308.

Comisky, Paul, Jennings Bryant, and Dolf Zillmann. "Commentary as a Substitute for Action." *Journal of Communication* 27, no. 3 (1977): 150–3.

"Contracts Signed between the Organizing Committee of the 1980 Olympic Summer Games in Moscow and Various Firms." 1980 1976. CIO JO-1980S-FIRM-CT. International Olympic Committee Historical Archives.

"Contracts Signed between the Organizing Committee of the 1984 Olympic Summer Games in Los Angeles and Various Firms." 1982 1979. CIO JO-1984S-FIRM-CT. International Olympic Committee Historical Archives.

Cook, Theodore Andrea. "Official Report Olympic Games of 1908." London:

British Olympic Council, 1909. http://library.la84.org/6oic/OfficialReports/1908/1908.pdf.

Coopmans, Catelijne, Janet Vertesi, Michael Lynch, and Steve Woolgar, eds. *Representation in Scientific Practice Revisited.* Cambridge, MA: MIT, 2014.

"Correspondence about Timing at the 1960 Olympic Winter Games in Squaw Valley, Omega." 1956. CIO JO-1960W-OMEGA. International Olympic Committee Historical Archives.

"Correspondence between the OCOG and Swiss Timing on Timing during the 1976 Olympic Winter Games in Innsbruck." 1975 1974. CIO JO-1976W-SWTIM. International Olympic Committee Historical Archives.

Creedon, Pamela J. *Women, Media, and Sport: Challenging Gender Values.* New York: Sage, 1994.

Daddario, Gina. *Women's Sport and Spectacle: Gendered Television Coverage and the Olympic Games.* Westport, CT: Praeger, 1998.

Daston, Lorraine, and Peter Galison. *Objectivity.* New York: Zone Books, 2010.

– "The Image of Objectivity." *Representations* 40 (1992): 81–128.

Davies, Richard O. *Sports in American Life: A History.* 2nd ed. Chichester, UK, and Malden, MA: Wiley-Blackwell, 2012.

Davis, Laurel R. *The Swimsuit Issue and Sport: Hegemonic Masculinity and Sports Illustrated.* Albany: State University of New York Press, 1997.

Del Riccio et al. v. Superior Court of California, In and For Los Angeles County, No. 19362 (California Court of Appeal, Second District, Division 3, 22 December 1952).

Del Riccio, Lorenzo. "Camera." United States Patent Office 2320350. Los Angeles, filed 20 March 1939, and issued 1 June 1943. http://pimg-fpiw.uspto.gov/fdd/50/203/023/0.pdf.

– "Method of Photographically Recording the Order of Passage of Moving Objects." United States Patent Office 2382617. Los Angeles, filed 20 March 1939, and issued 14 August 1945. http://pimg-fpiw.uspto.gov/fdd/17/826/023/0.pdf.

– "Method of Photographically Recording the Order of Passage of Moving Objects." United States Patent Office RE22881, filed 20 March 1939, and issued 20 May 1947.

"Die Spiele: The Official Report of the Organizing Committee for the Games of the XXth Olympiad Munich 1972. Volume 1." Munich, 1974. LA84. http://digital.la84.org/digital/collection/p17103coll8/id/25059/rec/40.

Dumit, Joseph. *Picturing Personhood: Brain Scans and Biomedical Identity.* In-Formation Series. Princeton, NJ: Princeton University Press, 2004.

Dumont, Guillaume. "The Beautiful and the Damned: The Work of New Media Production in Professional Rock Climbing." *Journal of Sport and Social Issues* 41, no. 2 (2017): 99–117.

Dyer, B. "The Controversy of Sports Technology: A Systematic Review." *SpringerPlus* 4, no. Article 524 (2015).
Dyreson, Mark. "Aggressive America: Media Nationalism and the 'War' over Olympic Pictures in Sport's 'Golden Age.'" *International Journal of the History of Sport* 22, no. 6: 974–89.
Epstein, David J. *The Sports Gene: Inside the Science of Extraordinary Athletic Performance*. New York: Penguin, 2014.
Fédération Internationale de Natation. *Constitution and Rules 2009–2013*. Lausanne, Switzerland: Fédération Internationale de Natation, 2012.
Fédération Internationale de Ski. *The International Ski Competition Rules (ICR): Book IV Joint Regulations for Alpine Skiing*. Oberhofen, Switzerland: Fédération Internationale de Ski, 2014.
– *Timing-Booklet: Alpine Skiing. Version 2.52*. Oberhofen, Switzerland: Fédération Internationale de Ski, 2014.
Fetter, C.H. "A New Way of Splitting Seconds." *Bell Telephone Quarterly*, October 1932.
"FinishLynx Sports Timers." https://www.facebook.com/groups/finishlynx/ (accessed 1 August 2018).
Finn, Jonathan M. *Capturing the Criminal Image: From Mug Shot to Surveillance Society*. Minneapolis: University of Minnesota Press, 2009.
Flash Results. "Flash Results, Inc." http://www.flashresults.com/whatwedo.htm (accessed 24 July 2018).
Fleming, Sydney W., trans. "Official Report of the Olympic Games of 1928 Celebrated at Amsterdam." Rokin, Netherlands: Netherlands Olympic Committee, 1928. http://library.la84.org/6oic/OfficialReports/1928/1928.pdf.
Fogel, Bryan, dir. *Icarus: Truth Is the New Banned Substance*. Netflix, 2017.
Foucault, Michel. *Discipline and Punish: The Birth of the Prison*. Translated by Alan Sheridan. New York: Vintage, 1979.
Fouché, Rayvon. "Aren't Athletes Cyborgs? Technology, Bodies and Sporting Competitions." *Women's Studies Quarterly* 40, no. 1–2 (2012): 281–93.
Fouché, Rayvon. *Game Changer: The Technoscientific Revolution in Sports*. Baltimore, MD: Johns Hopkins University Press, 2017.
Fuller, Linda K. *Sport, Rhetoric, and Gender: Historical Perspectives and Media Representations*. New York: Palgrave Macmillan, 2006.
Galton, Francis. "A Rapid-View Instrument for Momentary Attitudes." *Nature* 26 (1882): 249–51.
– "Conventional Representation of the Horse in Motion." *Nature* 26 (1882): 228–9.
"The Games of the XVII Olympiad Rome 1960: The Official Report of the Organizing Committee. Volume 1." 1960. LA84. http://digital.la84.org/digital/collection/p17103coll8/id/20106/rec/26.

"Games of the XXI Olympiad Montréal 1976: Official Report. Volume 1." Montreal, 1976. LA84. digital.la84.org/digital/collection/p17103coll8/id/28525/rec/42.

"Games of the XXII Olympiad Moscow 1980: Official Report. Volume 2." Moscow, 1981. LA84. http://digital.la84.org/digital/collection/p17103coll8/id/29539/rec/47.

Gilman, Sander L. *Difference and Pathology: Stereotypes of Sexuality, Race, and Madness*. Ithaca, NY: Cornell University Press, 1985.

– *Seeing the Insane*. Lincoln: University of Nebraska Press, 1996.

Goldstein, Jeffrey H., and Brenda J. Bredemeier. "Socialization: Some Basic Issues." *Journal of Communication* 27, no. 3 (1977): 154–9.

Goodwin, Charles. "Professional Vision." *American Anthropologist* 96, no. 3 (1994): 606–33.

Gruneau, Richard. "Aesthetics and the Politics of Representation: The Making of Modern English Sport." *Amodern* 3 (October 2014). http://amodern.net/article/aesthetics-politics-representation/.

– *Class, Sports, and Social Development*. Amherst, MA: University of Massachusetts Press, 1983.

Gruneau, Richard S. *Sport and Modernity*. Cambridge, UK, and Malden, MA: Polity Press, 2017.

Guttmann, Allen. *From Ritual to Record: The Nature of Modern Sports*. New York: Columbia University Press, 1993.

– *Sports: The First Five Millennia*. Amherst, MA: University of Massachusetts Press, 2004.

Guye, René P. "Modern Timing Instruments for the Olympic Games and Other Important International Sporting Events." *La Suisse Horlogère*, special issue, "The Measurement of Time and the Olympic Games," no. 4 (March 1955): 21–8.

Guyot, Edmond. "Evolution in the Timing Methods of the Olympic Games." *La Suisse Horlogère*, special issue, "The Measurement of Time and the Olympic Games," no. 4 (March 1955): 18–20.

Hemment, John C. *Cannon and Cameras: Sea and Land Battles of the Spanish-American War in Cuba, Camp Life, and the Return of Soldiers*. New York: D. Appleton and Company, 1898.

– "My Search for the Missing Link." *Motion Picture Magazine*, August 1914.

– "Photography Applied to Sports." *American Annual of Photography and Photographic Times Almanac* 5 (1891): 198–202.

– "Rapid Photography." *American Annual of Photography and Photographic Times Almanac* 6 (1892): 215–16.

Hervey, John. *Racing in America 1922–1936*. New York: Scribner Press, 1937.

Horowitz, Ira. "Sports Telecasts: Rights and Regulations." *Journal of Communication* 27, no. 3 (1977): 160–8.

Howell, Maxwell L., and Reet A. Howell, eds. *History of Sport in Canada*. Revised edition. Champaign: Sipes Publishing Comp, 1985.

Huggins, Mike, and Mike O'Mahony. "Prologue: Extending Study of the Visual in the History of Sport." *The International Journal of the History of Sport* 28, no. 8–9 (2011): 1089–1104.

– "Special Issue on Sport and The Visual." *International Journal of the History of Sport* 28, no. 8–9 (2011): 1089–1374.

– *The Visual in Sport*. London: Routledge, 2012.

Hundley, Heather L., and Andrew C. Billings, eds. *Examining Identity in Sports Media*. London: Sage, 2009.

Hutchinson, Alex. *Endure: Mind, Body, and the Curiously Elastic Limits of Human Performance*. 1st ed. New York: William Morrow, 2018.

Hylton, Kevin. *Critical Race Theory in Sport*. London: Routledge, 2008.

"Instantaneous Photography." *Science* 15, no. 366 (7 February 1890): 83–6.

Ivins, William Jr. *Prints and Visual Communication*. 7th ed. Cambridge, MA: MIT, 1989.

Jasanoff, Sheila. "The Eye of Everyman: Witnessing DNA in the Simpson Trial." *Social Studies of Science* 28, no. 5–6 (1998): 713–40.

"Les Jeux de La VIII Olympiade, Paris 1924: Rapport Officiel." Paris: Comité Olympique Français, 1924. http://library.la84.org/6oic/OfficialReports/1924/1924.pdf.

Jhally, Sut. *Playing Unfair: The Media Image of the Female Athlete*. Northampton, MA: Media Educational Foundation, 2002.

– "The Spectacle of Accumulation: Material and Cultural Factors in the Evolution of the Sports/Media Complex." *The Insurgent Sociologist* 12, no. 3 (1984): 41–57.

Jordanova, L.J. *The Look of the Past: Visual and Material Evidence in Historical Practice*. Cambridge: Cambridge University Press, 2012.

Joyce, Kelly Ann. *Magnetic Appeal: MRI and the Myth of Transparency*. Ithaca, NY: Cornell University Press, 2008.

Kellner, Douglas. *Media Spectacle*. New York: Routledge, 2003.

King, Richard C. *Sport and Race*. Basingstoke, UK: Berg, 2006.

King, Thomas. *The Inconvenient Indian: A Curious Account of Native People in North America*. Toronto: Penguin Random House, 2013.

Kolkka, Sulo. "The Official Report of the Organising Committee for the Games of the XV Olympiad, Helsinki, 1952." Translated by Alex Matson. Helsinki, Finland: 1955. LA84. http://digital.la84.org/digital/collection/p17103coll8/id/4950/rec/21.

Latour, Bruno, and Steve Woolgar. *Laboratory Life: The Construction of Scientific Facts*. 2nd ed. Princeton, NJ: Princeton University, 1979.

Layden, Tim. "Tim Layden: Photo Finish Examiner Details Dead-Heat Determination." https://www.si.com/more-sports/2012/06/26/track-field-photo-finish-felix-tarmoh (accessed 24 July 2018).

Lucas, Charles J.P. "The Olympic Games 1904." St Louis: 1905. http://library.la84.org/6oic/OfficialReports/1904/1904lucas.pdf.

Lynch, Michael, and Steve Woolgar, eds. *Representation in Scientific Practice*. Cambridge, MA: MIT, 1990.

Magdalinski, Tara. *Sport, Technology and the Body: The Nature of Performance*. London and New York: Routledge, 2009.

Manovich, Lev. "The Paradoxes of Digital Photography." In *The Photography Reader*, edited by Liz Wells, 240–9. New York: Routledge, 2003.

"Marketing (Official Suppliers – Timing) of the 1994 Olympic Winter Games in Lillehammer: Correspondence, IOC Approval Form, Contract and Information Kit Concerning Seiko (OS 6)." 1994 1990. C-J02-1994/145. International Olympic Committee Historical Archives.

"Marketing (Official Time Keeper) of the 1988 Olympic Summer Games in Seoul: Correspondence, Agreements and Press Kit Concerning Swiss Timing, Official Timekeeper." 1988 1985. C-J01-1988/076. International Olympic Committee Historical Archives.

"Marketing (Official Time Keeper) of the 1992 Olympic Summer Games in Barcelona: Contract Concerning Seiko." 1990. C-J01-1992/240. International Olympic Committee Historical Archives.

"Marketing (Official Time Keeper) of the 1992 Olympic Summer Games in Barcelona: Correspondence and IOC Approval Form Concerning Seiko." 1992 1989. C-J01-1992/243. International Olympic Committee Historical Archives.

McChesney, Robert W. "Media Made Sport: A History of Sports Coverage in the United States." In *Media, Sports, and Society*, edited by Lawrence Wenner, 49–69. London: Sage, 1989.

McClusky, Mark. *Faster, Higher, Stronger: How Sports Science Is Creating a New Generation of Superathletes – and What We Can Learn from Them*. New York: Plume, 2014.

Mérillon, M.D. "Concours Internationaux D'Exercices Physiques et de Sports: Rapports." Paris: Ministère du Commerce, De L'Industrie Des Postes et Des Télégraphes, 1901. http://library.la84.org/6oic/OfficialReports/1900/1900.pdf.

Messner, Michael A. *Out of Play: Critical Essays on Gender and Sport*. Albany: State University of New York Press, 2007.

Miller, Toby. *Sportsex*. Philadelphia: Temple University Press, 2002.

Mitchell, W.J. Thomas. *Picture Theory: Essays on Verbal and Visual Representation*. Chicago: University of Chicago Press, 2007.
Mnookin, Jennifer. "The Image of Truth: Photographic Evidence and the Power of Analogy." *Yale Journal of Law and the Humanities* 10, no. 1 (1998): 1–74.
Morozov, Evgeny. *To Save Everything, Click Here: The Folly of Technological Solutionism*. New York: Public Affairs, 2014.
Morrow, Don, ed. *A Concise History of Sport in Canada*. Toronto: Oxford University Press, 1989.
– ed. *A Concise History of Sport in Canada*. Reprinted. Don Mills, ON: Oxford University Press, 2000.
Mumford, Lewis. *Technics and Civilization*. Chicago: University of Chicago, 2010.
Muybridge, Edward. "A Dead Heat." *Nature* 26 (25 May 1882): 81.
Nafziger, J.A.R. "Avoiding and Resolving Disputes During Sports Competition: Of Cameras and Computers." *Marquette Sports Law Review* 15, no. 1 (2004): 13–27.
Nike. "Nike Introduces Breaking2." https://news.nike.com/news/2-hour-marathon (accessed 18 June 2019).
– "Just Do It. Breaking2." https://www.nike.com/ca/en_gb/c/justdoit (accessed 18 June 2019).
Nlandu, T. "The Fallacies and Assumptions Behind the Arguments for Goal-Line Technology in Soccer." *Sport, Ethics and Philosophy* 6, no. 4 (2012): 1–16.
"The Official Report of the Organising Committee for the XIV Olympiad." London: 1951. LA84. http://digital.la84.org/digital/collection/p17103coll8/id/5717/rec/19.
"Olympic Games Antwerp 1920: Official Report." Belgium Olympic Committee, 1957. http://library.la84.org/6oic/OfficialReports/1920/1920.pdf.
"Olympic Games Official Report Los Angeles 1932." Los Angeles: Xth Olympiade Committee, 1933. http://library.la84.org/6oic/OfficialReports/1932/.
OMEGA Watches. "Great Moments!" 23 August 2008. http://www.omegawatches.com/press/press-release-detail/1049.
– "Olympic Games: A Race Proudly Won by Omega." https://www.omegawatches.com/planet-omega/sport/olympic-games/ (accessed 18 April 2018).
O'Neill, Jerome P., Jr. "The History of Race Photo Finish Photography." Interim report of the Photo Finish Research Project. Rochester, NY: August 1971. Keeneland Library.
"Only the Photographer." *Technical World Magazine* 19, no. 6 (1913): 812–13.
Oudshoorn, Nelly, and Trevor Pinch, eds. *How Users Matter: The Co-construction of Users and Technology*. Cambridge, MA: MIT, 2005.
Parente, Donald E. "The Interdependence of Sports and Television." *Journal of Communication* 27, no. 3 (1977): 128–32.

Peirce, Charles Saunders. "What Is a Sign." In *The Essential Peirce: Selected Philosophical Writings Volume 2 (1893–1913)*, 4–10. Bloomington, IN: Indiana University, 1998.

Photochart et al. v. Del Riccio, No. 15293 (California Court of Appeal, Second District, Division 2 September 4, 1946).

Photochart v. Del Riccio, No. 17115 (California Court of Appeal, Second District, Division 1 October 27, 1949).

Prodger, Phillip, Iris & B. Gerald Cantor Center for Visual Arts, and The Cleveland Museum of Art, eds. *Time Stands Still: Muybridge and the Instantaneous Photography Movement; [Cantor Arts Center: February 6 – May 11, 2003 ; Cleveland Museum of Art: February 15 – May 16, 2004]*. New York: Oxford University Press [u.a.], 2003.

"Race|result Timers Group." https://www.facebook.com/groups/1646733288908445/ (accessed 1 August 2018).

RaceTech. "About RaceTech." https://www.racetech.co.uk/racetech/ (accessed 1 August 2018).

– "History of RaceTech." https://www.racetech.co.uk/racetech/history-racetech/ (accessed 1 May 2018).

Rafter, Nicole. "Criminal Anthropology in the United States." *Criminology* 30, no. 4 (1992): 525–45.

Real, Michael. "Reflections on Communication and Sport: On Spectacle and Mega-Events." *Communication & Sport* 1, no. 1/2 (2013): 30–42.

Real, Michael R. "Super Bowl: Mythic Spectacle." *Journal of Communication* 25, no. 1 (1975): 31–43.

Rosenblum, Naomi. *A World History of Photography*. New York: Abbeville Press, 1984.

Rowe, David. *Sport, Culture and the Media: The Unruly Trinity*. Berkshire, UK: Open University, 1999.

Schot, Johan, and Adri Albert de la Bruheze. "The Mediated Design of Products, Consumption, and Consumers in the Twentieth Century." In *How Users Matter: The Co-Construction of Users and Technology*, edited by Nelly Oudshoorn and Trevor Pinch, 229–45. Cambridge, MA: MIT, 2003.

Sekula, Allan. "The Body and the Archive." *October* 39 (1986): 3–64.

Sherwin, Richard. "Visual Literacy in Action: 'Law in the Age of Images.'" In *Visual Literacy*, edited by James Elkins, 179–94. New York: Routledge, 2007.

Siegfried, John J., and C. Elton Hinshaw. "Professional Football and the Anti-Blackout Law." *Journal of Communication* 27, no. 3 (1977): 169–74.

Simon, Mary. *Racing through the Century: The Story of Thoroughbred Racing in America*. Irvine, CA: BowTie Press, 2002.

Snyder, Joel. "Picturing Vision." *Critical Inquiry* 6, no. 3 (1980): 499–526.

Speed River Timing. "Speed River Timing." https://speedrivertiming.com/ (accessed 1 August 2018).

Steen, R. "Going Upstairs: The Decision Revew System – Velvet Revolution or Thin Edge of an Ethical Wedge?" *Sport in Society* 14 (2011): 1428–40.

Swatch Group. "Swatch Group Annual Report 2017." Switzerland: The Swatch Group, 2018. http://www.swatchgroup.com/en/investor_relations/annual_and_half_year_reports.

Tagg, John. *The Burden of Representation: Essays on Photographies and Histories*. New York: Palgrave Macmillan, 2002.

Thorpe, Holly. "Foucault, Technologies of the Self, and the Media: Discourses of Femininity in Snowboarding Culture." *Journal of Sport and Social Issues* 32, no. 2 (2008): 199–229.

"Timekeeping at the 1972 Olympic Summer Games in Munich: Correspondence Concerning Longines, Junghans and Omega." 1970 1969. CIO JO-1972S-OMEGA. International Olympic Committee Historical Archives.

"Timers Talk." https://www.facebook.com/groups/225542597606939/ (accessed 1 August 2018).

"Timers Talk Sales." https://www.facebook.com/groups/183969700626785 8/ (accessed 1 August 2018).

"Timing (Swiss Timing) at the 1992 Winter Olympic Games in Albertville: Correspondence, Contract and Form," 1991 1989. C-J02-1992/261. International Olympic Committee Historical Archives.

Underwood, Tom R. *Thoroughbred Racing & Breeding*. New York: Coward-McCann, 1945.

United States of America Track and Field. *2012 Competition Rules*. Indianapolis: United States of America Track and Field, 2012.

– "USA Track & Field – Dead-Heat Procedures Announced." http://www.usatf.org/News/Dead-heat-procedures-announced.aspx (accessed 24 July 2018).

Vanvolsem, Maarten. *The Art of Strip Photography: Making Still Images with a Moving Camera*. Lieven Gevaert Series, v. 11. Leuven, Belgium: Leuven University Press, 2011.

Veder, Robin. "Seeing Your Way to Health: The Visual Pedagogy of Bess Mensendieck's Physical Culture System." *The International Journal of the History of Sport* 28, no. 8–9 (2011): 1336–52.

Vera, Julio. "J.C. (John Charles) Hemment." Lexington, KY: Keeneland Library, March 2010.

Von Borries, Philip. *RaceLens: Vintage Thoroughbred Racing Images*. Gretna, LA: Pelican, 2014.

Wade, Nicholas J. "Capturing Motion and Depth Before Cinematography." *Journal of the History of the Neurosciences* 25, no. 1 (2015): 3–22.

Watson, Rebecca, and Sheila Scraton, eds. *Sport, Leisure Identities and Gendered Spaces*. Eastbourne, UK: Leisure Studies Association, 2000.

Wenner, Lawrence, ed. *Media, Sports, and Society*. London: Sage, 1989.

– ed. *MediaSport*. London: Routledge, 1998.

Whannel, Garry. *Fields in Vision: Television Sport and Cultural Transformation*. London: Routledge, 1992.

Whitson, David, and Richard Gruneau, eds. *Artificial Ice: Hockey, Culture, and Commerce*. Peterborough, ON: Broadview Press, 2006.

Williams, Brien R. "The Structure of Televised Football." *Journal of Communication* 27, no. 3 (1977): 133–9.

"World Beaters! Satisfaction Givers! Prosch Photographic Shutters. Storage Flash Lamps." *American Annual of Photography and Photographic Times Almanac* 6 (1892): 24.

Zemper, Eric D. "The Evolution of Track and Field Rules During the Last Century." Presented at the USA Olympic Team Trials for Track and Field, Eugene, Oregon, 4 July 2008. http://www.usatfne.org/officials/ruleshistory_zemper.pdf.

Index